*Women Mystics
and Sufi Shrines
in India*

*Studies in Comparative Religion*
*Frederick M. Denny, Series Editor*

# Women Mystics
and Sufi Shrines
in India

## KELLY PEMBERTON

The University of South Carolina Press

Published by the University of South Carolina Press
Columbia, South Carolina 29208

www.sc.edu/uscpress

Manufactured in the United States of America

19 18 17 16 15 14 13 12 11 10
10 9 8 7 6 5 4 3 2 1

*Library of Congress Cataloging-in-Publication Data*
Pemberton, Kelly.
Women mystics and sufi shrines in India / Kelly Pemberton.
p. cm. — (Studies in comparative religion)
Includes bibliographical references and index.
ISBN 978-1-57003-919-5 (cloth : alk. paper)
1. Sufism—India—Rituals. 2. Sufism—India—Customs and practices.
3. Women mystics—India. 4. Women in Islam—India. I. Title.
BP188.8.I4P46 2010
297.4'460820954—dc22

2010013179

This book was printed on Glatfelter Natures, a recycled paper
with 30 percent postconsumer waste content.

To Jack, who got me started on this journey,
and
to the women of the Gudri Shah Chishti and
Firdausi *silsila*s, for showing the Way

Gently, she walks, yet the anklet jingles with her beloved's love;
she looks at herself in the mirror and feels shy.

Embracing the female form,
the entire world throbs.

Excerpt from "She Adorns Herself," by Parveen Shakir
(translation by Sydra Raza Junaid)

# . Contents .

# . Illustrations .

# . Series Editor's Preface .

Sufism, the richly diverse mystical-devotional dimension of Islamic religion, is one of the most popular and appealing fields of discourse and practice in both global spirituality and the comparative study of religion. This new book in the Studies in Comparative Religion series is the eighth to address some significant topic pertaining to Sufism, 25 percent of all the titles that have been published in the series since its founding in 1985.

*Women Mystics and Sufi Shrines in India* is the substantial and original product of Kelly Pemberton's intensive, multiyear, field-based and historical research. She describes her "central focus" for the study as "how Muslim women's participation in the world of Sufi shrines in North India challenges but also sustains prevalent ideals of Islamic womanhood." Her richly detailed, theoretically discerning, and multilayered accounts of Muslim women's participation in quite diverse Indian Sufi communities is an important contribution to our understanding of their lives in today's developing social, political, economic and cultural landscapes. These accounts also help us to comprehend more fully how important women's participation in the diverse and complex local contexts of Sufi, as well as general Muslim life, has been in past centuries.

Frederick M. Denny

# . Preface .

In the summer of 1994 I traveled to India for the first time as a graduate M.A. student at the University of Washington. The journey came at the end of three years of studying Hindi and Urdu and was intended to improve my Hindi and Urdu speaking skills. During my stint at the Landour Language School in the town of Mussoorie, located at the foothills of the Himalayas, I became aware of the existence of a number of small, locally renowned Sufi shrines, but what intrigued me was the adulation ordinary people I encountered lavished on deceased and living Sufis. While many people described them as true seekers of God, others praised the work living *shaikh*s did for the most unfortunate members of society, in part through *langar khana*s, or "free kitchens" established at some shrines to feed the poor. I returned to the States at the end of the summer and scoured the bookshelves of my university's library for more information about shrines and Sufis in South Asia but found surprisingly little on the "lived experiences" of Sufis and the pilgrims who patronized Sufi shrines.

### Women and Sufi Shrines in Contemporary India

By the time of my second sojourn in the Subcontinent in the summer of 1996, now as a Ph.D. student at Columbia University, I had decided to investigate the question of contemporary Sufis by looking at a number of shrines in northern and central India. After three months spent traveling in sweltering, dusty government buses from the northwest corner of Rajasthan down through Madhya Pradesh and northeast to Bihar, I had amassed a large body of notes, tape-recorded interviews with Sufi men and women, and experiences I could not have imagined beforehand, but had no clue how to make sense of all this information. After my return to academic life, Professor Jack Hawley suggested, in light of what I had seen and reported to him, that I focus on the question of women's roles in Sufi orders today when I returned to India the following year. The thought of pursuing this topic was daunting.

I had broached the subject of women's participation with most of the Sufis I met that summer, but their responses to "the woman question" were discouraging. While many of them eagerly discussed the subject of female saints[1] who had lived in the distant past—most often people brought up the example of the eighth-century saint of Basra, Rabi'a al-'Adawiyya—they were reluctant to discuss the place of women in the Sufi communities to which they themselves belonged. Women, I was repeatedly told, had no significant role to play in Sufism today, except as disciples of a *pir* or *shaikh,* and women could never become *pir*s themselves. For some reason I wasn't quite ready to accept these opinions at face value, and what I had seen at three Sufi shrines that summer convinced me that there was a significant gap between what most people said women did at shrines and women's lived experiences. While visiting the town of Ajmer in Rajasthan, I had visited the burial shrine, or *dargah,* of the thirteenth-century Sufi master Mu'in al-din Chishti and was introduced by a young teenage boy, a servant of the shrine (*khadim*), to a few of the men—highly placed in the hierarchy of the shrine's functionaries—who claimed descent from the saint. I had been looking for primary sources about the shrine and saint and knew from prior research that the *dargah* contained a library, of which the *nazim dargah,* a government-appointed functionary, was in charge. I wasn't able to gain access to the *dargah*'s library or to meet with the *nazim dargah,* who was out of town at the time. In any case the library was in such a state of disrepair that I would have been unable to use it even if the *nazim dargah* had consented.

This disappointment proved to be a boon in disguise, since during the course of an interview with two *khadim*s that day, I was told that on the other side of the *dargah* there lived a family that had an extensive library, and that they would probably be willing to let me use it. That family was the Gudri Shah Chishtis, an order of Sufis locally considered "newcomers" to the area. The Gudri Shahs were established in the mid-1800s, and settled in Ajmer in the early part of the twentieth century. The former head of the order (*pir, shaikh*) had passed away two months previously. A prolific, multilingual, and widely respected scholar, he had amassed an impressive library, of which his son and successor was in charge. My first meeting with the Gudri Shah Chishtis was solemn—the *pir* was out that morning, but I was invited into the women's quarters (*zanankhana*), where I met his sisters, maternal aunt, and mother, who were still mourning their loss. Later that day I did speak with the *pir,* and was impressed by his efforts in the local community. He had founded a school, aptly named the Sufi Saint School, which provides education and financial aid to local children from disadvantaged backgrounds and seeks to instill in its students a respect for

their differences, as Hindu and Muslim children both attend. The school's principal was one of the *pir*'s younger sisters. She, like all of the Gudri Shah women of her generation, was highly educated and worked outside of the home. The Gudri Shah women also played a significant part, the *pir* told me, in ensuring the smooth functioning of the order, by helping out with the many programs, ritual events, and ceremonies it sponsored annually, although the women did not attend the large public ritual ceremonies. The Gudri Shah Chishtis were open to the idea of my returning to Ajmer to carry out research and assured me that they would help in whatever way possible.

If the atmosphere in Ajmer was warm and welcoming, such was not always the case in Bihar, which I visited almost three months later. Bihar has an unfortunate reputation as the "most backward" state in India, one in which law and order is largely absent. In 2000 the state of Bihar was divided. The more prosperous and resource-rich land to the south became Jharkhand. Because crime and violence are rampant, many people are wary of strangers, whether Bihari, Indian, or foreign. On the other hand, Bihar offered insights into the nature of Sufi ritual life, and women's roles therein, that had not come to light in previous contexts. I also had an advantage in Bihar that I had not enjoyed elsewhere: a friendship with Father Paul Jackson, a Jesuit priest who lived and worked at the St. Xavier School in Patna. Father Jackson had translated the *Maktubat-i sadi,* or *The Hundred Letters,* of the fourteenth-century saint Sharaf al-din Maneri, aside from writing several other books about Muslims in India and shrines in Patna, Bihar's capital city. He was also widely respected within a number of Sufi communities, including two branches of the Firdausi order, one based in Bihar Sharif and the other in Maner. Because of him I was welcomed into the inner circles of these orders as an honored guest. Graciously accompanying me and my husband on a journey to shrines in Maner and Bihar Sharif, Father Jackson enabled me to witness how ritual life in this Sufi milieu was unlike any other form of saint veneration I had come across until then. It was also in Bihar, and because of Father Jackson's advice, that I became aware of something that would be central to my study of women mystics: the existence of many other shrines that, apart from the *dargah,* or burial shrine, formed part of a larger network of devotion to deceased Sufi saints and their living representatives.

Studies of Sufi shrines and their patrons tend to focus on the *dargah* and the Sufi lodge (*khanaqah*) as the central venues for ritual performances. While the presence of women is noticeable at these two types of shrines, their activities, to all appearances, are the same as those of other pilgrims. The key to understanding that women can and do play a very significant

part in Sufism today—not only as pilgrims but, in many cases, as "ritual specialists" who mediate the power of the saint or, less often, as de facto *pir*s—lies in the smaller spaces that are not always readily apparent to the public. These smaller, ancillary spaces are part of a network of shrines where the (deceased) *pir*'s power has manifested itself, and they are often considered holy in their own right. They defy precise classification. Locally they may be referred to as *astana*s, *chilla gah*s, *maqbara*s, and *hujra gah*s, but in fact these terms can mean different things in different contexts and locations. Most of these auxiliary shrines are affiliated with a *dargah,* whether they are physically attached to it or located at a distance from it. While the *dargah* and *khanaqah* tend to be the primary sites of ritual activity for pilgrims who visit during major festival occasions, auxiliary shrines are often important sites of activity for pilgrims who reside nearby, particularly women. Often women come to pray at these smaller shrines, as others do, seeking to petition the saint and request his (or her) aid. Sometimes, however, they come to mediate the saint's power (*barakat*), working on behalf of other pilgrims who seek their services in such matters.

One of the keys to understanding the ways in which women can exercise spiritual authority as de facto *pir*s or "ritual specialists" is becoming acquainted with the "lesser-known" spaces in which they operate. Although in many of the large *dargah*s, the daughters, mothers, and wives of the saints buried within are venerated alongside them, the smaller Sufi *dargah*s, as well as the auxiliary shrines affiliated with large *dargah*s, provide more scope for women to operate autonomously on behalf of their disciples or clients. Women's ability to do so depends in part upon prevalent perceptions about the importance of these sacred places and the degree to which they are controlled by shrine management. Those shrines that are perceived by Sufis and pilgrims as being key centers of Sufi life outside of the immediate locality, those that are well-endowed, and those that draw pilgrims from a wide spectrum of classes, castes, and religious communities often fall under the cooperative jurisdiction and management of the head of the order and servants of the shrine.

In the town of Bihar Sharif, my husband, Father Jackson, and I visited a shrine that appeared to be a place of primarily women's ritual activity. The shrine, a private prayer chamber (*hujra gah*) used by Sharaf al-din Maneri, is part of a complex of institutions and buildings located in Bihar Sharif, all belonging to the Firdausi Sufi order, which, according to S. A. A. Rizvi, is a collateral line of the Suhrawardi order. The Firdausi order established itself in Bihar in the fourteenth century and is popular there. Thanks to Sharaf al-din Maneri, the order is also well-known in other parts of

India and in Pakistan, though it has not flourished outside of Bihar and Bengal. Sharaf al-din's *hujra gah* is part of a larger complex of buildings managed by the Bihar Sharif branch of the Firdausi order. It is located near the *khanaqah-i muʿazzam*, where the Shah Sahib[2] and his family live, and where he receives clients and disciples, the majority of whom are local women. Also included in the complex is an Islamic institution for higher learning (*madrasa*); a large building that was, on my first visit in 1996, still under construction and that, I was told, would be a kind of dormitory or hospice for visitors and for students at the *madrasa;* and a small, locked prayer chamber that had been used by Sharaf al-din's mother, which few pilgrims seemed to know about, and fewer still could visit, as it required special permission from the Shah Sahib. Of all these buildings, Sharaf al-din's *hujra gah* stood out clearly as a shrine that was important to local women pilgrims. It was a place where they could operate unsupervised in their activities, a place where some women—I would later find—could act as ritual agents on behalf of clients, sometimes in conjunction with and sometimes in contrast to the "work" carried out by the Shah Sahib.

The distance between discourses about the role that women play in the orders and the "lived religion"[3] that women experience daily was marked in Maner. There we were taken on a tour of the *khanaqah* complex belonging to the Maner Firdausi order. Part of the *khanaqah* also houses the Shah Sahib's family, which consists of his wife, son, and six daughters. The complex contains the room in which Sharaf al-din was born as well as a number of other chambers used by local pilgrims and disciples of the Shah Sahib for group prayer. The chambers are all considered sacred sites inscribed with the charismatic power (*baraka*) of Sharaf al-din and important members of his family. These include Sharaf al-din's mother, Bibi Raziya, who lies buried by his side in Bihar Sharif; his brother, Khalil al-din, the oldest son, who established the *khanaqah* and succeeded his father, Yahya Maneri, as head of the order; and Yahya Maneri, who lies buried beside his own mother in a nearby *dargah* complex that draws hundreds of pilgrims from Bihar and Bengal each year.

The burial of Yahya and Sharaf al-din beside their mothers drew these women into the orbit of daily supplications to and in the name of these Sufi *shaikh*s, thus marking their importance as focal points of devotion intimately connected with the spiritual development and guidance of their saintly sons. The importance of the mother of Sharaf al-din as a source of spiritual guidance and comfort to him intrigued me, but would not become clear until long after I returned to Bihar in the winter of 1998. What did emerge that day in early August 1996 was the complicated nature of

gendered discourses surrounding the roles of Bibi Raziya and her female descendants in participating in and sustaining the institutions and practices that defined the Maner Firdausi order.

To my question of why women couldn't become *pir*s or *shaikh*s, our young host replied it was because they were in *parda*. The answer surprised me all the more because our host was herself a young woman observing *parda,* the third-youngest daughter of the Shah Sahib. This was her first time meeting Father Jackson in person, although he had been a frequent visitor to the *khanaqah* during his thirty-odd years of living in Bihar and enjoyed a close friendship with her father. From our first meeting, this woman, Naila Firdausi, struck me as unusually confident and poised in mixed-gender company, aside from being impressively knowledgeable about the history of the order, the lives of the Firdausi saints, and the day-to-day ritual activities that took place at the *dargah* and *khanaqah* complexes. As was the case with the Gudri Shah women, she would become a valuable source of insight into how women's participation in the world of Sufi shrines in North India challenges but also sustains prevalent ideals of Islamic womanhood, the central focus of this study.

## The Research Setting: Sufi Shrines and Circles

My observations of women suggested that questions of dominance, subordination, power, agency, and authority; resistance and sovereign consciousness; and the relationship between ideas about Islamic "authenticity" and "lived" Islamic traditions as these play out in the lives of women who are active in the world of Sufi shrines were germane to any inquiry about the discrepancies between prescriptions for and descriptions of women's activities. Thus my discussion of colonial-era perceptions of Sufis, shrines, and women in chapter 1 draws upon approaches found in subaltern studies, praxis theory, and recent studies in South Asian Islam, particularly those that use deconstructionist and postmodern critiques to develop an analytical model for understanding some of the operational aspects of relationships of dominance and subordination. While exposing some of the difficulties with such analyses in relation to the articulation of ideals of Islamic womanhood and the gendering of the body, this study attempts to move beyond facile binary oppositions to a pragmatic hermeneutics that allows for interplay between the cohesive force of universalizing symbols (such as as Islam, Shari'a, Sufi "tradition," or *parda/hijab*) and specific, context-driven constructions of gender identity that are being shaped by ongoing sociocultural processes.

Drawing on two ideas elaborated in the next chapter, namely that it is possible for subaltern groups to develop a sovereign consciousness that both imbibes and rejects elements of a dominant framework of reference, and that the source for such a dialectic may be located in the inherent instability of that framework, this study takes a constructivist approach to the question of how women are able to exercise authority in the shrine setting despite a lack of "official" sanction for that authority. However, far from denying the viability of some essentialist claims to "Islamic authenticity," I investigate the give-and-take between this ideal and Sufis' own individual explanations of why women's actions do or do not contradict it.

Since this study is concerned with the impact of dominant or prevalent beliefs upon articulations of Islamic (and Sufi) tradition and the ways in which these articulations can change the boundaries of dominant pre-scriptive ideals for women, it was important to develop some sense of what individuals considered to be the "Islamic" core of their actions and iden-tifications and how they saw these in relation to women's participation in Sufi shrine cults. My sense of this "core" is informed by the development of what Fazlur Rahman has called neo-Sufism or, more generally, a Sufism that has been shaped by movements of reform and revival as they unfolded throughout the Muslim world in the late nineteenth and early twentieth centuries. Though such expressions remained heterogeneous, making it difficult to classify them or their adherents according to a unified set of criteria, they all generally emphasized the need for centering practice on Islamic Shari‘a. According to Barbara Metcalf, the reform movements of this period served to orient Muslims on the whole toward the founda-tional scriptural sources of Islam.[4] These sources, then, may be seen as a crucial component of the idea of Shari‘a as a measure of the "authentic-ity" or "inauthenticity" of Islamic expression. They constitute important elements of arguments for and against women's participation in the Sufi milieu.

## Islamic Shari‘a as Reference Point

The question of what constitutes Shari‘a-based faith and practice remains problematic in debates over Islamic authenticity. In practice Shari‘a often functions more as a system of ethical precepts drawn from the foundational sources of Islam—especially the Qur’an and *sunna* of the Prophet Mu-hammad—than as a closed, strictly codified compendium of legislation. In the realm of jurisprudence Hanafi law remains the standard in South Asia, but quotidian discourses about Shari‘a are usually not centered on Hanafi

legalistic concerns. Rather, as Armando Salvatore and Muhammad Qasim Zaman have pointed out, the idea of Shari'a is often reworked to refer to multiple conceptual and contextually constituted references of Islamic faith and practice.[5] Nathan Brown's and Talal Asad's descriptions of an ongoing Islamic "discursive tradition,"[6] and Brinkley Messick's argument for Shari'a as "total discourse" representing the "core of Islamic knowledge" for Muslims of the "social mainstream,"[7] effectively capture the fluidity and dynamism of Shari'a as an operational, rather than fixed, aspect of institutionalized Islam. Alternatively Shari'a may be understood from a metaphysical perspective as an Islamic social order that prioritizes equilibrium over imbalance, sexual complementarity over rivalry, and awareness and actualization over ignorance and neglect of God's will, as Seyyed Hossein Nasr points out. This vision of Shari'a centers itself on the self-fulfillment of human beings and culminates in the realization of Unity (as both a human and a divine state of being).[8]

For reform-minded men who were closely connected with the institutions of Sufism in colonial India, men such as Ahmad Riza Khan Barelwi (d. 1921), Shari'a's practical fulfillment centered on the practice, or *sunna,* of the Prophet Muhammad.[9] For Maulana Ashraf 'Ali Thanawi (d. 1943), the renowned scholar of the Deoband school, Hanafi *fiqh,* as well as the foundational sources of Islam—the Qur'an and *sunna* of the Prophet—provided the basis for what Metcalf has referred to as an "ethical Islam of individual responsibility,"[10] a phrase that captures the balance that Thanawi saw as each believer's duty to strike, between reception and interpretation of the sources of faith. This idea is recaptured in the work of the contemporary Karachi-based scholar, jurist, and fellow Deobandi Mir Taqi 'Usmani, whose advocacy of *taqlid* (following past precedent) as the mainstay of Islamic jurisprudence belies a much more flexible position on the practical implementation of Shari'a law in light of contemporary circumstances and concerns.[11]

All these conceptions of Shari'a may be applied at some level to the understandings of the Sufi men and women who contributed their views to this study, even where their understanding of the Shari'a's prescriptions for gender roles and relationships were presented as singular. In one sense their collapsing of the idea of Shari'a into a homogeneous whole can be understood as a mnemonic technique intended for my benefit as an outsider and as an individual who has not been raised with Islam as a major reference (and self-reference) point. Yet the idea of Shari'a as a critical framework of reference for self-identification and action, a framework that exercises persuasive force on the belief of many Muslims that it is an unequivocal category with an essential reality, should not be dismissed.[12]

Following Gilmartin and Lawrence, this study investigates the interplay between such universalisms and the everyday, situational, and "living" expressions of belief and practice that produce diachronic discourses (and often, ambivalent perceptions) of the self-as-Muslim. One of the ways in which it does so is by looking at the material conditions that give rise to such productions. In particular these conditions may be partly understood within the context of key historical "sites" of sweeping socioeconomic change.

Although Sufism in north India is historically and (in many cases) culturally connected with Sufism in other parts of India, Pakistan, and Bangladesh, it is also very distinct. The development of North Indian Sufism coincides with the rise of Islamic empires in the Subcontinent from the thirteenth century onward. While Sufism (and Islam) had arrived in South India centuries earlier, it did not enjoy the widespread influence that it did in the north and the Deccan, where substantial imperial patronage under the Delhi sultans, Mughals, and later the British; the settlement of prominent and charismatic *shaikh*s of the Chishti, Suhrawardi, Qadiri, Naqshbandi, and Firdausi orders, coupled with the efforts of their followers in spreading the influence of these orders; and the greater numbers of Muslims in the northern and Deccani regions (Muslims who, even if nominally, identified with the foundational symbols of Islam, which the early *shaikh*s of these orders emphasized as the cornerstones of Sufi belief and practice) all contributed to the enduring influence of Sufi institutions in these regions.

The shrines that I chose to survey are closely connected with what I think of as the "mainstream" or "establishment" Sufi orders; that is to say, those orders that have existed for many centuries, that have a widely recognized lineage of spiritual authorities, and that have historically produced the kind of *shaikh*s who emphasized Islamic foundational sources as the path stones to God. Although there are a number of shrines called Sufi that are connected with legendary heroes (such as the shrine of Salar Mas'ud in Bahraich) or mythical figures (such as the shrine of Shaikh Saddu in Bihar or Bon Bibi in Bengal), or that are administered by local government agencies rather than Sufi orders, I chose not to include these types of shrines in my survey, even if evidence pointed to a greater scope for women to act autonomously in these settings. Aside from the Qawwali singers who performed in the *mahfil-i rindan,* discussed in chapter 3, and the encounter with the woman I have described as a "ritual specialist" in chapter 4, the women who make up the subject of this study represent, more or less, the "spiritual elite" of Sufism, and so my interaction with the women pilgrims who frequent these shrines was limited. Since my interest was primarily in

the women who are able to perform the work of *pir*s, even to the point of being considered de facto *pir*s by many of their followers, it was necessary to limit most of my discussion to those women I could readily and consistently observe and converse with, and the women of Sufi families (and the female disciples of *pir*s) provided the most consistent opportunities to do this.

The primary reason for selecting the shrines that I did—those affiliated with Mu'in al-din Chishti in Ajmer Sharif and Sharaf al-din Maneri in Maner and Bihar Sharif—is that I wanted to be able to integrate both historical and ethnographic data into my analysis of contemporary Sufi shrines. This approach, I felt, would enable me to demonstrate the role of major historical events in transforming Sufi praxis and thus creating new opportunities for women's involvement. It would also help me clarify a number of issues germane to my investigation of women and Sufi shrines in contemporary India. First, focusing on shrines belonging to these establishment orders would allow me to use the rich historical, administrative, literary, and philosophical data available about them and their patrons, thus giving me a sense of how women—and questions about gender roles and relationships—figured into these accounts over time. Second, it would convey some sense of the history of women's involvement in Sufi institutions and thus situate my ethnographic data within a wider historical and institutional context of social, theological, economic, and political developments. Third, by comparing my data with historic and contemporary anthropological accounts of women and Sufi shrines in Middle Eastern and North African countries, I could get a better sense of how women's roles were distinct in the setting of Indian Sufism and what they shared with Sufis (and Muslims) elsewhere in the world. Finally, looking at the ways in which the idea of "normative" Islam was being articulated by the people I interviewed and observed (often with reference to Islamic and Sufi didactic texts), in conjunction with their explanations of women's participation in, or exclusion from, Sufi practices or ritual events, would give me a sense of how tensions between local cultural practices and transcendent Islamic values informed the experiences of Sufis, their families, and their followers. This last point underscores the importance that some scholars have accorded to the integration of "micronarratives" of lived religion and classic sacred texts as an indicator of the back-and-forth movement between the local and the transcendent that typifies the lives of most Muslims.[13]

In order to investigate the discrepancies between articulated ideals and lived experiences as these relate to the role of women in Sufi ritual life today, I decided to rely on a method of participant observation. In practice

this meant that I would try to be as flexible and adaptable as possible. Although I did conduct many formal, tape-recorded interviews, my efforts to do so often proved frustrating, since some people felt uncomfortable having their words recorded, while others were so busy that I could not interview them at any length. Much of the time, I simply had to spend many hours in a shrine or *khanaqah*, sitting, talking informally, observing, and listening to people. Afterward I would rush home to write down the information I had collected or would use a tape recorder to document my notes between the time I left the site of research and the time I arrived home. I had decided early on that I would not only observe what was going on around me, but also personally participate in as many rituals, events, and ceremonies as possible. I also tried to develop a relationship with the saints whose shrines I was investigating, not only by spending time in these places but also by praying at the shrines I visited, using prayers from my own Christian tradition as well as Arabic prayers I had learned over the years, like the *fatiha* and the recitation of the *ayat al-kursi.*

As I saw it, participant observation meant that, to the extent that it was possible, I would try to become a part of the society being observed. It meant building friendships with the *pirs, pirzade, khadim*s, and disciples of the Gudri Shah and Firdausi orders,[14] living in their environment, and spending as much time as I could sitting in shrines—sometimes talking to the women who had gathered there, sometimes praying alone, unobtrusively, making myself inconspicuous. In order to facilitate this process, I dressed as an Indian Muslim woman would, in tunic and pants (*shalwar-kamiz*), with a long scarf (*dupatta, chadar*) wrapped around my head and upper body. This facilitated my entry into shrines, and as a fairly light-complexioned African American with straightened hair who (eventually) spoke Hindi and Urdu well enough to be mistaken for Indian by many people (particularly those who had had little direct contact with foreigners, or even with Indians from outside their region), I was able to move around relatively unnoticed, simply a woman among other women pilgrims. Sometimes I think I went overboard in my zeal to show respect for the environment. Strictly speaking, one is expected to cover the head when inside of the shrine (and this is true for both men and women). This is not always the case, however. For instance it is not necessary to cover one's head while in the *khanaqah* (unless the *khanaqah* is located inside the *dargah* where the saint's remains lie), but I often did. On one occasion I was interviewing a *pirzada* man at the Mitan Ghat *dargah* in Patna City. We sat in an open area in the outer courtyard, adjacent to the mausoleum. I had covered myself with my *dupatta* carefully so that it would not slip when I moved. At one point in the conversation, he asked me why I was

covering myself; it was unnecessary to cover my head in the courtyard, he assured me. I declined to remove my *dupatta,* which only seemed to amuse him. I was eager, however, to convey the impression that I was not "loose," which is what many Indians believe about Western women. Since many of their impressions about the West are negative, based (at that time) largely on American television shows such as *Baywatch* and *The Bold and the Beautiful,* I felt I had to be extremely modest in my dress and behavior to counter the weight of assumptions about my morality.

Despite these efforts, forging friendships with the Sufis I wanted to observe was not always easy. Many of them were university-educated and keenly aware of the negative stereotypes of Muslims portrayed in the Western media. They were also (justifiably) wary of Western scholars, who they felt were not sympathetic to Muslims and, worse, portrayed Muslim women as oppressed victims of a misogynistic religion. This was not the case with the Gudri Shahs, who took me in as though I was family and with whom I have forged a deep friendship that has endured. In Bihar, however, my inquiries often met with suspicion. Why did I want to know about women? What was I going to write about them? Although I did establish friendships with the Firdausis of Maner, especially the Shah Sahib's daughter who had first taken Father Jackson, my husband, and me on a tour of the *khanaqah* complex of Sharaf al-din Maneri, I was not able to develop genuine friendships with many people in Bihar Sharif, and most of the *pirzade* women very politely avoided answering my questions. There were two exceptions, however. One of the sisters of the Shah Sahib of Bihar Sharif [15] was very open and warm. The first time I met her was in February 1998, after being invited into the women's quarters at the Bihar Sharif *khanaqah* during Sharaf al-din Maneri's *'urs.* I entered the room to find a large group of women staring intently at me. None spoke, and no one smiled. The atmosphere was extremely tense. The *pir*'s sister (who at the time was visiting from Patna, where she lives with her husband at Mitan Ghat *dargah*) took my hand and talked to me gently, then introduced me to her mother. She disappeared for a minute to retrieve a sweet dish for me to eat. As I ate it, trying not to look too uncomfortable with so many women staring at me, one of the women told me the name of the dish I was eating was *makuti.* I misunderstood. "Kutti?" (which means "bitch"), I asked, surprised and a little shocked. The women all burst out laughing, but thankfully the ice was broken by that faux pas. Later the *pirzada* woman who had shown me such kindness would answer many of my questions about women and Sufism, as would her husband, a scholar of Arabic and son of the *pir* of Mitan Ghat *dargah.*

One challenge in speaking with the *pirzade* women of Bihar, I soon found, was that I had to go through the men first. I would interview the men, then after a few days ask if I could meet with the women, if they had not already invited me into the women's quarters themselves. Many of the men I interviewed did not believe I could comprehend the more difficult aspects of Sufism and tended to talk to me accordingly. True, in the first few months of research, my language skills were not what they should have been, and it took me some time to get used to different accents (which vary widely from state to state). Even after I had become accustomed to the way people spoke in Bihar, however, men tended to address my inquiries by going off on long tangents about subjects I had not asked about. It was difficult at times to turn the conversation back to where I had begun. On the other hand, women's answers were always straightforward and unpretentious. Sometimes they would tell me to go talk to the men, insisting that they knew nothing. After some careful prodding, however, I was able to convince them that their opinions were valuable to me, since my project was about women and not just about what men thought of women. After a few initially awkward attempts, I found that some of the women I interviewed were willing to speak more frankly and at length. Indeed they knew much more than they had at first been willing to admit, although they tended to censor themselves whenever a male relative came into the room. This was not merely out of modesty—if men were present, they often dominated the conversation, wittingly or unwittingly.

While making general observations about the interactions between shrine servants and pilgrims was not difficult, I was not easily able to enter the "inner circles" of the orders I chose to work with (except in the case of the Gudri Shah order). Yet in some ways my gender and appearance gave me advantages that many other researchers did not have—as a woman I had access to the world of the *zanana,* or the women's quarters, from which the *parda*-practicing women of the family (particularly older women) were shielded from the eyes of the general public. Perhaps because I was not always immediately identifiable as a "foreigner," I found that many women pilgrims were willing to open up to me. As a person who was interested in Sufism both personally and professionally, I found that men and women were willing to engage me in lengthy discussions of faith and religion. On the other hand, my ability to blend in with the people I wanted to study sometimes proved to be a stumbling block, and I felt compelled to assume a much more subdued, modest, and quiet disposition than I typically demonstrate. At times I was asked not to turn up in Muslim neighborhoods without a male escort—the danger of hooligans was the explanation I sometimes

received, but I later realized that it also could damage the honor (*'izzat*) of my male hosts to have a lone, strange (presumably Indian) woman showing up at their door. As many of my colleagues have mentioned in conversation, white women researchers' ready "visibility" can sometimes act as a counterweight to everyday restrictions their female Indian subjects and colleagues faced, since foreign women are generally not expected to abide by the same rules of social interaction as most Indian (local or foreign) women. On the other hand, I rarely faced the kind of sexual harassment that my white (particularly blond) colleagues did. As psychologist and writer Sudhir Kakar has noted about a large percentage of men in India, "The Indian woman is a maa, a beti or a bahu for these men. The white woman, on the other hand, is fair game. She is a whore."[16]

A reasonable compromise solution seemed to be to find a female research assistant, at least for the Bihar portion of my study. This, however, proved ultimately unsatisfying. I did not want to hire a male research assistant because I felt that women pilgrims would be intimidated by the presence of a man asking questions and would not open up to me as readily as if I were alone or with another woman. I sought out female research assistants in Patna, where I was based. (I traveled every week to Bihar Sharif or Maner, staying for days at a time, then returned to Patna for more interviews and archival research.) For a long time, no one would let his wife or daughter accompany me to my research sites, since it was considered inappropriate and too dangerous. Finally a friend introduced me to one woman, Sa'ida Varsi, a local radio personality who was willing to assist me in visitations to shrines and interviews with their servants. What was nice about this arrangement was that like me, Sa'ida was married (and therefore more "respectable" in the eyes of the men I was interviewing), and she also had a personal interest in Sufism, which meant that she would be sensitive and thoughtful in asking questions. However, this arrangement did not last long, because Sa'ida developed serious health problems and could no longer assist me. Nevertheless I was grateful for her presence, for if I neglected to ask an important question, she would remind me of my omission or bring up the point herself.

I often felt constrained in asking insensitive questions of women and did not always want to broadcast my "outsideness" by so doing. Because of this I was sometimes forced to choose between digging deep for answers and letting go of my desire to obtain information about a particular issue because it clearly made some people uncomfortable. I often had to decide between maintaining the trust I had built with my subjects, thus foregoing information that at the time seemed important, and taking the risk of offending my subjects by prying into areas they were reluctant to discuss. I

eventually learned a very important skill: how to get the answers I needed without asking direct questions. Here subtlety and assuming the deferential and modest stance of other women I observed was important, for it communicated that I was willing to try to enter into the cultural universe of my interviewees, even if we both knew that someday I would leave and return to my own, very different, world. Sometimes I was surprised to find that people who had formerly been reluctant to discuss the subject of women with me suddenly opened up with a torrent of information. To this day I'm not sure how I managed to get some of the answers I did, and I certainly did not always succeed in getting answers at all. There were many frustrating hours and days talking with *pirzade* women about the weather, the latest news reports, politics—anything but the kind of information I really wanted to get at—and during the first six months of residence in India, I often felt I would not be able to obtain enough information to complete my research.

Luckily I did get enough information—more than I could use, in fact. The real breakthrough came with the friendships I developed with the Gudri Shah Chishtis and the Maner Firdausi *pirzade* women. Despite these friendships, however, many people I interviewed within the two orders were reluctant to discuss the issues I brought up. The shortcoming of interviewing, I quickly found, was that people often express their ideal, or what they would like the interviewer to believe. When it came to the question of women, most people I interviewed took a moral or theological stand (referring to the Qur'an, Sufi, and Hadis traditions) to show how Islam "forbids" certain roles to women or to show that what they hold as "normative" (that is, that women and men must not mix in the ritual setting or that women must observe *parda*) exists as an absolute truth. I found that the veracity of such claims could only be tested by direct observation over a substantial period of time. For example I was told by a few of the Gudri Shah *pirzade* women that women could not attend communal ritual events. Yet I was invited, along with some of the other visiting women pilgrims, to several musical assemblies during the death-day anniversary festival for Mu'in al-din Chishti. I pointed this out to the *pir*'s sisters. "Yes, but it is wrong!" one of them insisted, and she explained that they themselves did not attend these assemblies. The one exception was their youngest sister, a girl of fifteen who regularly sat with me and other female *murid*s and associates in these events. Months later, and for many years afterward, I returned to Ajmer to attend the death-day anniversary festival of the *pirzade* women's father, the former *pir* of the order, which a number of disciples, associates of the order, and their friends also attended. I found that the women all did indeed attend the *'urs* ceremonies held on this occasion,

though they managed to convey—through body gestures and their placement in the *sama'* assembly—that although they were in attendance they were clearly separate from male pilgrims.

Considering these examples of women's involvement in Sufi circles, and in light of the historical and ethnographic evidence that will be discussed in subsequent chapters, I suggest that women have always, on some level, participated in Sufi ritual life in ways that may seem to challenge or contradict prevalent religious and cultural ideals about gender segregation and women's subordination to male authority. The difference today is their increasing visibility—both physically and in contemporary narratives that seek to correct the misperception of these women as being essentially "hidden" and undervalued within the hierarchical structures of the Sufi orders. It is only with time and long-term acquaintance that such revelations become possible, and the boundaries between discourse and practice are revealed to be more fluid than might initially be assumed.

# . Acknowledgments .

Many people and organizations have helped me in this lengthy endeavor. Funding for the initial research was made possible by grants and fellowships from the Mellon Foundation, the Fulbright Foundation, the Charlotte Newcombe Foundation, and the University of California, Berkeley. In India the Asian Development Research Foundation, the ARCE music archives in New Delhi, the Asiatic Society of Bengal Library in Calcutta, and the Khuda Bakhsh Oriental Public Library in Patna allowed me access to valuable archives and other materials. Thanks to all the employees of these institutions, who were most generous with their time, encouragement, and assistance. The final stages of this effort could not have been reached without the help and guidance of the staff at the University of South Carolina Press. I am especially grateful to Jim Denton and Karen Rood.

This book has undergone many transformations from the first draft to its present form. It is a much stronger piece of work thanks to the comments and advice given to me over the years as I struggled to hone it into something that would do justice to the women Sufis whose lives are discussed, and to the men who support them. Suggestions by Jack Hawley, Fran Pritchett, Joyce Flueckiger, Carl Ernst, Richard Eaton, David Gilmartin, Shahid Amin, the late Qeyamuddin Ahmed, Mohammad Talib, and Tony Stewart were especially important to the early stages of the book's development, while it benefited in no small way from close readings of later chapter drafts by Barbara Metcalf and Amy Bard. Gail Minault, Art Buehler, Katherine Ewing, Rob Rozehnal, Anna Bigelow, Francis Robinson, and Leslie Peirce also provided valuable advice through successive revisions, while Elizabeth Buettner, Jenny Takhar, Diya Mehra, Arun Ranganathan, Huma Dar, Janet Chawla, M. Sivanesin, and other friends in India and the United States provided moral support, a place to stay, and encouragement. Zahurul Miyan, Inam Miyan, and Apa have been sources of guidance, hope, and love to me over these long years, as have Mahnur, Meher, Bahar, and Sajid, with their much-appreciated blend of good-natured teasing and serious lecturing. Along with them I thank the Gudri

Shah *murid*s, especially Faiz bhai, Hamu bhai, Akhtar Miyan, Radha, and Jamil bhai for their friendship (and occasional clarifications) over the years. I also want to thank the Shah Sahibs of the Maner and Bihar Sharif Firdausi orders, Pir Shamim ud-din Munammi (and family) of Mitan Ghat *dargah,* the Firdausi women, and the *khadim*s of the *dargah*s of Mu'in al-din Chishti and Sharaf al-din Maneri, for their hospitality and willingness to entertain my sometimes naive questions. Thanks are also due to the families who shared their homes with me during my visits to India—J. P. and Asha Singh, Bimal and Vina Chadha and Ammi, and especially Subhash and Niki Arora (and Raju and Lakshmi), with whom I have developed a dear and lasting friendship over these years. Last but not least, I want to thank Jeff, who was with me during the greater period of research for this book. Although our marriage did not last, our friendship has endured, and for that I am grateful.

This project has involved more work than I ever could have imagined, and it is a big relief to see it finally come to fruition. I hope I have done some justice to the subject of Sufi women. Whatever glitches, misunderstandings, errors, or omissions still remain in the text are, in the end, my full responsibility. To anyone else who helped and whom I may have inadvertently omitted in these pages, you know who you are. *Thank you.*

# . Note on Transliteration .

Aside from the 'ayn (represented by ') and the glottal stop or hamza (represented by '), diacritical marks have not been used in the text of this book, but as an aid to the scholar, they are included in the index. Using a transliteration system that will satisfy all readers of Hindi, Urdu, Arabic, and Persian at the same time is a daunting task. I have in most cases prioritized the Urdu spelling of words, and in doing so I have followed, more or less, the system of transliteration used in John T. Platts's *A Dictionary of Urdu, Classical Hindi, and English*. For Hindi I followed the system used in R. S. MacGregor's *The Oxford-English Hindi Dictionary*. All non-English words have been italicized, except for the word *Sufi* and other words that have become common usage in English, such as *Qur'an, Hadith, Imam, jihad,* and *Shari'a*. The *izafa,* whether Persian or Urdu, is represented by *–i,* except in the case of book titles whose original language has been transliterated by the translator. The Arabic words that end with *ha* or *ta marbuta* are marked with a final *–a,* except in the following words: *khanaqah, Shah Daulat,* and most words ending in *–qah* or *–gah*. Following convention, I have used the Arabic article *al-* in all cases, instead of eliding it with the succeeding "moon" letter, as would be warranted in the spoken forms of Arabic, Persian, and Urdu. Dates are given as c.e. to avoid confusion. In most cases plural forms are represented by the addition of an *s* at the end of a word instead of using the plural Arabic forms, which is not common in spoken Urdu.

# Introduction

## Women's Activities and
## Sufi Shrines—Some Perspectives

A number of ethnographic studies conducted since the late 1970s[1] have suggested that there is a substantial gap between discourses about women's participation in ritual life and women's lived experiences in the world of Sufi shrines. While this issue has produced several promising studies of the role women play in contemporary Sufi praxis, the subject remains largely unexplored. Historical, theological, metaphysical, and philosophical studies of the question of gender in Sufism have yielded a rich tapestry of discussion about its ultimate ephemerality in the search for God. However, the question of living, flesh-and-blood women—particularly those considered saintly, possessed of divine attributes, or capable of mediating the power of a deceased Sufi *shaikh* (*barakat*)—has helped to fuel stereotypes about the "dubious" nature of Sufism today. At the same time, the relationship between women and Sufi shrines is cited as evidence of Sufism's greater regard for women than "orthodox" or "scripturalist" Islam. Alternatively, and particularly among feminist scholars, women's activities in Sufi shrine settings are characterized as a manifestation of resistance to an Islamic patriarchy that is threatened by women's power, agency, or increasing public presence. None of these paradigms effectively answers the question of how women figure in contemporary Sufi praxis, nor can they address the question that is the central concern of this book, namely, how women can operate in the world of Sufi shrines as spiritual authorities and be recognized as such, even by those who otherwise condemn or criticize their activities.

### Women as Participants: A Disconnect
### between Discourse and Praxis

While women frequently appear as pilgrims, clients, and disciples in written narratives about saints and shrines, much less is known, or reported,

about those activities in which they are able to exercise a greater degree of agency and autonomy. As members of the family of a *pir* (*pirzade*), they are privy to information and knowledge about the shrine and its saints that the average pilgrim does not possess. As "ritual specialists" they may act on behalf of other women by petitioning the saint, and as healers and wise women, they may serve as the advisers and spiritual guides for male and female clients, although with few exceptions they are denied official recognition as *pir*s and *sajjada nishin*s. They appear sometimes as storytellers and composers, and less frequently as performers at the *qawwali* musical assemblies held on major commemorative occasions. As the relatives of particularly prominent Sufi masters, they may be buried in shrine complexes, widely considered as saints, and venerated as such alongside their pious male relatives. A few have had shrines erected solely in their honor, as in the case of Bibi Kamalo, the maternal aunt of Shaikh Sharaf al-din Maneri, or Bibi Fatima Sam, whose tomb now lies in obscurity in the old Indraprastha section of Delhi but was at one time frequented by such notables as the fourteenth-century Chishti *shaikh* Nizam al-din Auliya.

These facts were revealed only with patient prodding, and even then only after I had spent many months among the Sufi families who became the subjects of this study. I came to believe that their initial reluctance to discuss these aspects of women's experiences did not simply come from a religious or cultural sense of the impropriety of doing so, but rather that it was rooted in deeply entrenched, socially constructed and mediated attitudes about how women's participation (or lack thereof) in ritual life at Sufi shrines reflects prevalent ideals about Islamic womanhood. Thus an important agenda of this study was to go beyond a description of how women's participation in the world of Sufi shrines challenges and contests some of these ideals by investigating the ways in which participants also internalize and project dominant discourses in Islam about male-female relationships and the proper place of women within collective ritual spaces. This would require an integrated approach to the questions of language, action, and meaning as these are embedded within social experience but also shaped by a shared sense of culture, (meta)history, and faith.

In the past quarter century there has been an increase in the number of studies being published (and republished) in English about women's lived experiences in the Sufi milieu. Studies that have taken the historical approach[2] have focused primarily on the biographical literature of Sufism (*tazkira, tabaqat*) or on poetry, oral histories, and legendary accounts as sources of information for women's lives. Ethnographic and anthropological studies have relied on methods of participant observation to paint a picture of women's religious beliefs and observations in local contexts.[3] A

few publications featuring autobiographical and didactic writing by Sufi women have also recently appeared.[4] Finally practitioners of Sufism have offered a glimpse into women's experiences through descriptive and theological treatments of their lives as practicing Sufis or as de facto *shaikha*s.[5] These studies have all made important and much-needed contributions to our knowledge of the historical, theoretical, and practical aspects of women's experiences in the world of Sufi shrines and have significantly informed my investigation of women's lives. Still, there is a need for studies that can situate women's experiences in both their wider religious and historical contexts and their particular, "lived" aspects, and in so doing convey an integrated picture of how women's activities in the Sufi context have changed over time and in response to historical, cultural, and socioeconomic variables. It is in light of this need that this book is situated; it investigates women's lived experiences as they relate to three Sufi families in India: the Gudri Shah branch of the Chishti order, the Bihar Sharif branch of the Firdausi order, and the Maner branch of the Firdausi order.

The history of the Chishti order is well known among scholars of South Asian Islam, while the fourteenth-century writing of the Firdausi *shaikh* Sharaf al-din Maneri, the writing of Hazrat Zahur al-Hasan Sharib of the Gudri Shahs, and the prolific literary output of other prominent *shaikh*s and disciples of these two orders provide valuable insight into their historical development. Using historiographic information produced by members of these orders and their chroniclers, including biographical compendia (*tazkira, tabaqat*), recorded discourses of important *shaikh*s (*malfuzat*), surveys produced by servants of the British Raj, and secondary sources produced by scholars since the 1970s, this study seeks to understand the role of major historical events and sociocultural processes in transforming Sufi praxis and thus creating new opportunities for women's involvement. Thus the data derived from observations at a number of Chishti and Firdausi shrines and from my interviews with members of these orders and their sympathizers appears within a comparative, interdisciplinary framework that suggests how discourses about women in the public sphere have shifted over time.

The ethnographic research for this study took place primarily in the western and eastern states of Rajasthan and Bihar, and intermittently between 1996 and 2002, with the longest stretch from September 1997 to August 1998. The women who contributed their stories to this study live, work, and pursue moral and spiritual development, as well as help others pursue their own, in the towns of Ajmer, where the famed Chishti *shaikh* Mu'in al-din Chishti lies buried; Bihar Sharif, site of the burial shrine of the Firdausi scholar-*shaikh* Sharaf al-din Maneri; Maner, birthplace of

Sharaf al-din and final resting place of his equally saintly father, Shaikh Yahya Maneri; and Patna, where several descendants of these *shaikh*s and their families reside today. In light of the paucity of ethnographic data on contemporary Sufi women in South Asia within the scope of the establishment orders, I also liberally incorporated into my study (and my interviews) the research conducted by others "on the ground," particularly the work of Joyce Burkhalter Flueckiger on a female Muslim healer in Hyderabad (now deceased), affectionately known as "Amma." This work helped me to gauge individuals' reactions to the existence of real-life examples of female *pir*s, to develop a taxonomy of praxis among such women, and to get a better sense of how common (and accepted) the phenomenon is.

### Dominance and Authority as Framework for Articulations of Selfhood

The idea of the subaltern as both victim of superior structural forces and as possessor of a consciousness outside of the influence of those forces, an idea that was germane to the earliest wave of scholarship on the topic, has been effectively challenged in many works of postcolonial and postmodern theory that have appeared within the past quarter century.[6] However, these initial forays into subaltern consciousness have opened up many promising avenues for further investigation of relationships of dominance, subordination, and power as expressed through social, economic, religious, and political structures of organization; cultural production; and the material conditions under which individuals, groups, and communities engage in processes of exchange. Ranajit Guha (1997), Douglas Haynes and Gyan Prakash (1991), and James Scott (1985), among others, attempt to derigidify the idea of structured power relationships between dominant/elite and subordinate/subaltern groups by looking at balance-of-power shifts. Rather than characterizing these shifts as great upheavals by subordinate groups bent on undermining a dominant structure (or dominant culture), they contend that dominant structures and hegemonies are inherently unstable mechanisms of organization and power that produce elements of "resistance" within them.[7]

In works on peasant rebellion, Guha (1983) and Prakash (1991) investigate the processes by which subaltern peasant and tribal groups, in imbibing, adapting, and rejecting elements of the dominant culture, developed a sovereign (though not autonomous) consciousness that enabled them to subvert and even fracture this culture. Prakash shows how, even while reproducing the language and principles of upper-caste Maliks, the Bhuniyas in southern Bihar used performances of traditional oral narratives to

problematize and reformulate their position as outcastes and laborers who are dependent upon the Maliks.[8] Ultimately, however, this did not lead to a break with the dominant culture, nor did it change the socioeconomic position of Bhuniyas. Rather it pointed to the ability of Bhuniyas to self-constitute in ways that contested the operation of power as "naturally" rather than historically and materially determined.[9] Drawing on paradigms of "resistance," Guha elaborates how peasant groups subscribed to ideologies of subservience rooted in such Hindu religious and social paradigms as *bhakti* (total submission to divine and human superiors as an indication of spiritual commitment) and the caste system.[10] Yet these paradigms contained—or accommodated—elements of negation or reversal that could be expressed in ritual observances as seen in the celebrations of social inversion during Teyyam in Malabar or Holi in much of northern and central India. While these observances represented temporary, prescribed reversals of the dominant order, they nonetheless harbored the potential for more sustained changes. Insurgency, on the other hand, was meant to disrupt and undermine such order. Together these strategies worked to alter the borders of the structure of relations between dominant and subordinate.[11] According to Guha, these relationships predated and outlived British colonial rule and manifested as a system of relations that contained, produced, and reproduced antagonistic elements that ultimately served to deny ultimate authority to any of its individual components.[12]

The production of counterhegemonic elements within a dominant framework of reference is also illustrated in Guha's later study of the colonial state in India. He characterizes this state as a "paradox" that wholly resembled neither the British colonial power, with its championing of democracy in Europe and support of both feudalism and capitalist-driven "improvement" among its Indian subjects, nor the Indian bourgeois elites who both accommodated and agitated against British imperialism on the one hand and what Guha calls "pre-capitalist values and institutions in Indian society" on the other. Guha stresses the inherent fragility of British claims to represent the Indian past, arguing that the production of colonialist historiographies was an "exercise in dominance"[13] serving to aid British efforts to exploit the resources of the land. However, its by-products, particularly programs of English education that sought to displace Indian "tradition," linked the educated Indian to the state apparatus and developed a class of Indian elites who wholly subscribed to the (ostensibly) Western values of self-determination and liberalism. It served, then, to produce an educated elite culture among Indians that resembled neither the liberal-bourgeois capitalist culture of late-nineteenth-century Britain nor the pre-capitalist culture of India. The educated Indian political elite imbibed, and

learned to manipulate, the language of democracy and democratic institutions for reasons of expediency, but they did so while also tolerating, participating in, and sustaining unequal relations of dominance and subordination with their subaltern neighbors.

The British ultimately failed to contain the resistance of the subject population by either force or accommodation, and the Indian bourgeois elite proved unable to cast off what the feminist writer Audre Lorde called the "master's tools" in order to dismantle long-held feudal and semifeudal practices and concepts of power and authority. Thus, in the postcolonial state, ruling Indian elites could not truly command the allegiance of subaltern groups who did not, on the whole, benefit from the expansion of capital that followed the demise of the colonialist state. It is this failure of the Indian elites to break away from the structures of control, order, and persuasion (dominance) established in the British colonial state, and to ensure the general consent of the subject population (hegemony) to its ruling authority, that Guha and, following him, Partha Chatterjee (1993) refer to as a "dominance without hegemony."

These dominant-subordinate, produced-producing paradigms are also evident within relationships among colonial-era and postcolonial European observers; secular, English-educated Indian elites; the Sufi orders and their male representatives; and the women who patronize Sufi shrines. Many of the essentializing discourses about women's participation in Sufi shrine and *pir* "cults" that were promoted by European and secular, English-educated Indian observers in the colonial era affected Sufis' own attitudes toward women. Both European and Indian observers weighed their sense of an "authentic" or "orthodox" Islam against shrine-based practices found among contemporary Muslims and found the gap between the two uncomfortably large. Sufis also had their own sense of "authentic" Islam, at least those among them who represented the elite, and this sense was often colored by their education in the Islamic sciences (in such institutions as the local *madrasa*), their familiarity with key texts written by respected and renowned Sufi *shaikh*s (such as Ahmad Sirhindi), or their participation in the Hajj and subsequent periods of study in Middle Eastern centers of Islamic learning such as al-Azhar,[14] though even those who represented the educated elites among Sufis remained ambivalent toward the question of how local beliefs and practices conformed (or not) to that sense of Islam. This is perhaps illustrative of Muhammad Arkoun's sense of Islam as a tradition that

> is informed and conditioned by changing backgrounds, teaching, guiding, and conditioning these backgrounds in return. This interaction is

translated into the self-entitlement of each Muslim community to incarnate and monopolize the authentic expression of the "orthodox" tradition. . . . there is no Tradition with capital "T," but traditions that are more-or-less influenced by the scriptural tradition developed under the impact of four ideological forces: a central state, writing, learned written culture and thought—orthodoxy. . . . The dialectic tension develops everywhere, in all contexts between the sacred Tradition and local, ethnographic traditions. . . . The affirmation, promotion, protection or oppression and negation of the person will then depend on the social structures, the collective representations and the scale of values enforced by each central power or leading authority in limited communities such as brotherhoods, clans and tribes.[15]

Among Sufi and non-Sufi elites in the Indo-Pakistan subcontinent, the pilgrimage of women to saints' shrines, their participation in mixed-gender assemblies, their observance of rituals involving possession, and their practice of making vows to a deceased saint have often been seen as evidence of either a general decline in Sufi practice or the illegitimacy of a particular order of Sufis. Yet as this study will demonstrate, women can at once subscribe to the general prescription that their participation in the institutions of Sufism (particularly where this involved their exercise of authority) should have limits and at the same time engage in behavior, including ritual behavior, that consciously or inadvertently undermines that prescription. This has been particularly true for the women of Sufi families and for female disciples of a *shaikh* who have come to be considered spiritually gifted. Their actions may be better understood within the context of important socioeconomic changes that have altered the views of Indian Muslims toward gender roles and relationships, particularly among the upwardly mobile, socially elite classes.

### Change and Continuity in India's Muslim Community

Prominent among these changes is the post-1857 state of Muslim intellectual elites in the northeastern swath of the country, particularly the area comprising Delhi, the United Provinces (UP), and Western Bengal (then comprising Bihar). In the wake of the Uprising of 1857, many of the UP-based *'ulama'* retreated to small towns such as Deoband, where a new phase of Islamic reform and revival was inaugurated toward the end of that century. While the initial reform movements, such as that led by Sayyid Ahmad Barelwi (d. 1831), were politically motivated (for example Sayyid Ahmad's role in the Pindari wars and his declaration of jihad against the

Sikh state), the reform movements of the latter part of that century focused more pointedly (though not exclusively) on the moral and spiritual reform of the Indian Muslim *umma*. Within those efforts of reform, the values of Islam came to be inscribed on the bodies of women as women's behavior in public and domestic spaces became a major subject of discussion by intellectual elites and the wider public. As such, women came to embody the values and fortunes of the broader Indian Muslim community, and that association acquired political currency in both the colonial and the postcolonial state. This was also true in the case of Hindu women.[16]

The connection could be readily observed in the literary output of Muslim men—many of them embodying dual sources of authority as both Sufi *shaikh*s and members of the *'ulama'*. In the first decades of the twentieth century there was a proliferation of didactic literature directed at the "improvement" of Muslim women. A number of these texts were written by men who had received training in the traditional Islamic sciences through the *madrasa* system, which itself had been undergoing systematic changes since the close of the preceding century.[17] Much of the literature they produced was initially modeled on older Persian *adab* literary forms and, as such, both enabled ties with older Islamic discursive traditions and forged new ones. Although Francis Robinson has effectively argued that print undermined the traditional sources of authority whereby knowledge was handed down from master to pupil in a prescribed manner that underscored the hierarchy of authority in Islamic circles of learning,[18] the reality was more complex. Print, coupled with a widening system of education in British India that targeted women as well as men, also helped to create new sources of authority, for those armed with education could avail themselves of Islamic (and/or secular) knowledge that opened their eyes to the wider parameters of Islam and contributed to a growing sense of Muslim selfhood that reached beyond local, regional, and even national borders. At the same time, these new forms of authority enabled some of the *'ulama'*—men who were the chief producers of demotic literature targeting women as objects of reform—to make the most of emerging cultural capital and extend their authority by means of these new technologies. Among their ranks were Sufi *shaikh*s. The willingness of these *shaikh*s and *'ulama'* to exploit the new textual technologies that print afforded them and thereby increase the awareness of other Muslims about their efforts toward Islamic *tajdid o islah*, renewal and reform, should not be underestimated.

Another important site of change lay within the shifts in orientation for some *shaikh*s who sought to expand the territorial boundaries of their influence. In so doing they also opened the doors for the women of their families to assume a greater amount of responsibility in ensuring the

proper functioning of the order. These *shaikh*s—described by Arthur Buehler as "traveling mediating *shaikh*s"—have been aided in their efforts by
innovations in transportation that made journeying vast distances, and
reaching large numbers of people, much more feasible from the latter part
of the nineteenth century onward.[19] Whether embarking on extended
"spiritual travel" tours or regularly departing their lodges (*khanaqah*s) for
journeys to different parts of the country to promulgate Sufism and meet
with disciples, admirers, and fellow Sufi leaders, they left the women of
their families behind to attend to the needs of disciples and petitioners at
home. At such times the wives and daughters of the *shaikh* often served as
"substitutes" in his absence, acting as counselors or go-betweens for the
pilgrims who came to the *khanaqah* seeking advice, assistance, or spiritual
guidance.[20]

Finally an emerging site of major socioeconomic change in contemporary Indo-Pakistan is the rise of a large urban middle class that increasingly
aspires to upward mobility.[21] Defining the parameters of this class is challenging, in part because of its social complexity. (In other words it com-
prises groups as disparate as former upper-class, upper-caste royalty,
divested of much of their wealth by the economic reforms of the 1950s, and
the most socially marginalized caste groups, some of whom became
wealthy in the economic boom decades of the 1990s.) However, in many
ways the values of today's middle classes in India mirror the social, cultural, and political orientation that Pavan Varma, Leela Fernandes, and
Sanjay Joshi all associate with the middle classes formed during the latter
part of British Raj.[22] This orientation is further demonstrated in today's
middle classes' awareness of (and verbal support of) social justice issues,
which often translates into political claims of representation for the general
public. It is also encapsulated by ethical and intellectual aspirations to
influence, change, or propose state policies. Finally it is characterized by
the pursuit of upward mobility through English-language education (at
the primary, secondary, and higher education levels). In recent years, with
the rise of global economies and mass media, middle-class aspirations in
most South Asian countries have further expanded. These aspirations are
manifest not only in the rise of income levels, consumerism, and activity in
the political and cultural arenas, but also in changing attitudes toward
women's roles and responsibilities in the home and the broader public
sphere. For example the education of daughters in areas that were once
considered traditionally male (as in the hard sciences and engineering),
particularly where that education is conducted abroad in British, American, Canadian, and Australian institutions or, alternatively, in the English-
medium higher education institutions of the Subcontinent, is increasingly

pursued by upper-middle-class and upwardly mobile families, whether Hindu, Muslim, Christian, Sikh, Buddhist, or secular.

According to Leela Fernandes, the Indian state has become heavily invested in producing dominant conceptions of middle-class respectability that define middle-class womanhood.[23] Muslim religious elites continue to play a significant role in these productions for Muslim women too—at least those women who understand Islam to be a primary mode of their self-identification. Within the heterogeneous ranks of the religious elites has emerged a kind of consensus on the cultural, social, and economic changes that compete with the notion of a transcendent, Shari'a-based vision of Islam to shape the values of middle-class, religiously observant Muslims. Their contemporary production and dissemination of an ever-growing body of didactic texts for Muslim women—many of which are modeled on Maulana Ashraf 'Ali Thanawi's famous 1905 work, *Bihishti Zewar*—speak to these changes in suggesting that a compromise in some areas of cultural and civic life is possible, without undermining the fundamental Islamic spirit of gender roles and responsibilities. Accordingly for many observant and traditional-minded Muslim families, middle-class aspirations have been marked by a relaxation, or reformulation, of the rules governing such cultural practices as *parda,* or modesty and sex-segregation.[24]

Far from being merely recipients of prescriptive discourses devised by male religious elites, Indian Muslim women also actively participate in constructions of Islamic womanhood. This is readily apparent in the ways in which women in the Sufi orders—particularly, but not exclusively, the female relatives of the presiding *pir*—can become the catalysts for change. Some women—as mothers, but also as wives and daughters—are able to exercise authority because of their relationship to the *pir* (here authority should be understood as influencing major decision-making processes and engaging in acts that sustain the ideology or ethos of an order or undermine it). Others are able to do so because the *pir* provides a way for them to participate in events or assume roles that had previously been denied them. A *pir* may allow a woman do to things that would otherwise contradict social, cultural, and religious norms: for example, as rare written records and occasional oral testimonies suggest, some *pir*s in the Subcontinent have named women as their successors. However, a woman who crosses the boundaries into traditionally male territory typically must cloak her influence with the mantle of female modesty and compliance to an ideal of female subordination to male authority.

If the *pir* does not explicitly demand it, cultural norms dictate that most women operating within the sphere of the establishment Sufi orders

demonstrate allegiance to this ideal as evidence of women's spiritual development and as a reflection of the values and honor of their families. In the Gudri Shah Chishti and the Maner and Bihar Sharif Firdausi orders, the behavior of the women of the family, articulated in terms of "honor" (*'izzat*) or "noble character" (*sharafat*), is linked to the preservation and protection of the social and spiritual status of the *pir*s and *khadim*. That women's actions are constrained by such linkages might be readily connected to a lack of agency and authority, but such an explanation does not take into consideration the ways in which dominant cultural prescriptions exercise hegemonic influence over the actions of *all* members of a social group, both male and female.[25]

### Islam and Discursive Productions: Women's Presence and Sufism's "Decline"

Women's increasing participation in the institutions and practices of Sufism provides a unique vantage point for reconsidering the idea of Sufism's supposed "decline" or "degeneration." While women's presence was not assigned sole blame for this decline, their increased visibility in communal public spaces of Sufi sacred sites after the late nineteenth century drew the attention—much of it negative—of Orientalist scholars, servants of the British Raj, and Muslim (Sufi and non-Sufi) observers alike. More balanced and sympathetic studies of contemporary Sufi praxis by Muslim and non-Muslim scholars—including Carl W. Ernst and Bruce B. Lawrence (2002), Pnina Werbner (2003), Claudia Liebeskind (1998), David Gilmartin and Bruce B. Lawrence (2000), Yoginder Sikand (1997), and Valerie Hoffman (1995)—have been especially helpful to my investigation of these kinds of discursive productions as they emerged from within contemporary Sufi milieus in the Subcontinent. In particular the emphasis on the "cyclical" character of the Chishti orders in Ernst and Lawrence's *Sufi Martyrs of Love,* one that demonstrates why they are best understood as "complex[es] of spiritual practice, historical memory, and ethical models" that have always evolved in response to contemporary "political, ideological, and technological" developments, has informed this study's presentation of the orders today.[26]

Using this interpretive framework as a point of departure for discussing the responses of Sufis to the question of women's participation, this book suggests some ways in which contemporary ritual practices, past precedent, and shifting social relationships among Muslim men and women can serve as either the means of or the main hindrances to acceptance of

women's spiritual authority in the Sufi setting. Werbner's sense of the "transnational" character of the orders[27] and Gilmartin and Lawrence's explanation of "mobile collective identities" have called attention to the necessity of reenvisioning the institutions of Sufism as reflecting a much wider complex of self-references, correspondences, networks, cultural matrices, practices, beliefs, and relationships with modernity than previously imagined.[28] Such conclusions about the development and character of the orders today highlight the inadequacy of textual studies alone for gauging contemporary attitudes about women. Rather, considering the interplay between textual evidence, ritual practices in the shrine milieu, contemporary discourses about women, methods of "training" the spiritual adept, and the "witnessed" language of the body (expressed through gestures, styles of dress, postures, and the use or avoidance of space) helps to reveal how attitudes toward the participation of spiritually gifted or ordinary women in the life of the orders can be equivocal, even within a single, regionally confined order.

The prevalent hermeneutic in modern scholarship on Sufism has been an essentially linear, male-centered, evolutionary model of development, with an emphasis on Sufism's "golden age," subsequent decline, and contemporary revival.[29] It is equally true of colonial-era scholarship, studies emerging from the secular academic milieu, and scholarship by Muslims emerging from the major centers of learning (both religious and secular) of the Muslim world. This hermeneutic has developed persuasive force in the study of Sufism, affecting the perceptions not only of scholars today but also of Sufis themselves. But it is not a modern hermeneutic; as early as the tenth century, 'Ali ibn Ahmad al-Bushanji lamented the transformation of Sufism from "a reality with no name" to "a name without reality." And from the period of Sufism's institutionalization—roughly the eighth or ninth through the thirteenth centuries, according to scholars such as Julian Baldick and J. S. Trimingham—women's participation in the ritual life at Sufi shrines (particularly where that participation seemed to circumvent traditional mores governing the segregation of the sexes or the subordination of women to the authority of socially and spiritually senior males) could serve as a marker of Sufism's purported decline.

Debates over the propriety and limits of women's participation in Sufi ritual life have, since the late nineteenth century, been influenced by a more general and widespread movement of women into the public sphere in greater numbers than before. Opportunities for women to participate in the life of Sufi orders, including their greater visibility in the shrine milieu, have expanded in the past century. This is in part because innovations in

print, communication, and transportation have facilitated the publication
and dissemination of knowledge about particular Sufi shrines and the functionaries attached to them, enabling the establishment and expansion of
thriving markets surrounding these shrines, and making it easier for pilgrims
to travel to these places—for healing, for participation in commemorative
events, or for purposes of tourism.[30] The correlation between women's
greater visibility in these public sacred spaces and the widespread belief in
Sufism's contemporary decline was often implicit: the men and women I
interviewed cited the impropriety of women and men mixing indiscriminately as a reason why women's participation in Sufi ritual life was, or
should be, restricted. Such explanations also served as a means for distinguishing between shrines described as being of "low moral character" and
those described as "authentic" in their observance of Islamic social and
moral prescriptions for behavior. And yet the *shaikh*s, *pir*s, and ordinary
Sufi men and women who opened their lives to my inquiries all realized
that women were an increasingly important, informed, and assertive clientele of the functionaries attached to shrines. They also eventually volun-
teered information about Sufi women from the recent and distant past,
women who had been recognized within Sufi communities as important
disciples, and as spiritually gifted individuals. The spiritual guidance of
some of these women was sought out by some of their fellow travelers
along the path to God. A few of them had been widely considered *shaikh*s in
their own right although it was very rare that such a woman would be
appointed *shaikh* and successor to the head of a Sufi order. Still, examples of
such women suggest a degree of flexibility within the establishment orders.
Ironically this flexibility is intimately tied to the relatively fixed hierarchies
of authority that exist within these orders.

The importance of affiliation with one of the establishment orders in-
vokes conformity to an ideal that seeks to link the teachings of widely
respected, Shari'a-observing, sober *shaikh*s with notions of conformity to
Islamic Shari'a, particularly where ritual practice is concerned. Conformity to the hierarchies of authority within the orders is also important
with respect to a woman's spiritual greatness being recognized. For Sufis
such conformity can serve as defense against critics' allegations of "un-
Islamic-ness" or inappropriate practices. Yet it can and does also operate as
justification for the greater inclusion of women in the ritual life of an
order. In particular the teachings of Sufi masters prominent within the
orders (as recorded in the biographical, epistolary, and homiletic literature
composed by and about such masters) figure significantly in this respect, as
examples of women participating in communal ritual events, performing

the work of *piri-muridi,* and/or being sought out by eminent Sufis as powerful teachers and intercessors with God can be found within these works.

Considering the evidence that emerged from this study for the recognition of women as spiritual authorities within Sufi circles, I surmise that the prevalent attitude among Sufis and other interested parties—that Sufism today is a pale shadow of its glorious past and that women's increased participation in Sufi ritual life reflects this decline—is tempered by the acknowledgment that there exists, within the "structures" and institutions of Sufism, a precedent for women's recognition as spiritual authorities. This is equally true whether that recognition is accorded unofficially, through oral reports, or "officially," with titles and other insignia bestowed by a *shaikh* upon a female disciple. Within the realm of Sufi praxis—specialized disciplines and ritual commemorations that are meant to foster the spiritual development of practitioners and the daily cycles of ritual and nonritual activities that occur within the precincts of shrines—a dialectic of exclusion and participation operates to reinforce the separation of the sexes that serves as a marker of *sharif* (noble, righteous, pious) identity. But it also creates and sustains the conditions whereby women are able to exercise authority in areas traditionally considered the preserve of the *shaikh* and advanced male adepts. Women's authority is most readily observed in the realm of ritual practice: the seasonal commemorations that draw large numbers of pilgrims to shrines and the everyday observances that underscore the importance of shrines for the locals who patronize them daily. Although the authority of women in this realm is acknowledged and even welcomed by locals and *shaikh*s alike, it is also a highly contested arena that carries implications for the kind of Sufism practiced and for its reflection of Islamic moral and social values. The ambivalence that characterizes attitudes toward contemporary women practitioners and its material expression can be read in the language of the body.

## The Embodiment of Ambiguity

Some of the recent and innovative developments in the field of praxis theory that have suggested how rituals and other types of performances can produce ambiguities in identity have also emphasized the *processes* by which these ambiguities are produced. An emphasis on process enabled me to accomplish two objectives. First, it helped me investigate how larger narratives about the propriety or impropriety of women in the Sufi shrine context are embedded within articulations of spiritual, moral, and behavioral ideals of Islamic womanhood and actions that are meant to underscore these ideals. Second, it provided a useful corrective to the "resistance"

paradigm that has driven so much subaltern and feminist scholarship.[31] This is not to suggest that resistance *never* occurs; instead it suggests the necessity of characterizing resistance where it *does* occur—not every act of contradiction, defiance, or challenge is evidence of resistance. Following Saba Mahmood's work on the motivations driving Muslim women's participation in what has been called the "piety movement" in contemporary Egypt, this study looks to subjects' own explanations for what they do to understand how they consider Islam a vital, though not *essentialized,* component in the "practical organization" of their everyday lives.[32]

Although the existence of a world of women who played important, and much more influential, roles in Sufi circles than had been acknowledged in academic scholarship opened up exciting possibilities for reconsidering the evolutionary "cycles" of Sufism and Sufi practice, the question of exactly how contemporary Sufi men and women acted upon the incentives afforded by past precedent remained problematic for this study. The idea that there exists a repertoire of symbols—hagiographic accounts, oral traditions, and Islamic moral and ethical precepts—upon which my interviewees draw to explain the propriety or impropriety of women's participation in Sufi ritual life seemed an important one for explaining the prevalence of certain ideals about Islamic femininity. For instance the belief that a "spiritually gifted" woman demonstrated adherence to Islamic Shari'a either through knowledge of the Qur'an and submission to its guidance, or through obedience to her husband, father, or other senior male relative, was often expressed. This idea was also reflected in many of the written accounts that offered details about Sufi women's lives: biographical (*tazkira, tabaqat*), epistolary (*maktubat, insha'*), and didactic (*malfuzat*), and contemporary demotic works written by Sufis and their disciples. More promising were some of the developments in anthropological and sociological theory that have investigated the impact of "symbolic capital" upon an actor's ability to fashion the perceptions of others and contribute to wider institutional changes. Yet I was wary of any facile Geertzian correspondences between symbols or "symbol systems" and meanings or conceptions.

Geertz's model of relations between symbols and religious behavior or other religious phenomena depends upon the idea of symbolic systems as coherent, closed, and containing fixed meanings, but it does not get at the question of *process*—that is, the mechanisms that facilitate action, and to what end. The anthropologist Talal Asad, among others, has convincingly argued the susceptibility of symbols to change. Moreover, in Asad's view, discerning how a symbol operates in conjunction with others (for example at a particular moment in time or under certain conditions of time, space,

and audience) can illustrate how relationships or configurations of power play out "on the ground," as it were. At the same time, he cautions against collapsing the distinction between discourse *within* practice and discourse *about* practice.[33] With that caveat in mind, I tried to distinguish between the ways in which individuals and groups draw from a repertoire of symbols, paradigms and modes of behavior within a given "snapshot" of time and how they may do so similarly or differently in reference to a particular performance event. As such, any repertoire may be understood to contain both "fixed" and "variable" points of reference that may be used or explained differently under different circumstances, sometimes for strategic reasons.

In using these terms I do not mean, however, that some of these points of reference are universally understood in the same way while others may be interpreted differently at different times. Nor do I mean to dichotomize the "universally Islamic" and the "locally Islamic" as oppositional modalities of a singular worldview, though tension may sometimes exist between them. Rather I consider the relationship between these two modalities in the dual sense of "tradition" elaborated by William Graham in his study "Traditionalism in Islam." As Graham explains, tradition may be understood more or less synonymously with "local custom" or authoritative "customary practices" that are passed from one generation to the subsequent one or recognized as having been passed down and possessing a kind of "normative" status, or it may be understood as a "cumulative tradition" linked with the distant past and containing within it the sum of collected "customary practices."[34] In other words my sense of the "fixed" points draws from interviewees' understanding of collective Islamic imperatives or explanations of things they understand to be "transcendentally Islamic," where these are referred to as forming part of, or being closely linked to, the foundational tradition (for example, Qur'an, Shari'a, the *sunna* of the Prophet Muhammad, *purdah/hijab,* or Sufi "tradition" in a collective sense), while my sense of the "variable" draws from those things that were explained as tools or methods for understanding (or used by my interviewees as didactic tools or methods to help me understand their explanations). These "variable" points highlight significant discursive and material markers of and for faith and include narrative accounts of women in the Sufi milieu, sacred spaces, *purdah/hijab,* and Sufi "tradition" in a particularized sense. The fact that some of these points overlap both frames of reference is meant to underscore the importance of local context and its perceived connection to broader Islamic discursive formations and material realities in understanding the strategic nature of their use by the Sufi men and women featured in this study.

Didactic Paradigms for Female Devotion: Classical Tropes

The work of Rkia Cornell suggests how such "fixed" and "variable" points of reference can offer a nuanced understanding of the role of women in the Sufi milieu that goes beyond the perception that very few extraordinary women were recognized as legitimate and gifted travelers on the Sufi path. Her explanation of *ta'abbud,* or servitude, in the work of Abu 'Abd al-Rahman al-Sulami of Nishapur (d. 1021), an early systematizer of Sufi doctrine and the author of the Sufi biographical compendia *Tabaqat al-Sufiyya* and *Dhikr al-niswa,* highlights the historical currency of didactic paradigms for articulating a particularly feminine model for devotion and the importance of both particularlized and broader institutional sources of authority in the development of Sufi discursive traditions. For al-Sulami, *ta'abbud* as disciplined practice represented the essence of women's Sufism, distinguishing women from their male counterparts and opening them to divine inspiration (*wahy*). As Cornell points out, servitude had become a common trope used among early Sufis to express the depth of an adept's commitment to the spiritual life and to exemplify a path to salvation. Yet when the term is applied by al-Sulami to female adepts, it takes on a particular nuance that emphasizes their unique status. Female adepts who practiced *ta'abbud* as a spiritual discipline were able to travel on their own, participate in Sufi assemblies alongside men, and pursue intellectual development and a "life of the spirit" without the encumbrances of marriage and family in ways that were not open to most other women.[35] According to Cornell, al-Sulami also sought to impart a corporate identity to Sufi women in other ways, in part by feminizing certain terms that were commonly used among groups of male adepts to describe their spiritual methods or individual designations as spiritual practitioners.[36]

Less than a century later, the theologian al-Ghazali (d. 1111) connected a wife's entry into Paradise with her ability to please her husband humbly and selflessly, understanding marriage to be for the wife "a form of enslavement; thus she is his slave, and she should obey the husband absolutely in everything he demands of her provided such demands do not constitute an act of disobedience."[37] This connection between servanthood, righteousness, and a woman's attainment of proximity to God is further underscored in the story of the *darvish* Rabi'a, as narrated by al-Ghazali in this same work:

Rabi'a [of Syria], the daughter of Isma'il, asked Ahmad b. Abu al-Hawwari to marry her. He declined because he was preoccupied with worship and said to her, "My preoccupations are not inclined toward

women, because I am too preoccupied with myself." She replied, "I am more preoccupied with myself than you are, and I have no [physical] desire. However, I have inherited much wealth from my husband and I wish you would spend it on your spiritual brothers, and that through you I should come to know the righteous ones, thus finding a path to God, may He be glorified and honored." He replied, "Wait until I seek permission of my master." So he returned to find Abu Sulayman al-Darani, who used to enjoin against his getting married and [who had] said, "None of our companions ever got married without being changed." But when he heard her words, he said, "Marry her, for she is a friend of God. Hers are the words of the righteous." Al-Hawwari said, "I married her; and there was in our house a container made of plaster which had become worn out through use by those who hastily washed their hands and left after meals, not to mention those who had washed with potash." He also said, "I married three wives in addition, but she used to give me the best to eat and used to perfume me. She would say to me, 'Go with energy and strength to your wives.'" Thus Rabi'a of Syria was likened unto [the famous eighth-century mystic] Rabi'ah al-'Adawyiah of Basra.[38]

Al-Ghazali's work points to the development of a discursive tradition that draws upon numerous sources of authority: the Qur'an, Hadis, philosophy, Islamic law, and an amalgam of earlier customs and practices, influences that remained evident in his literary output even after the famous existential crisis described in his work *al-Munqidh min al-dalal.*[39] Is al-Ghazali, like al-Sulami, drawing here upon an established didactic paradigm for female seekers of God, or did such portraits of women merely reflect predominant social attitudes? The question is particularly significant at a time when the institutions of Sufism were beginning to acquire permanence[40] and methods of spiritual attainment systematized and connected with particular chains of authority (*silislas*). In the tenth and eleventh centuries, Nishapur, where both al-Ghazali and al-Sulami worked, was a nexus of intellectual activity in which Sufism, along with Islamic schools of law, theology, and philosophy, flourished and also jockeyed for influence and power in the region. Several scholars have effectively demonstrated that the type of Sufism discussed by al-Ghazali and al-Sulami had been developing in the tenth and eleventh centuries among circles of urban religious scholars and Sufis, particularly those form Khurasan.[41]

Sufism in this period was marked by several developments that bear implications for the development of didactic paradigms and methods for female adepts. Two in particular are addressed here. First was the fallout

from the breakup of the 'Abbasid empire in the mid-tenth century, which resulted in the emergence of local regimes and new elites, and the clustering of communities along lines of ethnicity, regional origin, tribal identity, or religious sectarian affiliation.[42] Religion in particular served as a cohesive force among an increasingly heterogeneous population, while the absence of effective central government control may have worked in favor of women who preferred to pursue the contemplative life.[43] Second, there seems to have been an increase in the numbers of *khanaqah*s, or spiritual retreat centers, accompanied by changes in the nature of the institution. As Jacqueline Chabbi has demonstrated, after the eleventh century, the *khanaqah* became increasingly associated with Sufism.[44] In a few Sufi chronicles composed during this period, including al-Sulami's *Dhikr al-Niswa,* wealthy women are mentioned as benefactors of these institutions and ordinary women as their residents, while in later chronicles spiritually gifted women are noted as managers or leaders of *khanaqah*s for women in places such as Aleppo, Baghdad, Cairo, and the Maghreb region.[45] The institution of the *khanaqah* also began to take on more formal overtones from the eleventh century onward, with rules for *khanaqah* life appearing in the works of a number of Sufis, such as the Khurasani mystic Abu Sa'id ibn Abi al-Khair (d. 1049) and 'Abdul Qahir Abu al-Najib al-Suhrawardi (d. 1168). In the rules established by Abi al-Khair, women's actions are addressed by implication as examples of what not to do: in Annemarie Schimmel's translation, Abi al-Khair's disciples are advised not to sit in holy places for gossiping, presumably because women were fond of visiting graveyards for both religious and social purposes.[46] While al-Suhrawardi's *Kitab adab al-muridin* does not address women specifically, it does contain a section on *rukha*s, or "allowances," that recognizes the desire of ordinary people who were not prepared for the rigors of the contemplative life to attach themselves nonetheless to Sufi masters and the institutions associated with them.[47] Margaret Smith's groundbreaking work on Rabi'a Basri, Cornell's translation of al-Sulami's *Dhikr al-niswa,* and Javad Nurbakhsh's translation of a number of documents in his collection *Sufi Women* confirm the existence of several such women in the central lands of Islam from the eighth to eleventh centuries.[48] It would not be far-fetched to imagine that al-Suhrawardi's recognition of the need for *rukha*s may have also coincided with his realization of women's desire to pursue the Path in greater numbers than before.

The production of didactic manuals and the establishment of more formalized structures of organization among Sufis from the tenth to twelfth centuries—particularly in centers of Islamic political and intellectual

ferment such as Baghdad, Nishapur, Egypt, and the Maghreb—also coincided with the growing support for Sufis by both government officials and 'ulama' and the need for Sufis to respond to non-Sufi criticisms of their practices by demonstrating that the practices were wholly in consonance with the Qur'an and *sunna* of the Prophet Muhammad. However, this was not their only motivation for so doing.[49] The establishment of precedents linking Sufi *tariqa*s (here incorporating both the earlier sense of "method" and the later sense of "brotherhood") with the earliest symbols of Islam drew heavily upon the foundational thrust of an Islamic ethical and moral worldview based on submission to God's will (*islam*) as the highest form of spiritual achievement. Institutionally the importance accorded to establishing chains of transmission of authority among the founders of Sufi orders—along lines similar to the establishment of sound *isnad*s in determining the authenticity of Hadis traditions—served to link *tariqa*s with the *sunna* of the Prophet Muhammad, who is himself referred to numerous times in the Qur'an as Allah's servant (*'abd*). In the works of early Sufis, servitude reflected the exhortation of the Prophet to humility as a hallmark of perfect faith, as seen in the *sunna* recorded in al-Bukhari's *Sunan*: "Narrated Haritha bin Wahb . . . al-Khuzai: The Prophet said, 'Shall I inform you about the people of Paradise? They comprise every obscure unimportant humble person, and if he takes Allah's Oath that he will do that thing, Allah will fulfill his oath (by doing that). Shall I inform you about the people of the Fire? They comprise every cruel, violent, proud and conceited person.'"[50]

The Qur'anic emphasis on humility underscores a threefold exhortation from Allah: lack of humility incurs God's punishment, while the lesson to be learned from suffering is humility before God (6:42–43, 7:94, and 23:76). Humble believers are rewarded with the fruits of Paradise (11:23, 22:24, 23:2, 33:35). The language used by Sufis to describe practices marked by an attitude of humility also reflected existing material realities. For instance the use of Turkish military slaves as trusted advisers, assistants, and managers by elite families in the central lands of Islam in the tenth century shaped the development of a terminology of servitude among Sufis,[51] while by the fourteenth century, the Sufi orders had become highly organized and specialized, Ottoman power had risen to the west of the Subcontinent,[52] and the Subcontinent itself had become a major site for the production of mystical love poetry, drawing from earlier Persian classical literary forms. By the sixteenth century, servitude had become a stock trope for expressing what was by then a predominant ideal of piety. The symbol of the woman-soul as metaphor for the perfect seeker of God had gained widespread currency in both mystic and literary circles and among the common populace in the Persian-speaking and Turkic lands of Islam,

which extended from Europe to Southeast Asia to parts of North and East Africa. Thus the term *ta'abbud* had much wider applications in Islam beyond the realm of the mystical. It also served as a means of expressing social realities, particularly relationships of dominance and submission as seen in gendered social hierarchies.

One must, however, beware ascribing any exclusively feminine meaning or significance to symbolic discourses about a particular female adept or group of female adepts. Sachiko Murata and Annemarie Schimmel have deconstructed the meanings of the (in)famous description given to exceptionally gifted women by Sufi and Sufi-minded men—"women in the shape of a man."[53] According to them such terms should not be unequivocally taken to signal the inadequacy of women as spiritual seekers (though undoubtedly some Sufi thinkers used it so), but rather to express a spiritual ideal in which "manhood" as trope was understood to be the highest form of spiritual attainment, in which even those men seen as "spiritually lacking" could be described as "not men" by adepts of either sex. With the development of Sufi poetry in the vernacular languages of Indo-Pakistan, the trope of the woman-soul as perfect seeker of God served as the highest spiritual ideal to which men and women alike aspired.[54]

Gender reversals, though not unknown among early Sufis, were increasingly used after the fourteenth century both to express spiritual ideals and as methods for annihilating the individual egos of Sufi adepts and engendering their nearness to or intimacy with God. Attachment to one or another gendered marker as expressive of reality[55] obscures the understanding of ultimate reality that Sufi adepts sought. As Murata explains, value-laden gender distinctions mark the limitations of human knowledge in the Islamic sapiential tradition and underscore humans' tendency to place themselves at the center of divine reality.[56] The relative nature of gendered markers is noted in the writing of classical Sufi thinkers such as Ibn al-'Arabi (d. 1240), particularly in their expositions upon the *jalali* (majestic) and *jamali* (beautiful) attributes of God. While such thinking cannot be said to characterize the actions and mind-set of the average *murid,* male or female, it does influence the thinking of many of those who represent the "inner circles" of disciples.[57]

Even so, the formal investiture of women as *shaikh*s or *pir*s has been and remains a contested practice in the world of Sufism, despite ample documentation of (largely isolated) precedents for this practice within several of the establishment and minor Sufi orders alike. For women seeking recognition as spiritual authorities within the hierarchical structure of the Sufi orders, as for the men wishing to acknowledge them as such, the paradoxes of nomenclature may be circumvented by investiture. This is achieved

through a number of representational practices in which a woman's status as de facto, if not de jure, spiritual guide is made to conform to dominant prescriptions for spiritual authority that draw upon culturally significant, gendered ideals of behavior, practices through which she is able to demonstrate knowledge of the outer (zahiri) and inner (batini) Islamic doctrines and practices; prove her mastery (and custodianship) of the traditions of the order to which she belongs; and show "results," as one *pirzada* man put it. In other words if her actions have effect (either tangible, as in the ability to manipulate the outcome of events, or subtle, as in the ability to affect the psychology, mind-set, or spiritual development of *murid*s and other affiliates of the order), she will be perceived as an effective spiritual guide. A number of external factors also shape the economies of meaning that affect the reception of women's roles as spiritual guides (within or outside of the purview of a Sufi order and its presiding *shaikh*), which are detailed in chapters 2 and 4 of this book. These chapters investigate ways in which women may exercise spiritual authority as de facto or de jure *pir*s.

### Discourse and Practice Revisited: Beyond the Resistance Paradigm

While a woman's position as spiritual authority may contradict the rhetoric of gender segregation, female subordination to male authority, and exclusion from the wider public arena as it is verbalized and explained within the framework of an "Islamicizing" discourse, she may not herself perceive any conflict between the authority she holds and Islam as the religious and cultural institution through which she defines herself. Despite this, such apparent contradictions in discourse and practice have often been characterized as "resistance," particularly by feminist scholars and cultural anthropologists.[58] One implication of challenging the resistance paradigm is that, in challenging the "truth" of the interpretive endeavor, one allows for the relationships between dominant and subordinate, paradigmatic and subjective modes to shift, changing not only the researcher's understanding of the relationship between these modes, but also their identification as *exclusively* one or the other. Relationships of power may be formulated in ways that deny ultimate authority—and by extension primacy—to any single mode. Applied to the Sufi shrine setting, my initial forays into the question of women's experiences suggested that these are shaped as much by women's understanding of the boundaries for expression as by their willingness to redraw those boundaries if and when they perceive this as necessary.

Both women and men tended to speak in terms of the ideal, and in so doing only gradually revealed stories about women in their families (or female disciples) who had in fact been considered spiritually gifted and

capable of guiding others. Such conversations were few and far between. I had to find a way to get at the discrepancies between the often-repeated claim that women could not assume spiritual authority because it was against Islam (or Islamic Shari'a) and the fact—as I witnessed it—that in certain cases, they indeed did. I decided that the best course of action would be to consider as wide a range of discourses as possible in order to address the question of how women's experiences in the Sufi milieu could reflect and sustain but also challenge prevailing attitudes about women's spiritual authority and "proper" place in mixed-gender settings. I use the term *discourse* in a number of senses here and throughout this study. First is the sense of "discursive formation" as developed by the French philosopher Michel Foucault—a system of "dispersions" that works to link together statements that are otherwise structurally, conceptually, or functionally disparate. Second is the later use of this same term by such subject-of-language thinkers as Émile Benveniste to index the relationship between language and the position of the human subject within it. While this usage leans toward a structuralist understanding of the relationship between language and social groups that attribute particular meanings to it (in the sense that language may be seen to structure experiences), my study strives to maintain a middle ground between the foundationalist claims of such terms as *Islam, Shari'a,* and *parda* and the material conditions that both shape the self-understanding of the individuals and groups discussed here and allow them to modify these understandings. Finally I use the term *discourse* to underscore the ability of the *unspoken* (such as gestures, symbols, and bodily practices) to mediate or transgress conflicting or disparate social realities as they are experienced by a social actor or group.

These multiple meanings enabled me to consider the discrepancies between dominant narratives about gender and observed practices as they reflected three senses of action: physical exclusion, attendance, or presence in same-sex or mixed-gender settings; the exercise of (spiritual) authority as a catalyst for change in established praxis; and the instrumentality of the language of the body—how saying nothing can be "doing something." On this last point, participation, as it reflects the exclusion of women from ritual spaces and the prohibitions on their participation in some ritual events, can communicate certain things about the ethos and orientation of an order. For instance it can serve to distinguish the practices in a particular order as *ba-shar'* (in conformity with Islamic Shari'a). Otherwise participation can signal the physical presence of women alongside men, or alternatively it can index those cases in which women engaged in the same kinds of activities as men, but in separate spaces. For example I observe the occasions on which women attend the musical assembly (*mahfil-i sama'*), a

major aspect of Sufi practice for Chishti Sufis and an important part of the ritual events observed during large public celebrations, such as the *'urs,* or death-day anniversary of a saint (even for orders such as the Firdausi, which otherwise do not usually sponsor *sama'* assemblies). In the wider public assemblies held at the Sharaf al-din Maneri *dargah,* women are prohibited from sitting inside the assembly, but some do gather around its perimeter to observe the performance, despite the protests of some of the shrine functionaries. In other cases a separate space outside the assembly is provided for women to observe and listen to the performances. Sometimes events are staged for women alone, from which all men except the presiding *pir* are excluded. In settings that were more strictly gender segregated, I considered those instances when women engaged in the same kinds of activities as the men in the ritual setting.

I also consider questions of authority and agency as they relate to the ways in which women are prevented from playing some roles. However, I do not prioritize the ways in which women are controlled and manipulated by patriarchal systems and dominant institutions such as Islam and the traditions of these Sufi orders. Nor do I assume an understanding of agency as an entirely autonomous mechanism by which women self-consciously assert their right to individual freedoms, self-determination, and choices. Although these sometimes play an important part in women's conception of themselves, I chose to steer clear of such issues of women's "status," which many studies—feminist and otherwise—determine by highlighting women's experiences of oppression or constraint. Instead I focus on how women may exercise authority within the confines of those boundaries that limit their self-expression while in effect straining and reshaping those boundaries. A woman who crosses the boundaries into areas that are widely considered "male" territory often must communicate her actions as being in conformity with prevalent cultural ideals of feminine modesty and subordination to male authority. In so doing some women are able to influence major decision-making processes, sustain the ideology or ethos of an order or undermine it, and ultimately reshape their social and cultural environments. Thus I operate from a notion of agency and authority that prioritizes their temporally embedded nature, meaning that the actions in which women engage are informed by the past, oriented toward future possibilities, and shaped by present situational contexts and their contingencies.[59]

As mothers, wives, and daughters, many women are able to exercise such authority because of their relationship to the *pir* or because the *pir* provides a way for them to participate in events or assume roles that had previously been denied them. Since the *pir*'s authority is paramount, it is no surprise that those whom the *pir* regards as important sources of authority

will be similarly regarded by others within the order. A *pir* may allow a woman do to things that would otherwise go against the grain—oral communications from my interviewees and some written evidence suggest that in rare cases, *pir*s had named women as their successors. In other cases ritual acts as a medium for conferring authority. For example, in the Gudri Shah order, the *mahfil-i rindan,* a musical assembly featuring women musicians, is a tradition instituted by the third *pir* of the order, who endured considerable censure from the servants and other functionaries in the Mu'in al-din *dargah* for allowing women to perform in the *mahfil* setting. However, it both responded to and opened up avenues for female performers to be recognized as important players in the fashioning of a Sufi cultural universe that was attempting to address ongoing social and cultural changes. At other times it is the women of the family who can become the active catalysts for change through strategic and self-conscious action, although there are a number of variables that determine how, and to what extent, they do. These variables include age, marital status, education, personality, *parda* practices, and social status, all of which affect the ways women may exercise authority over others in the shrine setting.

Finally I consider what "ambiguous" speech and nonspeech (that is to say, the language of the body—body movements, gestures, deportment) reveal about participants' internalization of dominant discourses on gender relationships in Islam and the proper place of women within collective ritual spaces at Sufi shrines. Publicly women are often obliged to assume a stance of deference to the authority of senior males. The placement of the body, gestures, and demonstrations of respect before senior men (such as refraining from speaking when a senior male is present unless asked to do so) are all informed by prevalent cultural ideas about female modesty. However, ambiguous words and movements of the body can also communicate defiance or disagreement. One day when I was interviewing one of the servants at the shrine of Sharaf al-din Maneri in Bihar Sharif, a woman pilgrim (dressed in a two-piece black *burqa'* with face veil, or *niqab*) joined our conversation. She had come to the shrine in connection with a vow and was residing in one of the cells (*hujra*) that servants of the shrine (*khadim*s) rent out to visitors. She approached, sat down across from both of us, and pulled her *niqab* over the back of her head so that her face was visible. For a while she agreed with everything the *khadim* said (at the time he was talking about the importance of maintaining *parda*). She concurred enthusiastically when he insisted that women should always defer to men's authority, then immediately began answering all the questions I asked him, cutting him off in midsentence, completely ignoring the annoyed look on his face! The stance of this pilgrim was perhaps one of the most obvious

forms of challenge to male authority I encountered. More often, however, the ways in which women could both challenge and uphold dominant discourses in a particular situation were subtle but effective nonetheless. These unspoken and "ambiguous speech" acts suggest a performative dimension to the communications between actors of different genders and pointed to ways in which these communicative acts are socially and culturally inscribed with meanings but also retroactively produce these (and other) meanings of their own.[60] Ultimately this is the predominant view driving my study. Each chapter in this book investigates these meanings and their articulation in different historical and living contexts.

This text identifies some of the prevalent colonial-era discourses surrounding the question of Sufi shrines and orders and women's roles therein, as it appeared in the climate of India in the early nineteenth to mid–twentieth centuries. In trying to avoid the problem of essentializing the discourses of British civil servants, Orientalist scholars, and Muslim religious reformers, this chapter considers the endeavor to represent the Indian "other" as one that is fragmented and heterogeneous, inherently contradictory (even necessarily so) and allowing for "counterhegemonies" to emerge and coexist with its self-assertion as dominant discourse, as Lisa Lowe has argued in her 1991 study of British and French Orientalism.[61] Here I do not want to overstate the claims to authority of colonialist and Orientalist discourses but, instead, to sort out some of the lines of thinking, the "persistent tropes" by which these writers and thinkers conceived of their subjects and through which their subjects were often inclined to view themselves, with varying responses. By looking at a cross-section of accounts that emerged during this period, in particular the firsthand reports of officers, employees, and subjects of the colonialist Raj, I hope to show the typical kinds of assumptions that are made about Islam, Sufism, and contemporary saint veneration in general and to demonstrate the prevalent images of women pilgrims at Sufi shrines in particular. These I compare to the treatment by indigenous writers of Muslims and their devotional traditions. Finally the chapter seeks to account for some of the social, economic, intellectual, and political projects that contributed to the development of these images and the effects of such projects. It asks, thus, how such portrayals of Indian Islam in the colonial period have influenced Indian Muslims' and Sufis' self-understanding, and how such self-understanding is manifest within discourses about women's participation in the institutions of Sufism.

The accounts that appeared during the colonial period of South Asian history were often tied to the interests of the British colonial administration

in solidifying their power over a subject population. European travelers, Orientalist scholars, and servants of the British Raj expressly promoted negative stereotypes about the "cults" of Sufi saints. The reasons for such treatments can be partly attributed to the need of the Raj to distinguish itself from and assert its superiority to its predecessors, the Mughals (thus serving the end of justifying British rule). In the eyes of many colonials and Indians alike, the Mughals counted not only as the former ruling elite but also as representatives of Muslim interests in the Subcontinent as a whole, thereby implicating the ordinary Muslim along with the Mughal aristocracy. As such, Sufis could be seen as collaborators with (as in the case of the Suhrawardi) or avoiders of (as in the case of the Chishti) the Muslim ruling classes. More often than not, British policy toward the establishment orders—as toward *pir*s and shrines—tended to operate on the assumption of necessarily preserving them as allies of the Raj, insofar as they could be co-opted as such. The unofficial policy of patronizing shrines and, as in the case of the Mu'in al-din *dargah*, of remaining actively involved in the administration of religious endowments[62] demonstrated this very assumption. At the same time, European accounts often ignored or failed to recognize distinctions among Sufism of the establishment orders, the veneration of local saints, and wandering *darvish* and *faqir* groups. This lack of distinction also applied to women's activities in the shrine setting, often characterized as "superstitious" practices and the antithesis of both Islam and Sufism, conceived as "classical" traditions. Most European accounts also promoted the view, which remains largely unchallenged today, that Muslim women's expression in the realm of the spiritual is chiefly relegated to the private, household arena and that the shrine is a place where women have little influence in shaping ritual life, except in their consultation of the *pir*. By investigating how such issues lay embedded within discourses of social, political, economic, and ideological control as these were generated within the literature written by servants of the British Raj, European travelers to the Subcontinent, Christian missionaries, and European and indigenous Orientalist writers, I hope to shed some light on how and why some images about women's roles in Sufi shrines and orders have endured, despite evidence to contradict those images.

Some of my objectives are twofold: first to assess the circumstances under which a woman may be recognized as spiritual authority despite "official" denial of such recognition, and second to look into the discrepancies between the commonly held idea that women cannot perform in the "public" setting of the shrine and my observations of women doing just that. I attempt a taxonomy of the master-disciple relationship, or *piri-muridi*, from its earliest institutional formulations to its current permutations. In so

doing it locates the master-disciple relationship at various points along a wide spectrum of possibilities, at one end of which is what some scholars have referred to as "classical," meaning the structured, hierarchical relationship between master and disciple formalized by the oath of allegiance (*bai‘at*) and located within the realm of the institutionalized Sufi orders (*silsila*s, *tariqa*s). At the other end of this spectrum are the loose, "associational" relationships between *pir*s and clients (who may or may not be formally tied to the *pir* and his order) based largely on the provision of ritual services on the part of the *pir* and payment on the part of the client. In this chapter I argue that while the loose, associational relationships of *piri-muridi* afford women the most scope to take on the role of a *pir*, even within the world of Sufi orders, women can be recognized as de facto (if not de jure) spiritual guides (*shaikh*s, *pir*s, *khalifa*s), as they have been throughout the history of institutional Sufism. By looking more closely at the role of women in two Sufi orders today—the Gudri Shah Chishtis of Ajmer and the Firdausis of Maner, Bihar—I investigate the factors that determine how and under what circumstances women may be recognized as or perform the functions of a spiritual guide.

I also consider women's participation in the Sufi musical assembly (*mahfil-i sama‘*) and highlight a *qawwali* performance I attended in Ajmer at the Gudri Shah *khanaqah* during the *‘urs* for Mu‘in al-din Chishti. Although women are not allowed into the performance hall (*mahfil-khana*) at the *dargah* during the *‘urs*, at the Gudri Shah *khanaqah* women may not only attend the privately organized *mahfil-i sama‘*, but are also lead singers in some of the *qawwali* troupes that are invited there each year to perform songs in praise of the saint. The propriety of this type of women's performance was hotly debated among those I spoke to—within and outside of the Sufi orders. What were the arguments for and against women's participation in the *mahfil-i sama‘*, whether as members of the audience or as performers? What aspects of "tradition" were recalled by my subjects as precedents for current attitudes regarding women's presence, and how do the discourses I encountered today index what is written in Islamic and Sufi literature about the propriety of women's performances in the company of men who are unrelated to them? I found that ideological positions on this topic varied widely, and that even with an individual interlocutor, notions of what constitutes "proper" (*sahih*) versus improper (*ghair-mazhab*) practice could shift according to the contexts, circumstances, and genres of performance.

I describe my encounter—as both researcher and subject—with a female ritual specialist at the *hujra gah,* or private prayer chamber, of Sharaf al-din Maneri in Bihar Sharif. In Bihar Sharif poor women of low social status

who are perceived as exceptionally close to God are asked by female patrons to present petitions to the saints, to Allah, and to the Prophet Muhammad on their behalf, by reciting *na't* (praise of the Prophet), *hamd* (praise of God), or other formulaic recitations. However, these women are compelled to operate outside the milieu of the "public" world of the major *dargah*s, since their activities are seen by many *pirzade* as contradicting the letter and spirit of Islam. What is the range of responses to people like the female ritual specialist I encountered, and how do factors of class or social location influence these responses? Most of the men and women I spoke with about the ritual specialists of Bihar Sharif took a dim view of the activities of the women who performed the work of petitioning at the *hujra gah*. I frequently encountered explanations from the men and women of the Firdausi order, as well as local residents of Bihar Sharif, that such women were mentally unstable, of questionable morals, or simply of low social status. I highlight the broader discourses that locate women's activities in the shrine setting as being within or outside the pale of "proper," "correct" Islamic and Sufi practice, focusing on the discrepancies and convergences between my observations of the ways in which women may perform specialized services for clients and what my interviewees told me about women's ability to perform such services. I distinguish among attitudes expressed in each of my case studies, with particular reference to the gender differences I encountered in the discourse of my subjects, and highlight the reasons given for why women cannot or should not perform such roles, despite the evidence that they indeed do. What surprised me most is how much those reasons resembled arguments against women's activities in the Sufi milieu in the late nineteenth and early twentieth centuries. In seeking to move beyond the facile condemnations of these activities encountered in the written records of British civil servants, Orientalist scholars, and Muslim religious reformers alike, I began to wonder about how the boundaries established by prescriptive (discursive) models of behavior for Muslims broke down in practice, and whether Islam's foundational symbols of and for piety provided a clear or an ambiguous organizing framework for the belief and practice. Those reflections appear in the conclusion of this book.

# Perceptions of "Women's Religion" in Colonial India

In a 1971 supplement to the *Patna District Gazetteer,* Nagendra Kumar wrote this telling portrait of the character of contemporary Sufi shrines and saints:

> The worship of *Pirs* has clearly been imbibed from Hinduism. Other-
> wise this concept is altogether alien to Islam. The worship of the tombs
> where the relics of venerated fakirs are enshrined are places of wor-
> ship not only for Muslims but for the rank and file of Hindus and in
> spite of the vertical division of the two communities, the attendance
> of Hindu mothers with their children has not much diminished at the
> *Dargah* of *Pirs.* Barren as well as expectant mothers and mothers with
> sickly children and such other members of the community including
> quite a few of those who are litigants, visit these places to receive the
> benediction of the priests who are supposed to invoke the spirit of the
> fakir to bring blessings on the devotees. One of the popular ways of
> devotees is to place new *chadars* to cover the tomb of the *Pir.*[1]

The attitude with which the author of this gazetteer approaches the subject of saint veneration approximates the views of many of the servants of the British colonial Raj, Muslim religious reformers, and Orientalist thinkers in nineteenth- and twentieth-century India. In the above passage, the veneration of Muslim *pirs,* conflated with the act of worship and linked primarily with women and Hindus,[2] stands in stark opposition to Islam's fundamentally monotheistic ethos, while his characterization of the belief in the power of *pirs* as being Hindu-influenced ignores the widespread popularity of *pir* and shrine veneration among Muslims outside the South Asian subcontinent. Kumar's depiction shares much in common with the portraits of contemporary saint and shrine veneration painted by three

groups of commentators on Islam and Muslims in the Subcontinent in the nineteenth and early twentieth centuries: British civil servants of the Raj, Orientalist scholars, and Muslim religious reformers. In the last half century of the colonial period, these groups began to address the question of women, producing a body of literature that, although widely divergent in its orientation, tone, aims, claims to moral authority, and target audience, suggests that the activities of women pilgrims at Sufi shrines could offer proof of shrines' conformity, or nonconformity, to normative prescriptions of Islamic faith and practice. This chapter aims to sort out some of the lines of thinking about "women's religion" in colonial India, focusing on the veneration of Sufis and pilgrimage to saints' shrines as such ritual practices are addressed in a selection of the literary output generated by these three groups of commentators. In the world of Sufi shrines in particular, women's ritual activities—the veneration of saints and the celebration of festivals associated with them; pilgrimage to shrines, particularly outside of the major festival occasions; and the patronage of living *pirs*—became the focus of debates among Muslim religious reformers and subjects of critique by commentators within circles of Orientalist scholarship and the British civil service. More important, these debates and critiques underscored the symbolic capital of essentialist claims to identity in the colonial state, claims that Muslim religious reformers were able to use to their advantage as they sought to represent the interests of India's Muslims—in the eyes of Indian Muslims as well as the colonial state.

These commentators shared generally negative views of the contemporary world of shrines and saints, although the works generated by Muslim reformers and Orientalist scholars suggest a kind of ambivalence toward Sufism as a moral-philosophical system. More important, such views were often counterbalanced against articulations of ostensibly normative parameters, or "transcendent" characteristics of Islam, as defined in opposition to culturally specific traditions, beliefs, and practices. Although the idea of a "normative" Islam with measurable and unalterable boundaries has retained persuasive force well beyond these debates, the parameters of the "normative," as this book seeks to demonstrate, remain stubbornly resistant to precise classification, notwithstanding continued efforts to homogenize religious identities—particularly among groups seeking political gain.

The connection between women's patronage of shrines, on one hand, and the distance between Indian Islam and its classical foundations, on the other, was thrust into the realm of public debate by British and Orientalist thinkers, but it had been reflected much earlier in the writing of Sufi thinkers and religious scholars (*'ulama'*) alike. However, until the late

nineteenth century, such writing was circulated chiefly among a select—and highly educated—audience. British civil servants—especially the land surveyors and census takers of the early nineteenth century who described the customs and practices of the groups they encountered—demonstrated little knowledge of the wider cultural and religious landscape of which Sufi shrines and *pir*s formed part. Instead they tended to view them as antinomian elements within Islam. Among the more erudite Orientalists, the characterization of Sufi shrine culture as curious "other," separate from and antithetical to an Islam whose prescriptive boundaries were taken for granted, drew as much from the Qur'an, Hadis, early Arabic and Persian historical writing, and legal compendia of the scholars of Islamic law as from early European travelers' accounts of their encounters with shrines and fakirs. For Muslim religious reformers, the moral authority of Sufi shrines and their representatives was closely connected to their perceived conformity to the Islamic foundational texts and traditions, particularly the *sunna* of the Prophet Muhammad, even if practice sometimes contradicted their letter. To the extent that women's activities in the world of Sufi shrines conformed to these foundational ideas, believed to embody "transcendent" Islamic values, shrines and *pir*s could be characterized as legitimate, even admirable expressions of faith. To the extent that women's activities contradicted these ideas, or worse, suggested a moral breakdown within Indian Muslim communities, they were condemned. As chapters 2 and 4 demonstrate, some women learned to accommodate certain aspects of the discourse of Shari‘a³ in order to exercise greater agency as spiritual authorities in the shrine milieu. Yet the mobilization of symbols only partially explains the interplay between such transcendent symbols of Islam and context-driven constructions of gender identity in the colonial state. For British civil servants, Orientalists, and Muslim religious reformers in colonial India, perceptions of Sufis and shrines and of women's activities within that milieu were also influenced by the particular social, economic, and political changes that drove—and challenged—the expansion of colonial Raj.

## The Colonial Administration: Shrines as
## Tools for Social Control

One of these changes involved redrawing the map of social arrangements and groupings. In the course of this reconfiguration, new classes of elites developed, and some existing elite groups were further enfranchised. For instance many of the families that previously had little connection to the

institutions of establishment Sufism in the Subcontinent but could produce documentation connecting them with a shrine were given land grants, settlements, subsidies, and other politically expedient privileges. This was particularly the case in the Panjab, United Provinces, the Northwestern Provinces, and, to a certain extent, Bengal.[4] In other cases existing Sufi families that were already recognized as spiritual and social elites enjoyed continued, or enhanced, privileges under the new rulers of India. In the case of landowning Sufis, such policies would seem to imply that the colonial Raj was well aware of the immensely influential role that Sufis played vis-à-vis the local population. In many cases they commanded the absolute loyalty of whole villages and served as mediators between local communities—of a variety of religious, class, and caste backgrounds—and local, regional, or central government representatives. In reality, however much this awareness might have served the pursuit of British hegemony, the colonial administration seemed—on the whole—curiously unable or unwilling to acknowledge the multifaceted roles that Sufis assumed. Instead, particularly in these four provinces, they came to view Sufis as (corrupt) landowning elites and political patsies or, in the case of wandering mendicants (often referred to in administrative literature as "dervishes" or "fakirs"), as threats to the social order, rather than recognizing their potential value as members of a spiritual elect. As most historians of colonial India concur, the Raj's flawed pursuit of co-opting these Muslim religious elites engendered mixed results.[5]

While the incorporation of living Sufis into the colonial administrative apparatus could at times serve as a counterbalance to the ever-present threat of defiance or revolt by the local populace, at other times the alliances between Sufis and the administration broke down completely. In other cases such alliances were never possible, particularly where they concerned wandering *darvish*es and others who had been displaced in the changeover from Mughal to British Raj. In the eyes of the colonial Raj, these wandering individuals and groups—and surveyors and census-takers recorded the presence of women among them[6]—posed a threat to the task of ordering the subject population. Attempts to control and settle them sometimes met with violent resistance.[7] The ruination of other groups that had ties to Sufis and shrines—office-holding aristocrats attached to the Mughal court in Delhi, weavers in Dhaka, soldiers of fortune, cultivators, and certain classes of landowners (such as *jagirdar*s) in Bengal—occasioned periodic revolts and military forays against the colonial administration and its (real or perceived) allies. In the case of the Muslim Pindari wars and the subsequent "Wahhabi" revolts of the early to mid–nineteenth century,[8] the

architects of and key players in these revolts were Sufi *shaikh*s and their disciples. If women disciples played any part in these movements, it seems not to have been recorded.

Since men—in all but a few isolated cases—were at the forefront of alliances with or agitations against the colonial Raj, the role of women within the world of Sufi orders and shrines was largely ignored by the majority of British administrators. This may be partly attributed to the fact that many of the women who played an influential role in the administration of shrines and ritual life remained in some sort of seclusion or *parda* and did not come into direct contact with British officialdom.[9] In contrast to examples recorded in the North African setting, British authorities seem not to have faced the question of how to mediate disputes among Sufi women and men who competed with each other over control of Sufi shrines.[10] If these disputes did occur, it is likely that they were resolved internally and without broader political implications. In other instances, as in the case of the Pir Bahor *dargah* in Patna, women who were in charge of shrines controlled only those shrines that had limited local influence and that were scarcely known outside their immediate location.[11] For the British administration, women *pir*s and female caretakers of shrines were insignificant anomalies in the contemporary world of Sufism, while the actions of female pilgrims who patronized shrines made their way into administrative documents chiefly as illustrations of the excesses of saint veneration. In the eyes of the British, such examples had little to do with the images of Islam they knew best. For most among them, women figured more significantly as objects of curiosity, sometimes of scorn, and at other times of pity, than as influential members of Sufi groups whose fortunes shifted in accordance with the improvement or decline of the Sufi families and shrines to whom they were tied. These attitudes were challenged only toward the end of the nineteenth century, when questions about women's enfranchisement, protection, and moral virtues moved into the wider public realm of discourse about cultural and religious expression.

British hegemony in the Subcontinent had brought not only the political and economic sovereignty (or in the case of the princely states and areas such as the Northwest Frontier Provinces, suzerainty) of a foreign power whose own outlook and orientation differed greatly from that of its subjects, but also a new kind of contact that introduced a broader range of cultural values into the Subcontinent. For the most part, the Mughal rulers, and even their predecessors, the Delhi sultans, had remained uninvolved in the religious lives of the vast majority of their subjects.[12] By contrast, after an initial hands-off approach (in theory at least), the British sought to encourage and influence the expression of religious identity. In part this

was fueled by political agendas: the implementation of policies and administrative apparatuses—the classificatory systems of census reports and territorial surveys, for example—gave primary recognition to subjects defined along the lines of religious identity. The first census, taken in 1853 in the Northwest Frontier Provinces, used the categories Hindu and Muslim rather indiscriminately, without inquiring about the meanings of these categories to the people they surveyed. It encouraged individuals and groups to see themselves as part of a larger community—Muslim, Hindu, Sikh, Buddhist, or Christian, for instance—and this identification came to have political repercussions as groups acquired representation in the institutions of government on the basis of religion or caste.

Religious motives also played a part: the question of religious identity was raised by European missionaries who sought converts from among the local populace and who denounced what they saw as harmful, ignorant, or misguided social and religious practices. Generally missionaries as well as the authors of the British gazetteers of the late eighteenth and early nineteenth centuries tended to speak and write disparagingly or condescendingly of the "cults" of Sufi saints, which to many of them smacked of polytheism.[13] Just how much these criticisms figured into the shift in Muslim piety "from the next world to this one" that Francis Robinson and, more recently, Armando Salvatore have highlighted[14] remains to be investigated, but we can assume that they did, indeed, play a role in generating new interpretative approaches to the question of community identity, and the impact upon women was profound.

By making religion the primary category of classification, the British focused attention on its formal characteristics—doctrine, creed, orthopraxy—as the mechanisms that determined the parameters of the "normative," or orthodox, and the heterodox. What the British shared with Orientalist observers and Muslim religious reformers in this regard was a fundamental bias toward what they believed to be paradigmatic texts of the religion. For Muslims the need for a reorientation toward the foundational texts of the faith could be cited from within the broader historical tradition of Islamic reform and revival. For many European observers, on the other hand, the essentialization of Muslim identity went hand in hand with intellectual projects derived from the European Enlightenment: in particular a preoccupation with "universal" and normative values within religious traditions and an appreciation of these values as they were conceived within Christian-oriented frameworks of belief and practice. The end result of the type of identity politics played both by the Raj and its subjects was the construction and definition of essentialized notions of community identities that have endured to this day, despite evidence suggesting that the

normative representational frameworks of which the colonized and colonizers sought to avail themselves stood in stark contrast to everyday cultural practice, such as was evident in the Sufi shrine milieu.

### The Raj's Perceptions of Islam's Antinomian Elements

Especially after the 1850s, the colonial administration came to believe that it should take up the task of strengthening what it understood to be Indian traditions,[15] which involved condemning what were believed to be some of their more "dubious" aspects. In this task it was aided as much by the works produced by Orientalist scholars as by the reports prepared by its own servants.

One of the more familiar images appearing in these works is the living holy man, particularly the mendicant (*darvish, faqir*), who often appears in these works as idle, lazy, burdensome, and fond of the use of intoxicating substances. Two kinds of descriptions of mendicant groups are discernible: on one hand company officials such as Sir Denzil Ibbetson identified whole "castes" as "*darvish.*"[16]

The disdainful attitude of many company officials toward such mendicant groups was the rule rather than the exception. Similar attitudes are evident in the many descriptions of *faqir*s as religious "fanatics" proffered in the census reports and land surveys conducted by servants of the Raj throughout the nineteenth and early twentieth centuries.

In the East-India gazetteers, Walter Hamilton describes the *faqir* as a devotee or mendicant who traveled around "in a palanquin, clad in silk, with numerous attendants to protect his sacred person." Moreover, he noted, "these fanatics are extremely proud, and in general insolent and abusive to Europeans."[17] More important, the portrayal of such groups as being resistant to control made it easier for the colonial administration to link the need to regulate, manage, and "settle" them with issues of state security.

For many company officials, the connections between the *faqir* and the institutions of Sufism were irrelevant. As Katherine Ewing points out, company officials often classified *faqir*s and *sadhu*s as criminal elements.

Sandria Freitag notes that these ideas were in part influenced by the existence of wandering bands of mercenaries who worked for Hindus, Muslims, and British alike and were known to engage in plunder, begging, and extortion, often during religious pilgrimages or fairs. That being the case, *sadhu*s and *faqir*s were seen by the British as groups needing to be regulated or suppressed. Such attitudes also influenced these groups'

self-images, as well as the ways in which they responded to British attempts to restrict and contain their activities.[18]

While the information that early generations of European travelers collected about Muslim saints and mystics was limited in nature and largely ignorant of how these figures shaped and were shaped by the religious and cultural landscape in which they lived, the literature produced by succeeding generations of Europeans sought not only to understand these questions, but also to see how the answers they derived could best serve the interests of the British Raj. The kinds of information that were sought out and recorded by company officials in the early nineteenth century—demographic data; preexisting systems of administration, law, taxation, and governance; the titles and roles of key functionaries (such as scholars, scribes, landholders, and revenue officials); scriptures, religious codes, beliefs, practices, and cultural mores; inter- and intracaste and class dynamics; local legends and oral stories; historiographies and imperial chronicles; works of literature, philosophy, grammar, and science; classical and vernacular languages and their systems of use; and archeological surveys—dealt with key areas in which knowledge was needed to facilitate the business of governing the land. In covering these topics, official publications such as census reports, territorial surveys, and district gazetteers encompassed the "investigative modalities of the colonial project" enumerated by Bernard Cohn: historiography, observation/travel, enumeration, museology, and surveillance, all of which sought to determine, order, and control information about India's past and contemporary present.[19]

Typically the district gazetteers and territorial surveys attempted to cover a broad array of subjects, and for this reason they dealt in a very cursory manner with devotion to saints. Much of the information they relied on about saints and shrines was anecdotal or collected by examiners within a very limited course of time. In some cases the authors of gazetteers and surveys relied entirely upon the information that their colleagues and subordinates furnished. Not surprisingly many of the facts they published about shrines, popular saints, and the legends surrounding these are flawed or altogether incorrect. For example one late-nineteenth-century source, Eastwick's guide to the Panjab, Western Rajputana, Kashmir, and Upper Sind, conflates descriptions of the Arhai din ki Jhonpra mosque and the *dargah* of Mu'in al-din Chishti, both located in Ajmer. Eastwick describes the mosque as the burial place of the saint, who is said to have been the son of "Khwaja 'Usman" ('Usman Haruni), the man who was actually his spiritual guide (*shaikh*)![20] By contrast the journals and territorial surveys of Francis Buchanan-Hamilton, one of the first company servants to notice

and take an interest in the large numbers of converts to Islam among the indigenous population,[21] provide a significant amount of information about the mausoleums built around the graves of Sufi saints in the areas he surveyed during the first decade of the nineteenth century: Bihar, Bengal, Madras, and the Northwest Frontier Provinces. His surveys mark the earliest detailed treatment of the phenomena of contemporary shrine and saint veneration by an East India Company official.

Buchanan-Hamilton's accounts of devotion to saints can hardly be called sympathetic. Like the reports of the East India Company officials who succeeded him, his descriptions of Sufi shrines evince an obvious disdain for the practices that took place on their premises. The presence of wandering holy men—long regarded with awe and respect as well as fear and suspicion by believers—is characterized in the journals he kept during a survey of Patna and Gaya as one of the more undesirable aspects of shrine life. He describes the mausoleum of Shah Daulat in Maner as being "in the most disgusting state":

> Fakirs have been allowed to boil their pots in the porticos, and have overwhelmed them with soot, to remedy which irregular patches over the pots have been whitewashed. One of the corner chambers is occupied by a beastly ascetic, who has shut up the doors and windows with old pots, clay, and cowdung patched together in the rudest manner, nor are any pains taken to keep the place in repair; yet the descendant of the saint has 6,000 bighas [3,750 acres] free of rent, and that of the richest quality. The whole is said to be expended in the feeding of idle squalid mendicants, vagrants who are in this country an intolerable nuisance.[22]

This vision of the "beastly ascetic" stands in contrast to that of the *sajjada nishin,* or saint's successor, whose possession of large tracts of land particularly interested the British colonial administration toward the close of the nineteenth century. While *faqirs* and the like were dismissed as rogue elements, the landed *sajjada nishin* was seen in an altogether different light. As landholder but also as a source of religious authority who could exercise considerable influence over the local population, the *sajjada nishin* proved a valuable ally for the colonialist project, and consequently the company began to adopt policies of cooperation, co-option, and control toward the more settled elements of Sufi authority—*pirs* and hereditary *shaikhs*—that they encountered among the subject population. The term *pir* was usually, but not always, used to designate Sufis who were attached to shrines (as such they could fall into the category of landed gentry), while the term

*faqir* was often applied to the figure of the wandering ascetic. These terms, however, were sometimes also used interchangeably.

British perceptions and treatment of Sufi shrines and *pir*s were closely tied to the colonial agenda of asserting economic, social, ideological, and political control over their subjects. In pursuit of this agenda, the company took steps to create pliable allies from among the ranks of those who were, or who were perceived to be, local elites. In reality the British colonial administration had multiple arrangements with Sufi shrines and their representatives in the Panjab. *Pir*s, local aristocrats, and tribal and religious leaders were given special privileges in return for loyalty to the Raj, which included cooperation in the job of administering large areas where European personnel and resources were lacking. From early on the Raj implemented policies that sought to understand, maintain, and replicate the types of patronage-based relationships that their predecessors had cultivated with local religious leaders. In failing to avail themselves effectively of the powerful symbolic value of human and nonhuman representatives of the sacred, they in effect reimagined the nature of the relationship between local and central structures of administration on the one hand and religious authorities on the other. British involvement in the affairs of shrine management and administration likely helped to legitimate colonial Raj in the eyes of many devotees of the shrines, as well as their caretakers. This worked to the benefit of the Raj, particularly in those cases where the involvement of some *pir*s with the local and central political system was so great that they could not develop much of an independent challenge to the colonial regime.[23] However, the sense of cooperation between *pir*s and the Raj remained ambivalent. The breakdown of this cooperation became evident in particular cases, such as that of the Pir Pagaro, and in a broader sense it was demonstrated in the ways in which revivalist Muslim religious leaders increasingly turned away from the British and toward the sources of Islamic tradition as the paramount symbol of moral authority after the late nineteenth century.[24]

The tombs of Sufi *shaikh*s attracted the interest of the East India Company in the nineteenth century because they represented powerful instruments of local and in some cases regional authority, as well as institutions to which were attached (in the cases of more prominent shrines) great amounts of wealth, chiefly in the form of limited-revenue or revenue-free *madad-i ma'ash, waqf, in'am, jagir,* and other types of land grants.[25] For many company officials in the nineteenth century, the descendants of these *shaikh*s, hereditary functionaries who owned (mostly in charitable trust) and managed Sufi shrines, were more important as landowning elites and

political power brokers who could exercise considerable influence over their followers than as religious authorities, and British treatment of them underscored their importance as such. In many ways, particularly where they possessed land and revenue rights that extended back through several preceding generations, these hereditary functionaries were perceived by the colonial administration to be the "natural proprietors" of land in India.[26] No doubt some of their claims to spiritual authority on the basis of descent from a Sufi saint were false. As S. A. A. Rizvi has argued, some landowning families deliberately forged links with Sufis both real and imagined in order to prove their superior ancestry and to establish proprietary rights.[27] This was particularly true in the first half of the nineteenth century, when the mechanisms for distinguishing true claims from false ones had yet to be refined. The problem was not particular to the colonial administration, however: Irfan Habib has shown how abuses of the system of land and revenue grants had also plagued the Mughal Raj.[28]

However real or spurious, these classes of religious leaders and the shrines they managed were incorporated into the apparatus of the colonial administration in such a way that, on the one hand, the most useful alliances between state and religious authorities could be preserved, and on the other, new ones could be created. However, this did not necessarily represent a departure from precolonial practices. Indeed in some cases it represented a continuation of policies followed by the Mughals, wherein grantees were chosen on the basis of their perceived ability to control or break the monopoly of other groups.[29] The effects of such policies were, in the Mughal as well as colonial era, to create new boundaries and shift old ones among certain castes and communities. As part of its endeavor to secure the cooperation of religious leaders and, through this, to aid in the task of legitimating the colonial Raj in the eyes of its subject population, the company implemented a policy of which there were three key features: the bestowal of endowments upon shrines and their functionaries; control of the administration and management of shrines, indirectly where possible and directly in those cases where such administration was crippled by corruption and/or debt; and the creation of an English-educated, loyalist contingent from among the ranks of the religious elite. A closer look at the workings of this policy is in order.

The Raj's policies of granting concessions to groups identified on the basis of religion had an underlying agenda aimed at creating an English-educated, loyalist, self-critical, and sympathetic contingent from among those whom the colonial administration believed to represent the elite. In these policies the aims of the state and the interests of Orientalist scholars were aligned. Lisa Lowe has identified three stages in this process. The

earliest stage of Orientalist education and the expansion of colonial Raj, through the eighteenth century, involved familiarizing Europeans with the cultures of the subject population in an effort to secure and expand their "cultural control." The second stage, up to the mid–nineteenth century, involved developing taxonomies of "Indian traditions" and "anglicizing" the upper classes, particularly the landlord and merchant-banker classes, by schooling them in British legal, administrative, and educational systems of knowledge. The third, post-1857, stage involved an expansion of these "anglicization" efforts among a wider cross-section of the population, through what the British perceived to be "traditional systems" such as caste- and patronage-based systems of exchange.[30]

## British Management of Shrines

Since the time of the Delhi sultans, endowments by wealthy patrons and by members of the ruling classes had greatly expanded the territorial holdings of many Sufi shrines. The functionaries attached to the wealthier shrines, most often on the basis of hereditary claims, owned and managed not only these institutions but also villages that had been granted them for the upkeep and support of their families. Although most hereditary caretakers of Sufi shrines eked out a living from the agricultural and manufacturing output of the villages they owned, as well as cash contributions from the pilgrims they serviced, others could and did profit handsomely. As early as the late eighteenth century, the East India Company began to take over the policies and patronage roles that had been implemented by their predecessors. At the same time, they became increasingly involved in the endowment and regulation of Hindu, Muslim, and Sikh shrines, religious festivals, and ceremonies. For example the Mu'in al-din Chishti *dargah* enjoyed a long history of gifts and endowments that had begun in the late fourteenth century and continued fairly regularly throughout the period of colonial rule. These endowments came from many sources: Delhi sultans and Mughal sovereigns, other Hindu and Muslim ruling families and wealthy elites. The devotion and generosity of many to Khwaja Mu'in al-din and his mausoleum—regardless of religious community, social position, or regional location—underscored the shrine's local, regional, and national importance. Despite the failure of some company servants to mention the shrine in their observations, on the whole the British East India Company did not fail to notice the shrine's importance in the region. That they continued the policies of their Muslim predecessors by appointing some of the *dargah*'s functionaries and by making substantial grants to it shows that they were, indeed, aware of its clout.[31]

The imposition of taxes upon pilgrims[32] accompanied the company's direct assumption of control in the administration of shrines. This process began with individual cases and quickly transformed into a broad policy. In the mid-1790s one Mr. Place, a collector in Conjivaram, donated jewels to a local Vaishnavite shrine, and a few years later had convinced the company to take over its administration. In 1806 the British passed an act enabling the company to assume control of the famous Hindu Jagannath temple in Puri (Orissa). Twenty-seven years later the Madras government alone was responsible for the administration of 7,600 Hindu shrines. Such control was also the case in the two other British-held territories, Bengal and the Bombay Presidency. However, not all company officials supported British involvement in the management of shrines, and objections were raised within the higher ranks of the administration about what was perceived as the state sanction of idolatry. Accordingly, by 1833 the directors sent out orders that company servants should desist from the management of temples and from participating in religious ceremonies, festivals, and pilgrimages. Moreover the pilgrim tax was abolished in principle that same year, although this abolition was not put into effect until 1840.[33]

Prominent Sufi shrines also came under the control of the colonial administration beginning in the early nineteenth century. After the annexation of Ajmer in 1820, the company came to know of the many problems plaguing the management of Mu'in al-din Chishti's *dargah*. Disputes erupted frequently over privileges, wealth, and succession to positions in the shrine's administration. Such disputes were often settled by litigation, and it was chiefly in this regard that the colonial administration initially became involved in the shrine's affairs. It soon became involved in other ways: over the years the Ajmer Commission had provided several generous loans to the highest-ranking functionary of the shrine, the *diwan,* and in 1887 it took over the management of his properties, citing mismanagement, debt, and corruption as the reasons.[34] Around six years later, the political agent for Bikaner, C. S. Bayly, also cited the debt of the *diwan*'s estate as a reason for its takeover but stated that its management had been turned over to the Court of Wards, an institution that was initially established to give financial backing to local intermediary groups.[35] Although Sufi shrines were not the only properties to come under the management of the Court of Wards, the fact that they were among the first targets for takeover by this institution testifies to the importance with which they and their hereditary caretakers had come to be viewed by the colonial administration.[36]

Through such mechanisms as the judiciary system, the government began not only to oversee the management of estates, but also to have a hand

in determining who would inherit them. Succession to the office of the *diwan* as it occurred at the Mu'in al-din *dargah* was one, but not the only, dispute in which the colonial administration found itself compelled to intervene. Removal from and appointment to the office of "trustee," or custodian of shrine endowments (*mutawalli*)—a post created in the sixteenth century, understood by the *dargah* administration to be secular in nature, and open to Hindus as well as Muslims—had rested with the Mughal emperor as late as the end of the 1820s.[37] Afterward the colonial government found itself thrust into this position of mediation, particularly as more and more candidates sought the intervention of British government officials in disputes over succession to the office. The authority of the government came to cover the appointment and dismissal of aspirants to this office and others, the redress of grievances among candidates, and the management of religious endowments, particularly where their holders had become debt-ridden. However, the company began to find its responsibilities in this regard burdensome. The passage of the Religious Endowments Bill of 1863 did little to dampen British involvement in the management of the *dargah*. After the enactment of this bill, the colonial government appointed a *dargah* committee, as well as an office called the *nazim dargah,* to oversee the management and proper functioning of the shrine's administrative apparatus. Despite these efforts the government was unable to extricate itself completely from direct involvement in the shrine, and the courts would be called in time and again to intervene in matters of succession and to respond to charges of corruption. Today the office of the *nazim dargah* remains a government-appointed post, and litigious disputes over succession, titles, and rights among the *dargah*'s functionaries continue.[38]

As viewed through the lens of its relationships with landed *pir*s and the shrines to which they were attached, the colonial administration's policies of appeasement, cooperation, and control only partially succeeded in legitimating the British Raj in the eyes of the subject population. Although overall the entanglement of *pir*s and shrines in the colonial machine limited the ability of the former to undermine it politically and economically, a subtle, and ultimately more dangerous, momentum began to gather by the end of the nineteenth century. It was predicated on a sense of community and national sovereignty and drew from, as much as it condemned, British understandings of both. The establishment of classificatory schema that drew from perceived religious differences and the promotion of scholarship on Indian Islam that alternately praised Sufism, condemned its contemporary manifestations, and—whether in praise or in condemnation—sought

to distinguish it from Islam conceived as a "normative" formulation were but two mechanisms by which European understandings of Indian Muslims were manifest. Such classificatory schema and descriptive paradigms quickly transcended the immediate colonial agendas of management and control to produce in the subject population (at least among its political and social elites) a much greater sense of itself as both "community" and "nation" entitled to its own self-determination and willing to reconceptualize its history in accordance with its own political and social aims. However many contradictions and ambiguities such understandings of sovereignty and selfhood entailed, for Sufi religious leaders, the stage was set for their emergence as players of importance to both sides, to the British who sought to maintain the state structure even as they began to realize its impending collapse and to the politically savvy nationalist and reformist groups who jockeyed for power and influence in the arenas of local, regional, and national politics. Perhaps most important, Sufis occupied a crossroads at which the question of community identity and its implications for the relationships among India's various groups, on the one hand, and the place of these groups within the nation, on the other, remained centrally important.

## Orientalist Scholars: Ambivalent Encounters

The literature that emerged during the colonial period of Indian history has contributed much to perceptions of the veneration of Sufi shrines and saints as anomalous characteristics of Islam in the Subcontinent. The bifurcation of Islam in its wider institutional sense from living Sufis and the shrines and circles to which they were connected is perhaps the most glaring feature of the works produced by the second generation of European colonialist, missionary, and Orientalist writers.[39] For some of these observers, however, the relationship between saint and shrine veneration and Islam in its broader perspective—particularly as seen in the Middle East and North Africa—was not unknown. As a result of increased access to primary sources in the mid–nineteenth century, which was preceded by European expansion into Muslim-ruled lands in the Mediterranean and Indian regions, writers such as the Austrian scholar Aloys Sprenger (d. 1893) and the scholar and British East India Company statesman Sir William Muir (d. 1905) had been able to compile historical biographies of the Prophet that departed significantly from earlier accounts. The works produced by them demonstrate a critical approach to the Prophet's life and earned them harsh criticism from the ranks of Indian Muslims, among

them the reformer Sir Sayyid Ahmad Khan.[40] These works fueled the composition of subsequent narratives on Muhammad and Islam by a number of European observers, including missionaries.[41] The veneration of the Prophet, in particular, served for many such observers as the most visible link between local saint veneration and the wider world of Islam. Writing about saint "cults" among the Arabs, Ignaz Goldziher (d. 1921) likened them to the worship of relics.

> The cult of Valis, or saints, has its counterpart and concomitant in the worship of relics in Islam. Though it has not been exalted in Islam to that universal importance which is accorded to other offshoots of the cult of saints, still it exhibits itself in the popular belief of the Mohammedans in extremely various forms. In the biographies of holy men we frequently see it noted that special value is attached to their "vestigia," so the Moslems call relics, and that enormous sums are offered for their possession. Even the manuscripts of saints belong to that category of hallowed vestiges. People acquire them for enhancement of inner religious faith, or *lil-tabarruk* as the Arabs express it, for a blessing. . . . Sufi adepts preserve in their chapels the clothes, especially the Khirka or the Sajjada and other articles, of the founder of the article. But the cult of relics finds expression among the vulgar in the interior forms of fetish.[42]

Noting the transformation of "cults" of relics from that of private use by individuals to a wider application in the general public milieu (and the particular devotion of women to such "cults"), Goldziher characterizes this shift as being indicative of the decline of Arab society. His assessment of the development of similar phenomena in India and Turkey, for which he draws from the criticisms of the "celebrated theologian of Medina, Sheikh Amin," is equally disparaging.[43] Yet he singles out the veneration of saints in India as "associated with the distinctive peculiarities of Islam in Hindustan. It has brought itself into line with the indigenous relic worship assimilating to itself many of the features of heathenism."[44]

Here especially, in connecting "saint worship" with indigenous beliefs and practices, Goldziher manages to disconnect the former from a broader sense of Islam that is—in his view—predicated on a "normative" vision of a religion of laws and statues that are taken as self-evident. Three biases emerge in Goldziher's assessments that Islam and the veneration of saints are antithetical and oppositional in their relationship to one another. Such biases implicate the wider ranks of early-twentieth-century Orientalist scholars. First, the interests of these scholars lay primarily with the study

of the "classic" texts, as had the interests of their predecessors. Second, they had even less cultural contact with indigenous Indians than had previous generations, and third, they tended to see evidence of the extra- or anti-Islamic in those cases where obvious reference to the laws and statues of a taken-for-granted Islam in "living" expressions of devotion was not forthcoming. Such views, however, were not limited to Orientalist observers, and in fact many among them took their cue from the opposition to the veneration of saints voiced by Islamic reformers, particularly the scholars of the law.

As cultural anthropologist Katherine Ewing has observed, another bifurcation is evident in the colonial period literature. Sufism is clearly distinguished from contemporary shrines and their saints, *faqirs*, and other types of ascetics, as well as a host of practices that were widely considered "Sufi." While the Orientalist idea of Sufism was partly shaped by notions of a "golden age" in which the highest ideals and most gifted individuals of philosophical-mystic thought predominated, shrines and their saints were treated as corrupt forms of a once-great tradition, where their connections with such were acknowledged at all. Women's devotional activities, in particular, were associated with some of the more dubious manifestations of saint veneration. Where writers dealt with the devotion of Hindu and Muslim women to Sufi saints and other sacred figures, this devotion could be couched in terms at once condescending and romanticizing. For example one work by the early-twentieth-century Orientalist scholar J. C. Oman reports on a procession during Muharram, the month of mourning during which the massacre of the Prophet's grandson Husain and his entourage in the desert of Karbala (Iraq) is commemorated. The devotion of female mourners to Husain is described in ambivalent terms, as evidence of women's "superior religiosity" as well as their "ignorance."[45] Such "ignorance" extended to the Muslim masses in general, who prefer—in Oman's reckoning—to venerate saints rather than to observe the basic obligations and tenets of Islam.[46] While Oman could reproach European and American women for their "unnecessary pity" for the "inmates of the harem" and claim that his "sympathies as a spectator were all with the dear [Muslim] women and their overfaith,"[47] he did not address the question of how such manifestations of piety and devotion fit into larger frameworks of religious observance. His portraits of Sufis, wandering ascetics, and other kinds of venerated saints fluctuate between romanticization of a religious ideal and criticism of its contemporary reality.

The ambivalence with which Orientalists and the elite among the company servants represented indigenous religious traditions owed much to

ideas that emerged from the European Enlightenment—a sense of historical and cultural relativism that sprang from the concept of tolerance, as historian David Kopf argues in *British Orientalism and the Bengal Renaissance*—even as it engaged in a search for normative and unchanging principles. On the whole the second generation of Orientalists and company servants evinced less empathy for "Indian civilization" than had their earlier counterparts,[48] but both generations shared a preoccupation with "universal principles" that prompted them to turn toward the so-called classical texts of religious traditions. For Hinduism these were primarily the Sanskrit Vedic corpus, including the *shastric* literature, the epics, and, later, the *Puranas;* for Islam the Qur'an, Hadis, and early Arabic historical accounts of the Prophet such as Ibn Ishaq's (d. 873) *Sirat Rasul Allah,* al-Waqidi's (d. 822) *Kitab al-maghazi,* and Ibn Sa'd's (d. 845) *Tabaqat;* and for Sufism the works of mystics such as Ibn al-'Arabi and al-Ghazali. Although British Orientalists did not share the same passion for the "classics" as did the Germans and the French, on the whole the fascination of European observers with Sufism lay primarily in its value as a vehicle for poetic and philosophical ruminations on such subjects as humanity, the soul, and the mystic's quest to know God intimately. That expressions of piety in the Sufi shrine presented quite a different picture from the images conjured in the texts written by classical Sufi authors figured heavily with Europeans writers' disdain for contemporary saints and their shrines.[49] The earliest narratives about such phenomena in the Subcontinent set the tone for these enduring biases.

## Early European Images of Sufism and Shrines in the Subcontinent, 1615–1835

Under imperial patronage Portugese travelers had established a conquering presence on the southwestern coast of the Subcontinent by the end of the fifteenth century. They did so partly through the aid, and then exploitation, of the Muslims (Moors) already established there. Although the accounts of such travelers had been recorded as early as Vasco da Gama's 1497 voyage around the Cape of Good Hope, they did not figure as significant sources of data for those servants of the British Raj who were initially entrusted with the task of information gathering in the early nineteenth century. One of the reasons behind this neglect involves the kinds of data that was collected by European voyagers before the nineteenth century: detailed lists of products, prices, and other information that was directly relevant to the business of commerce and trade. This data, as well as political information

about the Mughal Empire, its ruling classes and functionaries, and their relationship to the East India Company tended to reflect the particular concerns of the latter about the task of conducting business in the Subcontinent.

As might be expected, these early accounts proffered limited depictions of Islamic spirituality. Within them Sufis—as *faqir*s or *darvish*es, the apparent epithets of choice for most early European travelers—and the shrines erected in their honor tended to appear insofar as they related to the interests of the ruling aristocracy or as they figured in direct encounters with travelers or their companions, while their relationship with institutional Sufism—and Islam—remained essentially unexplored. Yet there had been a long history of exchange between Europeans and Muslims, and the mystical dimensions of the latter were not unknown to the former. In Marshall Hodgson's estimation, the direction of cultural exchange between "Islamdom and the Occident" prior to the seventeenth century (in which the latter, he argues, more often than not was the beneficiary) was "drastically one-sided," and the medium of such exchange tended to be indirect sources. These included not only texts that were originally composed in Greek, such as Aristotle's *Ethics* and Plato's *Republic,* and translated from their Arabic recensions, and natural science materials (mathematics, astronomy, medicine, and chemistry) translated into the European languages, but also translations of philosophical-mystic texts of "speculative Sufism" such as the works of ibn Rushd (Latin: Averroës), ibn Sina (Latin: Avicenna), and Ibn al-'Arabi.[50] In many cases early European travelers' awareness of the history of exchange between Islam and the Occident was confined to Islam's confrontations with Christianity, as in the cases of the Crusades and the rise of the Ottoman Empire, or in stories about the Prophet Muhammad, or fanciful tales of *1001 Arabian Nights*–style wandering *darvish*es and secret societies such as the Assassins. The narratives about encounters with Sufism produced by sixteenth- and seventeenth-century British and French merchants and political envoys in Persia and Mughal India had also piqued the interest of Europeans in Islamic mystical literature and philosophy.[51] In 1798 Napoleon's invasion of Egypt and his tactical (though short-lived) sponsorship of scholarship afterward also figured as important sources of information about Islam and its mystical dimensions for early European travelers.[52]

Notwithstanding the history of Islamic-Occidental interaction, the relationships between institutional Islam and the forms of Sufism that early European travelers encountered in the Subcontinent seemed to have been a subject that the latter did not feel necessary to explore in any depth, and it would be up to the servants of the East India Company who followed them in the nineteenth century, particularly the land surveyors and census

takers among them, to develop a more pointed interest in these subjects. Indeed, despite the disdain that many nineteenth-century East India Company officials felt for early European accounts as valuable sources of information for the colonial project, travelers' stories of wandering holy men and the shrines that housed their remains provided some of the fabric of colonialist narratives about contemporary shrine and saint veneration as they were translated and republished throughout the nineteenth century. The information in these travel accounts also served to shape ideas about the sometimes romanticized, sometimes maligned figures of "native" devotion.

Descriptions of Sufis and shrines in such accounts as those written by Sir Thomas Roe, sent as ambassador to the court of Jahangir by King James I in 1615; Jean-Baptiste Tavernier (1605–89), the French merchant; and the Italian soldier and doctor Niccolao Manucci (1639–1717), read as little more than curiosity pieces in narratives of travel and adventure. Yet even in these short descriptions, we are able to glimpse something about the ways in which these early voyagers conceived of the relationships among Sufis, shrines, and the local element in which they existed and how these conceptions were reflected in the memoirs, letters, journals, and reports of succeeding generations of European observers in the Subcontinent. While Roe does not mention the shrine of Mu'in al-din Chishti in his account of his visit to the Ajmer-based court of the emperor Jahangir (r. 1605–27), he does note the emperor's journey to "Ugen" (Ujjain) to visit a *darvish* reputed to be three hundred years old.[53] The interest of the princess Jahanara (1614–80), daughter of the emperor Shah Jahan (r. 1628–58), in Sufi mysticism, and her burial in the mausoleum of Shaikh Nizam al-din Auliya (d. 1326) in Delhi is mentioned by Tavernier within a larger narrative of life at the Mughal court.[54] Both Tavernier and Manucci mention the interest of the emperor Aurangzeb (r. 1658–1707) in "*faqiri*," although this interest was portrayed by both men as a political ploy to mask the emperor's political ambitions.[55] Their impression of the role of *faqir*s vis-à-vis the wider public suggests astonishment at the devotion with which the tombs of Muslim holy men were approached by pilgrims of many faiths.

Indeed Sufis were part of a cultural and religious landscape in which they, Hindu holy men and women, individuals such as the fifteenth-century mystic and poet Kabir (who did not fit neatly into any category of Hindu or Muslim, *faqir* or *sadhu*), and legendary, semidivinized, or heroic figures were highly revered, their aid in matters spiritual and mundane sought out by supplicants from a broad cultural, social, and religious spectrum.[56] Most of the early European travelers did not recognize their importance and wide-ranging appeal: for instance Manucci expressed surprise

upon learning of a tomb—widely believed to contain the remains of a *faqir* by the name of Malik Dinar—that was reputedly patronized by Christian women on behalf of their sons and grandsons. According to Manucci's account, Aurangzeb proved that the tomb contained nothing more than the body of a horse, which had been buried by its owner, a *faqir* who sought to reap financial gain by establishing a shrine, with eventually disastrous consequences for the *faqir*.[57] This revelation only served to confirm Manucci's opinion of *faqir*s as an untrustworthy lot, though it is Tavernier who hints at a distinction that had already been made within the ranks of Sufis themselves: that between "true" and "professional" Sufis. His comments about "professional" *faqir*s and others like them who became ascetics for reasons of expediency highlights the precarious nature of religious identities: "You may see in India whole provinces like deserts, from whence the peasants have fled on account of the oppression of the Governors. Under cover of the fact that they are themselves Musulmans, they persecute these poor idolaters to the utmost, and if any of the latter become Muslim, it is in order to escape work; they become soldiers or Fakirs, or people who make a profession of having renounced the world, and live upon alms; but in reality they are all rascals. It is esteemed that there are in India 800,000 Musalman Fakirs, and 1,200,000 among the idolaters."[58]

Equally telling in their implications for the opinions of succeeding generations of Europeans are the contradictions inherent in the author's portrait of wandering mendicants. Tavernier's uncertain depiction of *faqir*s illustrates the kind of ambivalence that baffled the colonial administration's efforts to categorize and order these particular subjects. Tavernier's condemnation of wanderers as "rascals," in part because of their failure to engage in productive activity, prefigures the attitude of East India Company servants and Orientalist scholars toward these most recalcitrant members of society. Katherine Ewing has analyzed their perceptions of wandering and begging as being a serious threat to the colonialist project. Two of her observations regarding Mughal and British colonial endeavors to understand, classify, and deal with the phenomena of wandering and begging are especially relevant here for the contradictory portraits they paint.

> First, although the wandering ascetic could also pose a threat to Mughal authority, the attitudes of the latter towards the phenomena of wandering and begging, and the violation of the social order that this represented, was tempered by the equally powerful notion of the wandering mendicant as saint and representative of religious authority. By contrast, for British colonial administrators, wandering groups were often associated with criminal activity, and as such, their religious

practice remained of little importance. Second, the colonial administration's awkward attempts to register them and regulate their activities produced randomly chosen categories that alternately sought to
highlight their status as a separate caste or tribe, or to distinguish,
within their ranks, Muslim and Hindu strands.[59]

Yet, as Tavernier's account hints, and as was indeed the case, these types of
wanderers often possessed identities that were neither unequivocally Muslim nor non-Muslim but that remained in flux. Although Tavernier apparently was aware that *faqiri* was by no means limited to the wandering,
begging mendicant, and that the *faqir* could occupy different spaces at different times (his somewhat more sympathetic portrayal of certain types of
*faqir*s as being schooled in the intricacies of Islamic law and striving to provide guidance to others of their faith is a case in point),[60] the overriding
image of the *faqir* in his accounts remained that of an imposter, rebel, and
violent fanatic. For later Orientalist writers, the figure of the Sufi could
embody something of a romantic ideal, the "retiring, self-contained ascetic" and "hero of the Far East," as opposed to the European "vigorous,
active worker for the good of others," obsessed as he was with the accumu-
lation of personal wealth.[61] Mrs. Meer Hasan 'Ali, a British woman who
married a Lucknow noble and wrote about her observations of Muslim
beliefs and practices during her twelve-year residence in India, distinguished between "the real Soofie" and the "hypocrites to the world, and
their Maker."[62] Of the former she noted two kinds "of the professedly devout
Soofies":

> the Saalik and the Majoob [*majzub*]. The true Saalik Soofies are those
> that give up the world and its allurements, abstain from all sensual
> enjoyments, rarely associate with their fellow-men, devote themselves
> entirely to their Creator, and are insensible to any other enjoyments
> but such as they derive from their devotional exercises.
>
> The Majoob Soofies have no established home nor earthly posses-
> sions; they drink wine and spirits freely, when they can obtain them.
> Many people suppose this class have lost the possession of their reason,
> and make excuse for their departure from the law on that score. Both
> classes are nevertheless in great respect.[63]

If the living saint seemed an object of contempt for many European observers, others—Muslim writers and Europeans who were in close contact
with Indian Muslims, as well as Indian converts to Christianity—did not
hold any simple, one-dimensional idea of the mystic. While the colonial
administration could associate living *pir*s primarily with economic and

social rather than spiritual authority and label wandering ascetics as degenerates, these views, promoted through the media, the courts, and manifest in administrative practices, were not hegemonic.[64] Indeed British endeavors to assess and explain the Indian past could serve to sacralize it for a subject population who used it to affirm their own identities and the merits of their religious traditions.[65] Such self-affirmation was inscribed on the bodies of women as the "woman question" became a key focus of debates about Islam in the Subcontinent.

### Muslim Reformers: Women as Symbols of Faith and Community

Within the first two decades of the twentieth century, women emerged as potent symbols of Islamic faith and community in colonial India. For Muslim spiritual elites and religious scholars, women's ritual performances, and indeed their observance of what was often referred to as "customary practices," reflected the moral ethos of the Indian *umma* and highlighted the need for reforming Islam in the Subcontinent. Adherence to what they saw as "excessive" and "un-Islamic" forms of devotion to *pir*s, particularly by women and members of the lower social orders, was another manifestation of Muslims' moral decline. Although *tajdid o islah,* Islamic revival and reform, had been a recurring theme throughout the history of Mughal India, as in the wider Muslim world, the reformist impulse that emerged in late-colonial India was also tied to changes in the social makeup of Muslims from the middle and upper classes. Moreover, as Gail Minault has demonstrated in her study of education among Muslim women in nineteenth-century India, Muslim religious reformers sought to counter what they saw as a decline in the moral fiber of the "respectable" classes, exemplified in part by the decadence of the Nawabi lifestyle.[66] The attention these reform-minded intellectuals gave to the question of women's participation in Sufi shrine culture marked an important shift in discourses about women toward the close of the nineteenth century, one in which the "woman question" took center stage in debates about the future of Muslims in the Indian Subcontinent.

This shift could be seen in the explosion of didactic texts written by members of the Muslim religious intelligentsia beginning in the last quarter of the nineteenth century. These texts initially targeted elite women but later cited the education and edification of ordinary women as being a key objective in the reform of Indian Muslim society.[67] Neither the writing nor the publication of such texts was entirely new, but their impact on the woman question from the late nineteenth century was major. The first printing press appeared in the Subcontinent as early as 1556, when it was

imported by Christian missionaries in Goa, though it did not become a viable means for the mass publication of texts until after 1830. The range of didactic publications, even in this initial phase of mass publishing, was wide. In the first half of the nineteenth century, works in Urdu such as Sa'di's *Gulistan* and *Bustan*, romances such as *Yusuf-Zulaikha* and *Majnun-Layla*, and the Bengali *Janganama* corpus were published. These works married well-known Arabic and Persian tales and themes with local folk idioms. Urdu *marsiya* texts extolled the virtues of the Prophet's martyred grandson Husain, his grief-stricken sisters, and the other victims of the Karbala massacre. Writers such as Nazir Ahmad (d. 1912) and Rashid al-Khairi (d. 1936) produced novels, short stories, and works intended to educate women about Islam and to provide a forum for topics of interest to them, such as polygamy, *parda,* and marriage.[68] Poetry and poetic narrative took on didactic tones as they sought to enlighten Muslims and change their perceptions about women: Altaf Husain Hali's (d. 1914) *Chup ki Dad* and *Munajat-i Bewa* highlighted the virtues of women in India while recounting their sad plight, while his *Majlis al-nisa'* called attention to the importance of education for Muslim women's social, religious, and moral uplift.[69]

Straightforward, comprehensive guides for Muslim women's edification appeared in works such as the women's journal *Tahzib al-niswan,* founded in 1898 by Mumtaz 'Ali, who was a product of the Dar ul-Ulum Deobandi *madrasa;* and in a book with the same title written by the Begam of Bhopal, a follower of the reformist Ahl-i Hadis movement. Other examples of this type of literature, such as the *Risala-i bagh-i niswan,* published under the patronage of the Nizam of Hyderabad, also featured collections of stories and poems illustrating ethical principles and emulated the style of classical Persian *adab* literature.[70] Mumtaz 'Ali's *Huquq al-niswan* addressed Christian missionaries' attacks on religion as a prime factor in the ignorance of women in India and marked the author's endeavor to change Muslims' adherence to false customs, which he blamed for the discrepancies between the legal status accorded to Muslim women in the Shari'a and their lack of rights in practice.[71] In addition to these, a small number of didactic manuals addressing the need for the reform of Islamic faith and practice were published before the 1870s. Karamat 'Ali Jaunpuri's *Miftahu'l-Jannat* (1827 or 1828) and Muhammad Qutb al-din Dihlavi's *Umdat al-nasa'ih* (1866; elsewhere noted as *Tuhfat al-zaujain*) spoke to women and men alike, while Dihlavi's later work, *Tuhfat al-ahibba fi ahkam tahrim an-nisa'* (1869), specifically addressed women's concerns.

Also during this period, a large number of reform-minded didactic texts for women were published in the regional languages. For example Bengali *dobhashi* texts, or narrative poems and religious discourses (also known as

*battala puthi* when printed in larger type), appeared widely in print. Muslim composers of *mangal-kavya, vijay-kavya,* and *panchalika* literature[72] sought to marry the cultural heritage of Islam (as represented by legendary and mythical heroes) with idioms that were particular to Bengal. Sometimes these works took on an anti-Hindu bias, as in the case of Muhammad Khan's *Maqtal.* In other cases Muslim personages were recast in terms familiar to Bengali aesthetics and religious sensibilities, as in the case of Shaikh Tanu's *Fatima surat nama* and the poetry of Pagla Kanai.[73] Tamil novelists and essayists of the second half of the nineteenth century such as Mayuram Vedanayakam Pillai, Subramania Bharati, Bharati Dasan, A. Madaviah, and R. Krishnamurthi married vernacular language styles and entertainment forms with moral and ethical messages that sought, among other things, to highlight the importance of women's rights.[74] New forms of literature in Telugu—novels, short stories, farce, drama, and essays—dealt with women's issues and concerns within broader frameworks of discussion about reform, and a large number of women's journals such as *Satihitabodhini, Telugu Zenana,* and *Stree Hitabodhini* emerged in the late nineteenth century to tackle women's concerns more directly.[75] Traditional romantic legends of the Panjab, such as *Hir-Ranjha,* were disseminated in chapbook format from the 1850s onward, while various renditions of and commentaries on the text, such as Abd al-Karim Na'at's *Na'at di Hir* (1880) and Roshan's work, published as *Hir Roshan* (1873), used the story as a springboard for juxtaposing the doctrinal aspects of Islam against Hir's beliefs, which often represented individual (and thus misguided) expressions of Islamic piety.[76]

From the latter half of the nineteenth century, a highly varied body of didactic works was being printed in increasing numbers by reformers throughout the Subcontinent. Within these works the question of revitalizing Indian Islam by targeting women as objects of reform loomed large. Thus by the time Maulana Ashraf 'Ali Thanawi's famous manual for women, *Bihishti Zewar,* was published in 1905, the genre had been well established. Several movements had emerged that would dominate the reformist impulse in Indian Islam—the Ahl-i Hadis; the Qadianis, or Ahmadiyya; the Tariqa-i Muhammadiyya and its offshoot, the Tablighi Jama'at; the Deobandis; and the Ahl-i sunnat wa jama'at (Barelwis) being among the most active and prominent. Of these the latter three would marry classical Sufi moral and philosophical teachings with Islamic Shari'a, embarking upon preaching and ceremonial activities in small towns and villages (through the auspices of voluntary associations, or *anjumans*). Not least of all, these groups produced a prodigious amount of didactic literature that exposed conflicting opinions about the permissibility

or proscription—from the point of view of Islamic Shari'a—of belief in the intercession of Sufi *pirs* or *shaikhs* and the efficacy of pilgrimage to Sufi shrines.

This tension reflected shifts in both the readership and the authorship of such literature. The early generations of didactic texts, written largely by locally prominent scholars expressing a diversity of legal opinions, sought the edification of Muslim women by appealing to their instructors: a male teacher (*ustadh*), a female teacher (*ustani*), a male Sufi *shaikh* in the cases of those with close ties to local shrines, or a husband. By the middle of the nineteenth century, independent publishing operations—a majority of which were connected formally or informally to the Islamic schools run by the reform movements named above (*dini madaris* or *madrasas*)—had begun to mass-produce demotic instructional literature on Islam and its contemporary practice in the vernacular languages for a female reader-ship.[77] By the end of the nineteenth century, it is possible to describe the production and dissemination of didactic works as an explosion fueled by the political climate of the times, in which the question of women's educa-tion was at the forefront of key public debates: the ignorance of Islam among the majority of India's Muslims and the concomitant lack of moral instruction among Muslim women; the connection of Indian Islam to the wider Muslim world, especially in matters of faith and practice; the British civilizing mission; the home-based *zanana* education being imparted by Christian missionaries; the role of the domestic sphere in a rapidly mod-ernizing India; the decline of traditional sources of patronage that sup-ported indigenous education; and the formulations of Shari'a law as these concerned the rights and freedom of Muslim women. The explosion of printed didactic materials for women can also be attributed to a major cul-tural shift between the first and last half of that century, during which occurred the establishment of girls' schools, the "normalization" of the case for women's education, the growth of a professional class of men schooled in the British system, and the rise in numbers of educated men who desired educated wives. Most significantly this era was a time of the evolution of Muslim scholars, *'ulama',* into a religious elite that saw them-selves at the core of the *umma,* vested with the authority to interpret the meanings of Shari'a for the community of believers. As they struggled to reassess the meanings of Islam and being Muslim in the wake of Mughal decline, British ascendancy, and the aftermath of the Uprising of 1857, these reform-minded elites began to express two dichotomous views toward the question of women's religiosity: on one hand they characterized women's patronage of *pirs* and shrines as evidence of the moral degeneration of Indian Islam and the ignorance of its adherents, and on the other they

idealized women's religious faith as representative of what was worth preserving in Islam.[78]

In a rapidly changing social and political climate, acquainting women with the classical sources and principal ethical underpinnings of the faith came to be seen as an important method of establishing stronger connections between the Indian Muslim community and a Shari'a-centered Islam. For religious reformers this was especially imperative in face of an existing educational system that in the late nineteenth century was largely funded by government agencies and staffed by missionary women from Britain, a system in which the education of Muslim women outside of the domestic arena did not have a specifically Islamic content.[79] And yet for many of those reformers with close ties to the institutions of Sufism, there was hardly consensus on which sources, aside from the Qur'an, were authoritative. The varied reactions of such men to the question of Shari'a—a concept poorly defined and increasingly articulated as a finite set of doctrines and texts—suggested ambivalence toward the idea of women's patronage of Sufi shrines and their belief in the intercessory power of *pir*s. For some the impropriety of women making pilgrimages to shrines was itself unequivocal in the eyes of the law, though many other acts of reverence for those widely renowned masters of Sufi thought and practice—such as reading the *fatiha* prayer in the name of a saint, for the transfer of merit from that act to the person's soul—in principle were not.[80] For others instruction by a Sufi *shaikh* who was both knowledgeable about Islamic Shari'a and a living model for the *sunna* of the Prophet Muhammad was an important ingredient in the perfection of women's faith.[81] For still others both pilgrimage and belief in the intercessory powers of a living or deceased *shaikh* or *pir* were well within the pale of Islamic Shari'a, but it was the manner in which these activities were carried out (particularly where this manner strongly suggested the influence of Hinduism) that was criticized as un-Islamic rather than any belief in the intercession itself.[82] Thus women's patronage of shrines and belief in intercession became for many Muslim reformers closely linked to the "legitimacy" of certain expressions of Sufism and the activities centered on Sufi shrines.

As part of a cultural and religious landscape that tended to witness the incorporation, rather than rejection, of local idioms of the sacred, Sufis and shrines often found themselves at the heart of debates about what represented true Islam and what constituted the "un-Islamic." The responses of living *shaikh*s and their supporters are often described as reformist or revivalist and shared common goals of solidifying the Muslim community by promoting those symbols that could serve to reinforce collective notions of Islamic identity and institutional Sufism's connection to these notions,

while criticizing or condemning those symbols that could not.[83] These responses had far-reaching implications for depictions of women as patrons of Sufi shrines and as devotees of saints. In his *Bihishti Zewar,* the Sufi *shaikh* and Deobandi scholar Maulana Ashraf ʻAli Thanawi portrayed women as the perpetrators of much of the superstition and ignorance within the Indian Muslim community (especially because of their veneration of saints and shrines). Like many other reformers who shared or opposed his general disapproval of rural shrine-based religious cultures, Thanawi turned to the ideal of Islamic precedent—the Qurʼan as ethical foundation and the *sunna* of the Prophet as moral authority for men and women alike—to restrict the participation of women in the setting of the general public *dargah,* citing Shariʻa law as a kind of self-evident and "normative" standard by which women's activities should be measured.

However, the focus on articulating women's proper conduct in light of Shariʻa-based norms also reflected a growing trend toward the consolidation of reformist "platforms." As Muhammad Qasim Zaman has argued, this consolidation marked a shift among the religious elite toward viewing Shariʻa more as an inflexible set of rules than as a "process" of legal thinking (whereby the legitimacy of multiple possible conclusions on many matters of jurisprudence was recognized).[84] Evidence strongly supports Zaman's contention that this increasing homogenization of Islamic legal discourses reflected a colonial discourse of legal authority that ultimately culminated in the establishment of Anglo-Muhammadan law. It was mirrored in the increasing rigidity with which religious identity was treated in the public realm by the British, Orientalists, and Muslim religious reformers alike.

## Oppositional Worlds, Women's Worlds:
## Sufism and Shrines in Colonial-Era Literature

A trend toward the homogenization of Islam and Islamic identity was also evident—though less obviously so—in the works of "cultural preservation" produced by Muslim writers such as Jaʻfar Sharif and European writers such as Mrs. Meer Hasan ʻAli and Garcin de Tassy. These works describe ceremonies, rituals, and various other acts of devotion to the memory of deceased Muslim saints. Like much of the Orientalist literature of this period, they served the interests of the Raj. For instance Jaʻfar Sharif's work on the customs of Deccani Muslims, *Qanun-i Islam,* was translated by the incumbent surgeon of the Madras Establishment, G. A. Herklots, subsequently edited by the former civil-service administrator William Crooke, and published under the patronage of the East India Company in 1832 and

**Fig. 1.1.** The *dargah* complex of Mu'in al-din Chishti. Plan based in part on P. M. Currie, *The Shrine and Cult of Ajmer,* 104–5

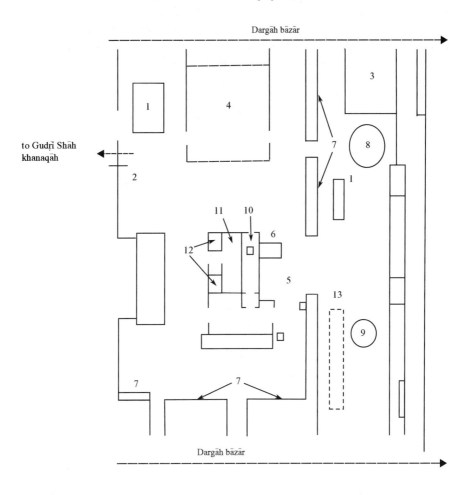

1. Reservoir for ablutions before prayers

2. Jhalra tank, a reservoir

3. maḥfil khāna for music and poetry assemblies

4. Shāh Jahān mosque

5. Auliya mosque

6. Ṣandal khāna mosque

7. hujra gāhs, owned by the servants of the shrine (khādims) and leased to pilgrims as lodging

8. large cauldron (deg) used to feed pilgrims during the 'urs

9. small cauldron (deg)

10. grave of Mu'in al-dīn Chishtī

11. Arḥat-i nūr, containing the grave of Bibi Ḥafiẓ Jamāl, daughter of Mu'in al-dīn Chishtī

12. enclosures said to contain the graves of Mu'in al-dīn's Chishtī's sons and grandsons

13. free kitchen (langar khāna)

again in 1921.[85] It was originally intended as an informative and educational reference for company officials and soldiers at a time when Europeans and Muslims in India, according to Herklots, were in close contact with each other, and when no counterparts to the study of Hindu history, religion, and customs existed for Islam.[86]

Such works on Indian culture were of two types. One type depicted the rituals, customs, and ceremonies surrounding the veneration of holy men and women as little more than curious vignettes divorced from any wider social, institutional context. Another type used "native" as well as European sources to portray the richness of Muslim religious life and, in so doing, evinced more sympathy for the religiosity of the Indian Muslims. One aspect of devotionalism that these writers focused on was the supposed "worship" of Sufi saints. Some company officials, such as Maj. K. D. Erskine, had characterized festivals as either "Hindu" or "Muslim" and ignored the ability of popular celebrations such as the Hindu festivals Durga *puja* and Holi and the death-day anniversary festivals (*'urs*) of Sufi saints to attract pilgrims from a variety of religious and sectarian backgrounds.[87] Others acknowledged, but expressed surprise at, the devotion of Hindus to Muslim saints. Around 1830 Garcin de Tassy, a professor of Hindustani at the University of Paris, wondered at the donations given by the "Mahaji and Daulat Rao Scindia . . . Hindus and strict followers of the Brahmanic cult" to the mausoleum of Mu'in al-din Chishti in Ajmer and to the functionaries attached to it.[88] De Tassy also noted the propensity of Muslims and Hindus of the lower classes and castes to seek the assistance of deceased Muslim saints.

A belief in the prevalence of syncretistic tendencies among the lower social orders of both groups was widespread. In fact many of the activities connected with devotion to Muslim saints and shrines were seen by the writers of the eighteenth and early nineteenth centuries as the preserve of the lower classes, rural dwellers, and women, all of whom are portrayed as ignorant and superstitious. De Tassy described shrine-centered devotion to the boy warrior Salar Mas'ud Ghazi (Ghazi Miyan) in Bahraich thus: "Around the shrine in which Mas'ud Ghazi is buried, fanatics tie themselves to trees and hang by their feet, hands and neck with the hope that through this vain act of penitence, they will get their wishes fulfilled. People, always from among the vulgar, call this great person Gajna Doulha, and the women devotees, Salar Chhinala. The reason for these appellations is that the woman who enters the shrine falls down faltering and imagines that the saint has sucked her. Cursed be such a thought!"[89] This attitude was shared by the Methodist bishop John A. Subhan, a lecturer in the Henry Martyn School of Islamics in Lahore and a Muslim who had converted to

Christianity. Subhan's thoughts on Sufism's contemporary incarnation, however, stressed its connection to Islam in a broader sense, despite the fact that

> its divergence from orthodox Islam started long before it began to deteriorate. In its course of progress it gathered elements which were foreign to Islam, and so now in its doctrine of God, in its outlook upon life, and in its conception of the relation of man to God, it differs to a very great extent from the early Islam preached by Muhammad. . . . Further, the practice of paying an excessive homage to the saints and worship at shrines cannot be reconciled with the religious duties based on the rigid monotheistic teachings of Islam. Nevertheless the extraordinary thing is that though the present form of Sufism is made up of elements many of which contradict the teachings of the Qur'an it has found an abiding place in Islam and is integrally related to it. It is now woven in the very texture of the orthodox faith of the Muslims.[90]

Indeed Subhan, a former member of the Qadiri Sufi order, could look at mystical Islam with a sympathetic eye. Bishop Subhan's work on Sufism in India presents a fairly comprehensive view of the development of Sufi institutions and philosophical systems in the Middle East and South and Central Asia and, to a lesser extent, its contemporary character. In this endeavor he was aided by the efforts of Reverend L. Bevan Jones,[91] Reverend J. W. Sweetman, and the Orientalist scholars L. E. Browne and Murray Titus. Like the accounts of most of his contemporaries, Bishop Subhan's account promotes an image of a "degenerate" Sufism in contemporary existence that, no matter how integrated into Islam as a whole, existed in opposition to both Sufism of centuries past and an Islam figured as a "normative" and coherent system of precepts, laws, and beliefs.[92]

If Subhan could claim to understand the connections between Sufism of the past and present, many of his contemporaries could not. Most tended to focus instead on the more bizarre manifestations of saint veneration. In the 1919 Bengal gazetteer for Gaya district, L. S. S. O'Malley describes practices at the shrine of the "mythical person" Bibi Kamalo, who was actually the maternal aunt of the fourteenth-century Firdausi *shaikh* Sharaf al-din Maneri. According to O'Malley's description, the mausoleum was renowned for exorcisms and the cure of infertility and illness. Women who desired children would gather there to present small offerings in the name of the saint. The faithful would smear oil on a special stone engraved with an inscription and then anoint themselves with the oil. Such an act was said to give the gift of tongues. A more graphic description of a ritual of possession during a festival held in Maner for the boy warrior Salar Mas'ud Ghazi

is given by the same author: "At a shrine on a mound east of the rest-house a strange sight is seen in the morning of the day on which the *mela* [fair] is held. Women and girls supposed to be possessed by devils prostrate themselves before the shrine in the hope of being cured. They get into an ecstatic state, and casting themselves into a trance, excite the fit to which they are liable; incense is then applied to their nostrils, and they recover."[93]

These kinds of vignettes typified depictions of the role of women in contemporary Sufism. In the literature of the nineteenth and early twentieth centuries on Indian Islam, women are often identified with the excesses of saint veneration. One of the more frequent images of women visiting shrines shows the devotee or pilgrim as manifesting an ecstatic state or possession by the spirit of a deceased entity (*pir* or *jinn*). Generally this possession is described as involuntary, having been imposed upon the woman through the "spell" of a rival or enemy. Sufi shrines often appear in these accounts as places where the possessed could find relief through the aid of a resident *pir*.[94] Sometimes, however, as in the descriptions of a ritual called *baithak* at the shrine of a legendary saint, Shaikh Saddu, located in Amroha, Moradabad district, possession was deliberately courted by women so that they could serve as oracles for those who sought out their services. The *baithak* ritual is described in Herklots's translation of Ja'far Sharif's *Qanun-i Islam* and in Mrs. Meer Hasan 'Ali's *Observations,* from which later Orientalist scholars such as Titus, gazetteer writers such as O'Malley, and the husband-wife missionary team of Violet Rhoda and L. Bevan Jones borrowed:

> Some impious women fix a day, dress themselves in men's clothes and have a night session (*baithak*). They collect flowers, betel, perfumes, and sweets, and get women of the Dom caste to play before them on the timbrel (*pakhawaj*) or the small drum (*dholak*). Then a woman becomes possessed by Shaikh Saddu, and as she whirls her head about foolish women who want something ask her how to attain it. For instance, a woman says "Master! (*miyan*) I offer myself (*sadqi*) to thee that I may have a child." Then if she pleases, the possessed woman gives her a packet of betel leaves, some of the betel which she has chewed herself (*ugal*) or some sweets, all of which she eats in perfect faith. . . . Should she fail to become in child she concludes that the Master is angry with her, and she repeats the rite with increased credulity. Sensible people have no faith in Shaikh Saddu, and hold that he is a devil.[95]

Not only is the rite itself considered "foolish" by the author, but the saint in whose name it is performed is said to be considered "a devil" by "sensible

people." Indeed little is known about Shaikh Saddu, and it seems that he is
a somewhat legendary figure who was not associated with a Sufi order.
Moreover the practice of *baithak* falls into the category of "popular custom" and "superstitious" practice, the antithesis of Islam in the view of
these authors. These kinds of practices, and belief in the powers of the legendary saints and martyrs (such as Khwaja Khizr and Salar Mas'ud Ghazi)
as well as devotion to saints of "dubious" merit, were often associated with
women and the "ignorant" masses rather than with the "respectable" and
educated, although even these latter are described by authors such as
Crooke (in reference to Ja'far Sharif himself) as prone to belief in the powers of saints.

One other image of women in the shrine setting that appears during this
period is that of the dancing girl. Unlike the *baithak* ritual, which seems to
have been practiced primarily at non-Sufi or "pseudo-Sufi" shrines,[96]
*mujra,* or performance in the name of the saint, could be observed at minor
shrines such as that of Loh Langar Shah in Mangalore, as well as the more
prominent Sufi shrines, such as the mausoleum of Mu'in al-din Chishti
in Ajmer.[97] Besides these images one encounters women making vows in
the name of a saint—these vows and the practices are often performed by
women to cure sterility, ensure the birth of a son, or fulfill some similar
goal. More often than not, women are depicted as undertaking these vows
on behalf of their husbands or children. Often these vows were performed
in the domestic setting, but they could also be undertaken at a shrine. In the
latter case, the supplicant relied on the services of a resident *pir.* In a few
instances, it was noted that these services were provided by the wife of the
*pir.* The Joneses' 1941 study of Muslim women describes the case of a
woman in a Panjab village, a *pir*'s widow who had acquired a reputation for
sanctity such that others sought her out for her power to work miracles.[98]
And on his 1811–12 tour of Patna and Gaya, the company officer Buchanan-
Hamilton noted one shrine, that of the saint Pir Bahor, which according to
the author was evidently in decline because it apparently attracted fewer
and fewer pilgrims each year. Yet what is interesting about this shrine is
that it was owned and managed by the widow of its former *pir.* This woman
is said to have acted as *pirzada* for supplicants since her husband's death.[99]
Such information about women as active players in the shrine setting is
rare. By and large women were depicted as supplicants seeking the aid of
living *pir*s and/or the deceased saint. Except when performing as oracles
possessed by the spirit of a *pir,* or when dancing in the name of the saint,
they are rarely depicted as taking an active role as ritual agents performing
or providing aid to others who seek them out. Indeed the women who provide these kinds of services are often portrayed as belonging to "low" caste

groups or to groups that exist on the "margins of society" (for example courtesans and prostitutes).[100]

Despite the disdain with which the literature regards many of the practices associated with the veneration of saints, what is implied in Orientalist accounts is that Sufism potentially afforded women more freedom than was accorded them by scripturalist Islam. A few of these accounts mention female saints, of which Rabi'a al-'Adawiyya, Bibi Fatima, and the mother of the Chishti *shaikh* Baba Farid are most often acknowledged. Mention is also often made of Muslim women who were well-known for their piety, such as the princess Jahanara and Bibi Hafiz Jamal, the latter the daughter of Mu'in al-din Chishti. Like all the saints of Sufism past, though, these female saints tended to be held up as an ideal that no longer existed, even as the veneration they were accorded by the faithful proved to these authors that, in the words of V. R. and L. Bevan Jones, "among Sufis alone does the distinction between male and female tend to disappear."[101] Such an ideal struck a few Orientalist scholars as an example of what was commendable in the religion of Islam, even as the practices in which some women engaged in the name of Sufi saints were questioned.

These practices were also addressed by Muslim religious reformers, in part through the medium of print. The promotion of the vernacular languages through print provided an important boon for the reformists of the late nineteenth century when there was a substantial increase in the production of "etiquette literature" in Urdu, particularly for a female readership. Many of these texts were written in a simple prose style to facilitate comprehension, while the juxtaposition of sections of Qur'an and Hadis in the original Arabic with local forms of Urdu (not to mention similarly formatted translations of the Qur'an in part or as a whole) became a favored means of spreading knowledge about the sources of the faith. Reformist *'ulama'* and Sufis exploited the new technology, printing and disseminating newspapers, tracts, pamphlets, and a host of demotic literature written in Urdu that spanned the range of translations of the Qur'an to the teachings of *shaikh*s to various other types of literature about the Muslim faith. At the beginning of the twentieth century, these publications numbered in the thousands.[102] As a survey of these texts demonstrates, Muslim religious reformers spread the idea that there existed "universal" or "transcendent" principles in Islam predicated upon the notion of Shari'a and, in the shrine milieu, upon an idea of spiritual inheritance—symbolized by the Qur'an, mosque, and Prophet—that sometimes clashed with the local identities of Sufi *shaikh*s and shrines.[103] This shift toward an ideal of "universality" in Islam was marked by efforts to instill among Muslims knowledge of the most fundamental obligations of the faith. Conceptually this meant that

each Muslim man and woman should become familiar with the Qur'an and Hadis—the latter inclusive of the *sunna* of the Prophet—as the foundation of belief and of the law. Practically it entailed the performance of the obligatory ritual duties and the affirmation in word and deed of the uniqueness of Allah (*tawhid*) as the sole deity worthy of worship. In some cases this shift to the foundational aspects of Islam entailed a wholesale rejection of the symbols of shrine and Sufi (as in the case of the Ahl-i Hadis), but in most others these latter connected with Islamic foundations. This was particularly the case with the orders themselves. One major aspect of the reformist Chishti Sufi platform was the tripartite scheme of *piri-muridi,* shrine, and *'urs,* all concepts infused with a deep concern for the propagation of the fundamental obligations of Islam.[104] In fact it is in part because so many of the most prominent leaders of reform were connected with the institutions of Sufism—the Deobandi scholars Rashid Ahmad Gangohi and Maulana Ashraf 'Ali Thanawi (members of the Chishti order), Sayyid Ahmad Barelwi, 'Abdul Hayy, and Shah Isma'il of the Tariqa-i Muhammadiyya (initiated into the Naqshbandi order), and Ahmad Riza Khan Barelwi (a Chishti Sufi) functioned as both *'ulama'* and *shaikh*s—that they sought to effect a rapprochement between the reformist organizations in which they actively participated and the establishment Sufi orders. Many of the practical guidelines for living in accordance with the rules laid down by Islamic law were generated within, and promoted by, *madrasa*s, which instituted new forms of organizing and disseminating information among Muslim religious notables and sought to bind them together in a renewed effort to improve the situation of Muslims as a community. In this endeavor the founders of *madrasa*s such as the Dar ul 'Ulum Deoband drew on old allegiances among the scholars of the law and Sufi notables in order to seek effective methods of addressing some of the most pertinent questions regarding the status and prosperity of Muslims. In so doing they pressed programs of Islamization that would change Muslims' perceptions of themselves as a community bound by a common tradition and shared symbols of authority that linked them in fellowship with Muslims outside of the Subcontinent. Armando Salvatore points out that, despite a trend toward "essentializing attitudes" in neo-Sufism with the intention of defining the "correct" Islamic path, such a shift did not entail a complete reification of the idea of Muslim community and its projection on the *umma* as a whole. One indication of the ambiguity with which community identity was (and is) articulated by reformists is the way in which Shari'a was "discursively reworked" to "match, influence, redirect, and normalize" manifold references to Islam at different levels of individual social life.[105]

The main lines of thinking about Islam and Sufi shrine culture that emerged from the colonial period of Indian history largely drew upon concepts of identity that were rooted in essentializing discourses. As Barbara and Thomas Metcalf have demonstrated, the "abstract categories" imposed by the British overshadowed, over time, their earlier endeavors to incorporate local modalities of self-understanding into the administrative apparatus of the state.[106] The modes of identification, classification, and characterization that emerged during colonial Raj have been briefly described here as they relate to the place of Sufis of centuries past, contemporary *pirs*, and the "cults" with which both were associated. These understood contemporary Sufis to be Muslims of a "different" sort, precariously linked to but still representing an Islam that could be construed in either favorable or pejorative terms. As peaceful missionaries they had claimed adherents by their spirit of openness, tolerance, and personal example, though these qualities, in the eyes of most European observers, set them apart from Islam in the formal, legalistic, and exclusivist sense with which it was "normatively" conceived.

A tendency to distinguish between Sufism of an ideal past and of the degenerate present characterized much of the literature that emerged in the colonial period, and it is not surprising that such a bifurcation also characterized depictions of women in the Sufi shrine setting. Saintly women of the distant past could be regarded with admiration by some scholars, but their contemporary counterparts emerged in the literature as "ignorant," "uneducated," and "superstitious," admiration of their "superior religiosity" (in Oman's words) couched in disdain for their belief in customs at which European observers looked askance. Such disdain would color the discourse of reform that began to emerge in the late nineteenth century, one in which the British staked out their position as protectors of women's virtues and sought to educate them (and Christian-led *zanana*-education programs took the lead in this) by dispelling the hold of customs that were perceived not only as contradictory to Islamic law, but also as impediments to the "progress" of Indian society.

This sense of normativity, predicated on an irreconcilable opposition between the letter of the law and local idioms of belief and practice, left little room for consideration of "counterhegemonies" as anything other than oppositional in nature. Thus the so-called syncretistic tendencies manifest in the veneration of local saints and shrines, for example, or the ritual activities of women in the shrine setting represented for most colonial observers abnormalities to be ridiculed and condemned. Such attitudes not only highlighted a preoccupation with social amelioration but underscored the inability of European—and some indigenous—observers to consider

that, particularly in its local incarnations, Indian Islam could make spaces for the coexistence of dominant discourses about what it meant to be Muslim and challenges to these discourses. The ways in which this coexistence is maintained can be seen in the interplay of ritual practices and belief systems, which is investigated in the next chapter. It will analyze the circumstances under which a woman may engage in *piri-muridi* as a de facto, if not de jure, *shaikh* or *pir.*

## . 2 .

## *Piri-Muridi*

*Piri-muridi,* which refers to the relationship between spiritual master ( *pir,* *shaikh*)[1] and disciple (*murid* ), evokes a wider range of associations than most of the academic literature on Sufism would suggest. In fact the didactic and historical literature produced by Sufis and their observers since the eleventh century suggests that a variety of models of *piri-muridi* has long existed, and that *pir*s have always incorporated two interconnected roles, tailored to different types of disciples at varying levels of spiritual development.[2] Perhaps because until fairly recently in scholarship *piri-muridi* has been examined primarily through the lens of institutional, formal, and male-centered Sufism, the presence of women—not only as pilgrims and devotees, but also as *pir*s in their own right—has been largely overlooked. Beginning in the 1970s, a number of studies on devotion to *pir*s of South Asia—including those by Rafiuddin Ahmed, Asim Roy, Richard Eaton, Catherine Champion, and Tony Stewart in Bengal, Bihar, and the Deccan; Joyce Flueckiger in Hyderabad, India; Sarah F. D. Ansari and Katherine Ewing in Pakistan; Victor C. de Munck in Sri Lanka; Katy Gardner in Bangladesh; Jackie Assayag in South India; Marc Gaborieau in Nepal; and Pnina Werbner among Pakistani Muslims in Britain—began to demonstrate the often fluid nature of *pir-murid* relationships, as well as the difficulties in placing these relationships squarely within or entirely outside the institutional framework of the establishment Sufi orders.[3]

### Historical Models of the *Pir-Murid* Relationship

The historical, historiographic, and ethnographic evidence for *piri-muridi* in its South Asian context suggests a tension between classical Sufi formulations of religious authority and local "micronarratives" of spiritual power. This tension is often couched in the language of "Islamic orthodoxy" by those among the establishment Sufis and their supporters who

seek to articulate what anthropologist Talal Asad has referred to as "relation[s] of discursive dominance" with rival claimants to authority in the
realm of Sufi belief and praxis. It is hard to overestimate the importance of
hierarchies of knowledge and experience in classical Indo-Muslim formulations of spiritual authority—measured in part by an emphasis on comprehension of the extrinsic and "inner" meanings of Islamic foundational
teachings and values and in part by a number of other moral and spiritual
qualities that are seen to demonstrate the *shaikh*'s possession of divine
grace. In many of the classical didactic texts of Indian Sufism,[4] religious
authority as represented in the person of the perfected *shaikh* is underscored by a number of qualifications, some of which have been identified
by the Indo-Islamic historians Annemarie Schimmel and Simon Digby.
These include control of the lower soul; piety; knowledge of Islamic foundational and Sufi canonical texts; adherence to Shari'a,[5] consanguine
descent from the Prophet Muhammad or one of his companions; participation in a lineage of recognized spiritual masters from one of the establishment Sufi orders (represented in part by the genealogical tree, or *shajara*);
understanding of the unseen world, *al-ghaib;* control over states of ecstasy
(in that the *shaikh* should not be frequently prone to such states); an ability to work miracles and the perspicacity not to showcase them; devotion to
the service of ordinary people; and possession of *ijaza,* or the sanction of
prior *shaikh*s (which, among other things, functions as a testament to the
*shaikh*'s training and spiritual development).[6]

These qualifications operate as a kind of "script" or "blueprint" for constructing relationships of spiritual exchange and also for recognizing spiritual greatness.[7] They are rooted in a fundamental belief in the *pir-murid*
relationship as one based on the power and authority of the *pir* and the subordination and obedience of the *murid,* the immediate goal of the relationship being the destruction of the individual ego and the spiritual
"awakening" of the *murid* to the infinite possibilities of the divine. While
some of these qualifications have worked discursively to exclude women
from exercising authority as recognized *pir*s of an establishment order,
they also serve as a mechanism for constructing new internal configurations that enable the individual believer, regardless of gender, to self-iden-
tify on a number of different levels. In this regard they have provided some
women with the means to wield spiritual authority and influence within
and outside of the establishment Sufi orders, despite a lack of "official"
sanction. An outline of three models of *pir-murid* relationships—as have
been described in the biographies, letters, and discourses composed by representatives of these orders; in the academic literature on Sufism; and in the
oral narratives of Sufis of the Chishti, Firdausi, and Naqshbandi orders of

Ajmer (Rajasthan), Patna, Maner, and Bihar Sharif (all in Bihar)—as I have encountered them over time can shed light upon a range of possibilities for performing the work of *piri-muridi,* possibilities that women have been able to exploit throughout the history of institutionalized Sufism, with or without the sanction of the establishment orders.

The most familiar model of *piri-muridi,* commonly found in the major lexicons of Sufi practice,[8] is one in which the bond of discipleship is established by a pledge of allegiance (*bai'at*) a disciple makes, vowing obedience and service to a spiritual guide who is the head of a Sufi order. In such an arrangement, the *murid* aspires to ascend the stages of spiritual perfection through a process of self-examination, discipline of the lower self (*nafs*), and total submission to the tutelage of the spiritual guide. A second model of *piri-muridi* indexes a relationship in which the spiritual guide holds a formally recognized position within a Sufi order, but the position is of lesser status than a *pir* or *shaikh.* The guide in this case is a *khalifa,* or delegate of a *pir,* who is designated by investiture to pass on the teachings of the master.[9] These two models reflect rather "standard" representations of the more fluid reality evident in everyday contexts. In a third model of *piri-muridi,* the relationship between *pir* and *murid* is associational, subsuming but not rigidly enforcing an obligation of allegiance on the part of the *murid* and guidance on the part of the *pir.* In this model the individual who is referred to as *pir* may or may not be actively involved with any of the establishment Sufi orders. A *pir* thus conceived may simply refer to a person who has acquired a reputation for sanctity, a scholar of the Islamic sciences (*maulwi, maulana*) who is also versed in occult or esoteric arts, or someone who has acquired forms of "secret" knowledge (such as how to interpret dreams, communicate with *al-ghaib,* or make amulets) and who can use this knowledge to provide spiritual and material services for others. This last form of *piri-muridi* has long occupied a morally ambiguous place in the history of Sufism, in part because of its lack of structure and its apparent absence of sanction or control by the formal institutions of mystical Islam. Perhaps not surprisingly, women who have come to be widely considered *pirs* are found within the ranks of this third model more readily than in the previous two.

All three models of the *pir-murid* relationship existed early on in the history of institutional Sufism. The third in particular did not necessarily presuppose a goal of ascent through the stages of the Sufi path to the ultimate conclusion of this mystical journey, union with the divine (*fana'*), although it may also be said that even within the formal institutions of classical Sufism, *fana'* was not necessarily the goal to which all adepts aspired. While master-disciple relationships evolved alongside the development of

Sufi orders, "ways," and the emergence of outstanding mystics from the tenth to sixteenth centuries, even the foundational treatises on Sufism bear evidence that some individuals sought to attach themselves to Sufi masters and institutions for reasons other than the quest for spiritual perfection. "Allowances," or *rukhas,* a section of the earliest written guide for novices on the Sufi path, *Kitab adab al-muridin* of Abu al-Najib al-Suhrawardi (d. 1168), addresses the dilemma faced by nonspecialist associates of an order. These associates had been formally initiated by the order's presiding *shaikh* but were not prepared or equipped to take on the difficulties associated with pursuing the Sufi way of spiritual development. The concept of *rukhas* developed by al-Suhrawardi for the "imitators" of Sufis (*mutashab-bihun*) constitutes a minimum ethical framework for members of a mystical order. For al-Suhrawardi *rukhas* was a tacit acknowledgment of the growing interest of ordinary followers in Sufism.

The image of spiritual brotherhoods organized around the fundamental teachings, traditions, and, later, burial shrines of powerful Sufi masters has endured; in scholarly treatments of the *pir-murid* relationships that emerged during the formative period of Sufism, this image has predominated, often to the exclusion of others.[10] Yet as is suggested by the letters, discourses, and pedagogical works of Indian Sufi masters, *piri-muridi* could also encompass relationships fostered by factors that varied according to the circumstances and motives of the seeker. This was as true for *pir*s and *murid*s of the establishment Sufi orders as for those who stood outside of these institutions. Regarding a disciple's question about why he had begun admitting people as his disciples without discrimination and without inquiry into their background and motives, the Chishti *shaikh* Nizam al-din Auliya (d. 1325) said:

> One reason is that I frequently hear that many people who join my dis-cipline abstain from sinful acts, offer prayers in congregation and keep themselves busy in litanies and supererogatory prayers. If I tell the conditions of initiation in the beginning and do not grant the Cloak of Repentance (Khirqa-i Tauba) and blessing upon them, which are equal to Khirqa-i Iradat (Cloak of Initiation), they will be deprived of whatever good thus comes to them. Secondly, I am permitted by a perfect Shaikh to initiate people without any recommendation, any intermediary, any hitch. When I find a Muslim approaching me with humility, eagerness, and submissiveness and he says: "I repent from all sins," I take him at his word and initiate him.[11]

In Nizam al-din Auliya's reckoning, then, nonspecialist members of the Chishti order were as deserving of the opportunity for spiritual instruction

as those who sought to reach the summit of mystical illumination, though some of his contemporaries disagreed with him. Attitudes about the different degrees of affiliation, as articulated by Sufis of the establishment orders today, reflect similar disagreements, as do opinions about some of the "magical" aspects of *piri-muridi*. The dilemma for Sufis, however, is that these very aspects—making amulets, countering the effects of black magic (*jadu torna*), and the like—are important means by which many *pirs* today are able to generate a livable income. Thus they come in direct competition with ritual specialists who may stand outside the formal hierarchies of the orders.

Although many Sufis today subscribe to theories of Sufism's "degeneration" in the present age, *pirs* seem to have always incorporated two interconnected roles.[12] First, as spiritual masters they offered moral and ethical guidance to their disciples. Second, they extended specific aid for illness, misfortune, and various other kinds of troubles. Referring to the earliest generations of Chishti *pirs* in India, the historian Mohammad Mujeeb elaborates:

> It is quite intelligible that the shaikh or pir, who undertook to give spiritual guidance and at the same time put himself and all that he said and did under the constant scrutiny of the murid should, in return, demand steadfast and unquestioning loyalty. But murids of whom this was expected were few. The vast majority of the people who came to the sufi desired to exploit his spiritual powers to cure an ailment or fulfil a wish . . . the writing of *ta'widh*s for this purpose began very early. Shaikh Fariduddin asked his pir, Shaikh Qutbuddin, what he should do about the large number of people who came to him asking for *ta'widh*. Shaikh Qutbuddin replied, "The matter is neither in your hands nor in mine. The *ta'widh* bears the name of God. Write it out and give it." Shaikh Fariduddin in his turn once placed the inkpot before Shaikh Nizamuddin and asked him to write out *ta'widh*s for people who had come to them. Seeing that his disciple was looking depressed because of the number of ta'widhs he would have to write, Shaikh Fariduddin said, "You are distressed already by having to write out prayers (*du'a*). What will your condition be when large numbers of needy people come to your door and ask you for a prayer?"[13]

Apparently such practices were not uncommon during the time of the *pirs* who helped to found and establish the Sufi orders in India. Other examples may be found in the letters (*maktubat*) and discourses (*malfuzat*) of the Firdausi *shaikh* Sharaf al-din Maneri (d. 1326). Despite his reputation for being a strict observer of Islamic Shari'a and his disdain for miracle mongering,

the saint's *maktubat* point to the fact that he did believe in the reality of enchantment (*sihr*) and the usefulness of amulets (*ta'wiz* and *naqsh*). One discourse has him referring to his use of certain verses of the Qur'an to cure a case of snakebite for someone who had requested his aid.[14]

Although discourses of authenticity surrounding establishment Sufi *pir*s have often de-emphasized the existence of multiple models of spiritual authority, some of the structural and historical forces that shaped the development of *piri-muridi* have also worked to expand opportunities for a greater number of adepts to claim *pir* status and develop circles of disciples. At times these circles have been able to attach themselves to the establishment orders and eventually be accepted as such themselves.[15] Three factors that significantly contributed to this development were the expansion of the orders into the general population, the proliferation of shrines that were reputed to be sites of miraculous events, and an increase in the numbers of people who styled themselves *pir*s or were so designated by others. As the renown of particular *pir*s and their shrines spread throughout the Muslim world from the fifteenth century forward—and in conjunction with changing social, economic, and political circumstances, particularly the expansion of patronage networks—whole clans or villages found it personally and politically expedient to attach themselves to these spiritual masters and their descendants. While this was especially true for *pir*s and shrines connected to the establishment Sufi orders, many of the *pir*s and shrines that enjoyed local but not regional or extraregional renown and had tenuous or nonexistent ties with the formal institutions of Sufism also commanded significant followings. This development is perhaps best chronicled in Bengal.

In the Bengal countryside—which developed, unlike the rest of the Indian Subcontinent, without distinctive nuclei such as villages and dominant clans to exercise cohesive authority and social control and without significant representation of "Sanskritized" Hindu upper-caste groups— patronage networks developed around locally defined sources of authority such as the guru, mullah, mosque, or *pir*. Following the Mughal conquest of Chittagong in 1666, mosques and shrines began to proliferate throughout the Bengal hinterland. A British report of 1770 found that most of the land in this region was held in charitable trust by religious elites who had been granted it by *sanad*s (court documents), which had been issued in the name of the Mughal emperor since the previous century.[16] Under such circumstances *piri-muridi* developed both as devotion to a spiritual leader and as the allegiance of groups of "client peasants" to the shrine as an effective unit of economic and social organization. Many of these *pir*s were cultivator-pioneers who, under the patronage of the local landowner (*zamindar*),

helped to open up jungle areas (particularly in eastern Bengal) to settlement from the late seventeenth to the mid–eighteenth centuries.[17] According to Asim Roy, this pattern of settlement followed massive changes in the
deltaic regions of Bengal, in which gradual shifts in river systems resulted
in the relocation of fertile areas from the western to the eastern and southern areas of the delta, drawing settlers from the older fertile regions to
the new ones.[18] As Richard Eaton has demonstrated, *zamindars* who came
to occupy this productive land became members of a religious gentry
endowed with tax-free lands that others worked as shareholders or ten-
ants.[19]

Expansion of the meanings of *piri-muridi* also occurred in other Islamic
lands, as association with a *pir* began to develop dimensions of political
expediency.[20] In Morocco *pir*s (called *shaikhs, murabit,* and *salih* in Arabic
and *agurram* or *amghar* in the Tamazight, or Berber, language) acted as
mediators between potentially hostile tribes.[21] In other parts of North
Africa (as elsewhere in lands colonized by the British and French), European colonial authorities tried to co-opt Sufis as mediators between themselves and local communities but also regarded Sufis with apprehension,
particularly when *shaikh*s refused to bow to the demands of service and
obedience made upon them. This tension was particularly acute in the case
of the *shaikha* of the Rahmaniyya Sufi order, Lalla Zaynab (1850–1904),
daughter, successor, and only surviving child of Shaikh Muhammad ibn
Abi Qasim (1823–97). As director of the Rahmaniyya *zawiya,* or lodge, Lalla
Zaynab provided religious, educational, and socioeconomic services for pilgrims, students, and scholars who came from Algeria and other parts of the
Maghreb region. She also acted as political agent, negotiating her claims to
authority over the order with the French colonial powers, who attempted
to undermine her position and install her (male) cousin as Shaikh Muhammad's successor.[22]

In West Africa, Sufis and other saintly figures have frequently engaged
in militant struggle and actively sought political power. For instance in
Hausaland and Borno, the Qadiri order has been long associated with the
ruling powers, while the Tijaniyya order, founded in Cairo by Shaikh
Ahmad at-Tijani (d. 1815), has been characterized by some historians as a
sort of political opposition to them.[23] The Sokoto caliphate arose simultaneously as a political, military, and spiritual movement, established by the
charismatic 'Uthman dan Fodio (1754–1817), a scholar and Qadiri Sufi who
was himself the son of a well-known Muslim scholar. Several of his daughters, including the prolific Nana Asma'u (1793–1864), and two of his four
wives were also renowned as *shaikha*s, here understood as women learned
in both Islamic Shari'a and the inner sciences of Sufism, with the latter

expressed as the refinement of the "qualities of the heart." They all played a major role in the day-to-day management of the community and the spiritual and moral education of its members.[24]

As the examples above suggest, changes in the nature of *piri-muridi* as well as the existence of multiple meanings of piety and sainthood meant that women too could occupy positions of authority within the institutions that produced and developed around the Sufi orders. Yet the historical evidence is rather more ambiguous on the extent to which these represented new developments. In the cases of the Qadiris and the Rahmanis, the *shaikh's* sanction and blessing (whether explicit or tacit) served as impetus for saintly women—believed to possess the requisite character, knowledge, *barakat* (charismatic power), and leadership qualities—to assume successorship of these Sufi orders. Other evidence suggests that kinship with a *pir* was indispensable to women's ability to become *pirs* themselves. For instance Amit Dey's study of Sufism in India refers to one *pirani* named Hazrat Sayyida Janab Khatun of Bengal, otherwise known as Raushan Bibi or Raushan Ara (d. 1342), whose brother, Pir Hazrat Gorachand Razi of Balanda, was well known in Bengal as a holy man. At her mausoleum in West Bengal, devotees celebrate each anniversary of her death in the month of Chaitra.[25] In other cases the roles for women of Sufi families seem to have become more diverse as the institutions of Sufism themselves expanded. As Ruth Roded's work on women in Islamic biographical collections has demonstrated, with the development of Sufi retreats for men and women (*ribat*s, *khanaqah*s) beginning in the twelfth century, particularly in Baghdad, Cairo, Mecca, and Damascus, women could become formally designated *shaikha*s. Yet there were some differences in the nature of these titles for men and women. For women the title did not mean that they officially assumed the leadership of Sufi orders, but rather were in charge of Sufi retreats; organizing prayers, Qur'anic recitations, and communal assemblies (such as *zikr,* or the ritualized repetition of the names of God); and instructing residents of Sufi hospices (*khanaqah, ribat, zawiya*).[26] In several documented cases, such women were the unmarried or widowed daughters, wives, sisters, or disciples of *shaikh*s.

While kinship with recognized Sufis has long facilitated women's acceptance as spiritual authorities in their own right, these vocations have been open to a much wider pool of women than those affiliated by blood ties with renowned *shaikh*s: some women were dubbed *shaikh*s or *pir*s because of the high degree of their spiritual knowledge and piety. This seems to have been a recurring theme in the lives of saintly women. The Firdausi biography, *Mirat al-kaunain,* names one woman, Bibi Maimuna, who achieved renown as a *hafiz,* or one who has memorized the entire

Qur'an, among a list of six "*shaikh*s of Islam in India."[27] Sharaf al-din Maneri himself referred to a saintly woman who was so great, and had received so many spiritual benefits, that she was called a *shaikh*.[28] In his seventeenth-century hagiography, *Akhbar al-akhyar*, Shaikh 'Abdul Haq Muhaddis Dihlavi names several women—among them Bibi Fatima Sam and Bibi Auliya—who were recognized as *waliyas* ("friends of God") and *salihat-i waqt* (righteous women of their time) by their most prominent Sufi and imperial contemporaries. Although the terms connote a number of forms of spiritual authority that the word *saint*, often used as a stand-in, cannot adequately convey, in these narratives the women are sought out for their counsel in matters of the spirit by men (and presumably women, since they are described as having a following), and their spiritual achievements are connected solely to their "perfected" faith, performance of austerities, and/or inherent spiritual power.[29]

The expansion of the orders after the nineteenth century further expanded opportunities for women's participation in the Sufi orders. Innovations in transportation, communication, and the development of print culture enabled *shaikh*s to travel more easily, widely, and for more extended periods, to meet disciples and other *shaikh*s, and to work to spread the influence of their orders. In their absence the women of the family, particularly the *shaikh*'s wife or mother, often "filled in," addressing the needs and concerns of pilgrims. The geographical spread of the orders outside of the lands of Islam—and particularly to Europe, North America, and Oceania—also introduced new patterns of female spirituality into the orders, as European, American, and Australian women became followers of *shaikh*s and, coming to the Subcontinent, participated in the public life of the orders in ways that their Indian counterparts rarely did. Thus the socioeconomic role of shrines and *shaikh*s took on new dimensions of authority, especially as growing movements for more scripturalist, rigid forms of Islam (particularly Wahhabism, Salafism, and similar movements inspired by them) on one side, and a secular nationalism that sought to confine religious expression to the private, individual sphere on the other, posed new and ongoing challenges to Sufism. Many Sufis have seen themselves as besieged on all sides and as charged with the task of ensuring the continued vitality of Sufi spirituality in the contemporary age. As Carl Ernst and Bruce B. Lawrence have demonstrated, some modern-day Chishtis have responded by adapting their spiritual discourses to a universalist message aimed at non-Muslims.[30] Others have broadened their inclusivist tone in order to reach out to the widest possible audiences, as the messages of brotherhood and universal fellowship contained within several of the Web sites of the custodians of the Mu'in al-din Chishti shrine demonstrate.[31] In

this the women of Sufi orders have also played a significant role as both promulgators and living examples of this new expansiveness. This is particularly true of the women of Sufi families, who are becoming increasingly visible in the struggle to ensure the continued vitality and relevance of Sufi spirituality, though controversy about the ways in which they should wield spiritual authority in mixed-gender settings continues.

Such controversy over the roles and place of Sufi women—particularly as attested by historical examples but also by recent anthropological studies—suggest that there are two crucial factors to consider in evaluating the ambivalence with which the subject of women-as-*shaikh*s is treated by Sufis in contemporary India and in the historical past. One of these is a structural constraint, namely the role of the order—and particularly its presiding *shaikh*—in approving which tasks a woman may perform in the spiritual context, how she may perform them, and with what precise designation or nomenclature (that is, what titles women may "officially" assume within the spiritual hierarchy of an order). The other is both discursive and embodied, namely, the ways in which women are able to draw upon, communicate, and effectively mobilize the symbolic capital of Islamic Shari'a, or "Islam at the center."

The importance of these criteria in contemporary Sufi praxis are suggested by two assertions made by Robert Rozehnal in his study of the contested nature of Sufism in Pakistan today. First he points out that, in dealing with critiques of contemporary Sufism from conservative elements in Islam, such as the Taliban and Wahhabis, on one hand, and secular nationalists in Pakistan, on the other, Sufis have learned to manipulate certain symbols of modernity and, in so doing, to cast Sufism discursively as Islamic orthodoxy and as a crucial aspect of modern Indo-Muslim life that inhabits core moral, social, political, and aesthetic dimensions.[32] Second, in his discussion of sacred biography, Rozehnal illustrates the dual paradigmatic and protean nature of sainthood in Sufi reckoning: that is to say, the lives of holy men and women from the past can function as paradigms for the ethicomoral behavior of contemporary "friends" of God, but these paradigms are also socially constructed and adaptive to the responses and needs of the wider public.[33] As I will demonstrate, within the Sufi circles discussed later in this chapter and in subsequent chapters, the ability of a woman to function—in name and/or in deed—as a spiritual authority depends in part upon her ability to position herself discursively as being wholly in accord with the traditions of her order as expressed in oral and/or literary narrative (in the case of women belonging to the establishment Sufi orders) and in conformity with Islamic orthodoxy. In some cases this requires denying any relationship between her work as de facto *pir* and her recognition as

such within the formal hierarchies of the order to which she belongs, except insofar as the *shaikh* has expressly accorded her this recognition and commanded his disciples to accept it. In other cases a woman is able to capitalize on the lack of consent—in Sufi circles as well as in the wider public discourse—on the precise meaning or connotation of terms such as *shaikh, pir,* and *khalifa,* all denoting degrees of spiritual authority in Sufism and all involving what my interviewees refer to as doing "the work of *piri-muridi.*" Either way women who operate as de facto (or de jure) *shaikh*s are compelled to position themselves as examples of Sufism's continued vitality, relevance, and centrality to Islam. Indeed, the acceptance of women's greater visibility in the public life of the orders can signal to others the success of an order in the face of intense competition for resources, prestige, and widespread—even global—renown.

While literary evidence is scant, it can provide some insight into how discourses about and arguments for women's ability to exercise spiritual power as de facto *shaikh*s operate in contemporary Sufi settings. The literature by and about the saints of Islam appears to confirm the understanding of my Sufi sources in Bihar and Ajmer that the role of *khalifa,* rather than that of *shaikh,* is more appropriately open to women. In Islam the general meaning of *khalifa* is "vice-regent," that is to say, someone who is invested with the authority to carry out the will of a superior, but precise meanings of the term vary, both in its Qur'anic usage and in its historical connotations.[34] In the earliest history of Islamic empire, the *khalifa*—Anglicized as *caliph*—was the successor of the Prophet Muhammad and the temporal head of the Muslim community, who also worked to uphold the spiritual lessons conveyed by the Prophet and expressed in the Qur'an. The caliph wielded temporal power that was (ideally) subject to the will of God, and symbolically he served as a model of the spiritual and temporal authority of the Prophet. This was the role played by *al-rashidun,* or the four "rightly guided" caliphs who succeeded the Prophet Muhammad; after them the spiritual dimension of the caliph's role declined in importance, and his role as political enforcer eclipsed those aspects of his role that emphasized the necessity of a caliph's ethical, moral, and spiritual probity. Yet even in these early formulations of caliphal authority, by no means was the caliph ever seen as equal to the Prophet; rather he was the Prophet's representative and the enforcer of his *sunna,* as well as God's law. He was bound and constrained by both God's will and the Prophet's authority.

Although there are obvious differences in the dimensions and type of authority wielded by the *shaikh,* and the precise meanings of the term have varied within different Sufi orders, there are also noteworthy parallels

between the political caliph's authority vis-à-vis the Prophet Muhammad and the Sufi *khalifa*'s authority vis-à-vis his/her *shaikh*. In much of the classical literature of Sufism, a *khalifa* is a designated successor to a *shaikh*, a steward or custodian of the traditions of the order, and someone entrusted with the task of spreading the order.[35] A *khalifa* also acts as spiritual guide and counselor of others in ways that are somewhat similar to those of a *shaikh*. For instance a *khalifa* may initiate disciples into the circle of her *shaikh*'s adherents and help them along the path of their spiritual development: in this capacity she promulgates the teachings of her *shaikh*. Yet she is not herself of the same spiritual level as a *shaikh*: a *khalifa* operates under the authority of her *shaikh* and as such may be authorized to bring other disciples into the order, as disciples of her *shaikh* or as her own disciples but within a faith community that is presided over by her *shaikh*, whether he is living or deceased. The general connotation is that within the hierarchy of the establishment orders, the *khalifa* is of subordinate status and always subject to the command of her *shaikh*. The *shaikh*—even if deceased—is understood to still have a commanding and enduring presence within the order, which he communicates in part through dreams. Thus, to say that the *khalifa* must remain subject to the authority of her *shaikh* is in complete conformity with Sufi cosmological and metaphysical understandings of the soul's existence and of the ability of the perfected soul to break through the veils of human perception at will.

Although in practice male *khalifa*s have exercised authority beyond that granted by permission of their *shaikh*s and have themselves acceded to the status of *shaikh*, the evidence for women doing the same is rather more ambiguous. Some women are said to have made their own disciples and subsequently promulgated their own teachings (sometimes in conflict with those of their *shaikh*), while others were apparently prohibited from doing so. Some female *khalifa*s also apparently guided men and women on the path to God, while in other cases they were restricted to guiding only other women. In Sufi biographical and epistolary literature, women who are ranked among the *shaikh*s of Islam are often listed as their *khalifa*s. In other cases the names of female *khalifa*s of renowned male *shaikh*s appear within the biographical narratives of the latter. For instance the naming of Bibi Hafiz Jamal, daughter of Khwaja Mu'in al-din Chishti, as her father's *khalifa* is narrated in the fourteenth-century biographical work (*tazkira*), *Dalil al-'arifin*,[36] in Ilah Diya Chishti 'Usmani's *Sair al-aqtab* (1647), and in the more recent *Bazm-i Sufiya* (1970). In all three works she is mentioned within her father's biography as the sole woman among his forty *khalifa*s.[37] She is also identified as a *khalifa* in two other sources for the life of Khwaja Mu'in al-din Chishti, *Mirat al-israr* (1654) and *Khazanat al-asfiya* (1865).

According to a few observers, Bibi Hafiz Jamal was one of the few Sufi women authorized to make disciples, but there appears to be some ambiguity about whether this authorization restricted her to members of her own sex.[38] Other women in Sufi literary sources were apparently permitted to make disciples of either sex as *khalifa*s but were restricted from exercising spiritual authority autonomously as *shaikh*s, even where their capabilities warranted this kind of recognition.

For instance a letter written by the fifteenth-century Chishti master Hazrat 'Abd al-Quddus Gangohi to his female disciple, Bubu ("elder sister") Islam Khatun, suggests that the formal appointment of women as *shaikh*s was problematic, even if the head of a Sufi order was so inclined. He writes:

> Chaste and modest sister, one who was prostrate in adoration and whose head was bent down in reverence and prayers, the pride of women of the two worlds. . . . You, my sister, have had the courage to put your steps along the men of God, the Most High, and *are worthy of running the stream of spiritual preceptorship. But as this is a missionary work and women have not done it, the "Jama" (robe) of the "Pirs" has not been sent to you and the special robe (khirqa) of the Shaikhs has not been made over to you, and you have not been authorised for initiation.* But if any sincere woman or man feels inclined towards you, you may give to women, either in presence or absence, and to men only in absence, the cap and the skirt (*daman*) as an agent for your spiritual guide. You may get "Shajara" (genealogical list of saints or holy predecessors) written out and give it and make her or him as the disciple of your "Pir."[39] (emphasis added)

In this letter 'Abd al-Quddus Gangohi does not specifically mention the term *khalifa*, but he implies that Bubu Islam Khatun is being granted a restricted kind of spiritual authority, indicated by the fact that he authorizes her to initiate women and men as the disciples of Gangohi and his successors. The saint's instruction that she initiate men only "in absence" enforces a physical separation of sorts between Bubu Islam Khatun and the men with whom she will come into contact in a relationship of spiritual guidance. Presumably Bubu Islam Khatun, following the advice of her *pir,* would have had to initiate men from behind some sort of physical barrier such as a curtain (*parda*) or designate another (perhaps a male relative) to perform the physical exchange of insignia while she herself guided the act from afar, as the wives and daughters of the Maner Firdausi Shah Sahib do today. The inability of 'Abd al-Quddus Gangohi to recognize his disciple's achievements through the ritual bestowal of the symbols of preceptorship

(the robes of the *shaikh*s) and the granting of authorization (*ijazat*) to initiate disciples is explained as being contrary to the practices of his time, but
such practices were not unknown among Gangohi's Chishti precursors.

## Women and *Piri-Muridi*

Some written sources suggest that women were given permission to make
their own disciples, although this apparently did not mean that they were
given the title of *sajjada nishin* or *shaikh*. For other Sufis the question of per-
mitting female *khalifa*s to make their own disciples seems not to have been
problematic. The preeminent eighteenth-century Naqshbandi master
Mirza Mazhar Jan-i Janan (d. 1781) named at least two women as his *khalifa*s and authorized them to make disciples of their own: his wife and Bibi
'Ajiba, the wife of one of his closest disciples and *khalifa*s, Qazi Sanaullah
Panipati. These women *khalifa*s stand among many of the Naqshbandi
master's other female delegates, and it is likely that these two were not the
only women among them authorized to make their own disciples. As
anthropologist John Bowen has argued in *Muslims through Discourse: Religion and Ritual in Gayo Society,* the tension between classical literary formulations and local cultural praxis is a central part of Muslim lives today as it
has been during other critical moments of sociopolitical transformation in
the wider *umma,* or Muslim community.[40] It calls attention to the historical
connections among Muslims across transnational boundaries and to the
persuasive force of transcendent symbols of collectivity in Islam. It also
points to a dialectic between formal structuring mechanisms and the conditions under which these mechanisms enable or inhibit action. Because
this tension underscores, in effect, the strategies, discourses, and creative
forces that enable the production of collectivities and individual voices, it
suggests that any discussion of the circumstances that allow for new perceptions of faith and praxis to develop among believers must take into consideration how symbols of and for faith may change, be manipulated, and
serve as mechanisms for mobilizing actors. This does not mean that symbols should be seen (as in the work of Clifford Geertz) as coherent and
closed systems of meaning, nor that there is necessarily a causal relationship between the emergence of particular symbols (or sets of symbols) and
shifts in cultural praxis. Rather the prominence of symbols of collectivity
with the power to coalesce or fracture reflects the practical aspects of language in its capacity to produce transformations in conceptions (and articulations of) the self. Here the work of Pierre Bourdieu and Marcel Mauss,
and particularly their elaboration of the Aristotelian concept of *habitus*
(which Aristotle located in the realms of moral character and virtue), may

be helpful in understanding how women in the Sufi orders are both constrained by external structures and structuring mechanisms (social rules, institutions, ingrained knowledge) in their ability to wield spiritual authority as *pir*s and capable of reconfiguring, restructuring, or reinterpreting those forces, in part through embodied actions.

In Mauss's work *habitus* refers to nondiscursive knowledge that is anchored in the body and expressed as gestures and body movements, conventions, learned habits, and tastes. Its variation from individual to individual and with "societies, educations, properties and fashions, [and] types of prestige" led him to see it as rooted in social institutions and in the realm of human reason. Ultimately, however, his model of knowledge posits a link between the training of the body and social control by empowered elites in ways that leave little room for the kind of self-reflexivity explored by later thinkers such as Bourdieu. Like Mauss, Bourdieu's notion of *habitus* as a "socialized subjectivity" includes socially conditioned dispositions and beliefs, but Bourdieu also locates a domain of "relative autonomy" wherein individuals may restructure the external forces that constrain them.[41] While, like Bourdieu, I do not want to accord an overly deterministic role to structuring forces in discussing the ability of social actors to act, I argue that it is possible to look to the relationship between symbols (specifically the economies of meaning they index) and the material conditions that shape the self-understanding of social actors as a window into how individuals may modify their sense of "correct," or morally acceptable, praxis within an Islamic framework of understanding. This modification, I believe, occurs both strategically and in "unreflected" ways. The "perceptual capacities" that Charles Hirschkind has investigated in his study of contemporary cassette culture in Egypt offers useful suggestions as to how the relationship between symbols and material conditions produces religious configurations that both compliment and challenge institutionalized structures of authority.[42] Applying Hirschkind's model to this study, I argue that these capacities largely determine which symbolic configurations of the sacred Sufi women will draw upon to buttress their own claims to spiritual authority and how they will do so.

Thus the institutions, representations, and practices that were discursively framed by my subjects as key to a woman's ability to wield spiritual authority—the family, ritual spaces, hierarchies of knowledge, and observance of obligatory practices in Islam (particularly prayer)—serve as the means by which women are able to assert their ability and right to practice *piri-muridi,* and the ways in which these are both articulated and embodied in ritual action form the primary focus of my investigation here. Yet there is also something to be said for a third realm of activity, existing beyond the

social and individual, which both highlights the power of structuring forces and transcends them: the realm of the metaphysical. The explanations of *habitus* as expounded by philosophers such as Ibn Sina, al-Kindi, and al-Farabi (drawing upon Aristotle's earlier work) have particular relevance to the classical formulations of Sufi praxis and thus to the examples provided by the Maner Firdausis and Gudri Shahs, who see themselves as representatives of these older strands of Sufism. In the work of Ibn Sina, *habitus* (*malakah*, '*adah*) is a faculty of the soul with which certain elect individuals are endowed by God for the purpose of comprehending and communicating his reality. Al-Farabi sees *habitus* as a type of reason that is rooted in experience, but one that enables us to judge, by means of intuitive acumen, right and wrong—it thus has a strongly ethicomoral dimension that is inscribed within the individual. In al-Kindi *habitus* is a stage of actualization of the intellect, distinct from the potentiality of thought.[43] Thus for these mystically inclined philosophers, *habitus* indexes the ability of the individual to draw upon internal embodied configurations—ultimately emanating from the metaphysical realm—that allow him or her to access realms of transcendent reality that can neither be grasped by the ordinary faculties in and of themselves nor be limited solely to the realm of the social.

My approach, then, privileges the transformative potential of discursive and embodied resignifications (conditioned socially but also determined in part by the peculiar ethicomoral faculties that a woman possesses) that in effect allow women to do the work of *piri-muridi* as de facto *pir*s—without having to claim that status for themselves. However, it also calls attention to the importance of actualization within that individual, and its recognition (and sanction) by influential members of the order and its affiliates. The difficulty of reconciling nomenclature with ritual action presents an especially paradoxical situation for women acting as spiritual guides and commanding a loyal following (aside from, or in addition to, facilitating ritual transactions such as providing amulets, performing healing prayers, and petitioning a saint on behalf of a client), since much of the opposition to women becoming *pir*s, evident in the hagiographic and didactic literature of Indian Sufism and in the discourses of the Chishti, Firdausi, and Naqshbandi Sufis I interviewed, revolves around their *formal designation* as such. Privately their spiritual greatness is acknowledged, sometimes in terms surpassing that of renowned *shaikh*s from the recent past.

In matters of spiritual authority and saintly succession, the ceremonial investiture of women as *pir*s remains a contested practice in the world of establishment Sufi orders and shrines, although the existence of multiple types of relationships that signify the *pir-murid* connection, as outlined above, gives women greater scope to take on roles and duties that are commonly

associated with the figure of the *pir*, even within the formal and hierarchical structures of the establishment Sufi orders. There are at least three capacities in which they may do this. First as the mothers, sisters, daughters, or spouses of *pirs*, women are privy to detailed information about the order and its members, and in many cases their knowledge of the sacred texts of Islam, the teachings of the saints, and ritual procedure enables them to take on some of the roles commonly associated with *pirs*, particularly where this involves counseling female members of the order. As the daughter and wife of the Shah Sahib of Maner explained, in reference to my question about whether a woman can do the work of *piri-muridi*:

> In the sense of a guidance role, yes. And she can prescribe *ta'wiz,* and this is the big thing: in every society she has the role of custodian. In our family, whatever customs, rituals, ceremonies, etc. there are, she follows them and preserves them. Especially in Sufism, the *pir*'s wife (*pir ma*) will have a lot of information about proper etiquette (*tahzib*), or if not that, she will have a lot of information about the *khanaqah*'s traditions. Like which *fatiha* will be read and when, and which *fatiha* will include which items, and when should it be read, and what kind of *fatiha* should be read.
>
> And if a female comes into the *khanaqah* to be made into a *murid* [of the *pir*], she will assist in the making of a *murid:* she'll have her ritually washed (*wuzu*), have her recite the *nafil namaz* [prayer], she'll apply the *'itr* (perfumed oil) on her, she'll give her the flowers, she'll set out the clothes [to be given to her by the *pir*]. She'll sit in front of the girl and give her guidance for becoming a *murid.* The whole role falls to the *pir-ma.*[44]

Second, a woman who acquires a reputation for saintliness or miracles is often sought out by others and may be referred to as *pir* or *shaikh* by them. Third, some women have acquired the requisite tools and knowledge—how to make amulets or perform "spells" for curing illness, for example—with which to set themselves up as *pirs*. This third kind of *piri-muridi* is generally frowned upon by Sufis of the establishment orders, and the women who practice it are considered by many of them to be acting in contradiction to the laws of Islamic Shari'a and the spirit of Sufism. On the other hand, as will be treated in greater detail in chapter 4 of this book, these women are also sometimes acknowledged as providing a valuable service to the poor and unfortunate, and (as several among the Sufis I interviewed noted) they may in fact possess a window into *al-ghaib,* the unseen world, which makes them more suited to mediate the power of saints than others may be.

The scope for women to act as *pir*s within the framework of the establishment Sufi orders investigated here—in the first two capacities mentioned above—depends in part upon their ability to project the outward signs of social respectability, moral uprightness, and the insignia of "proper" behavior, and upon their complicity in upholding an ideal that women's authority is subordinate to that of men's. As the cases below will demonstrate, the behavioral signs by which a woman may outwardly convey subordinate status are articulated as Islamic prescriptions of womanhood, but they are also mediated by local economies of meaning that work to fashion the boundaries that restrict or permit scope for women to be acknowledged as powerful spiritual authorities in their own right. Where women have the greatest scope for becoming *pir*s in practice, if not in name, is often outside of the purview of the wider public, though not always outside of public view. Many women have wielded great power from "behind the scenes," so to speak—for instance as custodians of the genealogies of imperial dynasties or as the mothers of prominent Sufi *shaikh*s who guided their sons' early spiritual and religious education. Often it was politically expedient for women to exert influence in this manner: the imperial Ottoman harem provides perhaps the best-known example in Islamic history.[45] On the other hand, many women have been able to exercise authority within the "inner circles"—including the intellectual circles—of Sufis, particularly if they demonstrated an aptitude for the spiritual life from a young age while refraining from participating in the ritual ceremonies that admit the general public or while restricting their interaction with people who are not intimate members or close associates of the order. In so doing they may remain active within mixed-gender circles outside of their immediate family, while appearing to be "hidden" from view in the broader public sense.

Although the investiture of women as *pir*s is frowned upon within the establishment Sufi orders, it is widely acknowledged among them that the women of the *pir*'s family ( *pirzade* )[46] may take on some of the roles of guidance, service, and instruction that are commonly associated with *pir*s, roles that become apparent within the context of activities that unfold within the "protected" spiritual territory that is presided over by the order to which they belong. Herein lies the most compelling evidence for women's ability to act as spiritual guides, for it is the *pirzade* women, with their access to privileged information about the orders; knowledge of their traditions, their orientation, and the lives of their representatives; and familiarity with ritual life who are in the best position to provide the kinds of services associated with the work of *piri-muridi*. The extent of *pirzade* women's participation in the ritual life of the Gudri Shah and Maner Firdausi orders nonetheless varies among them. But by operating within

established paradigms of authority, status, and conformity to accepted hierarchies of knowledge, they are able to maintain their status as members of a social and spiritual elite while exercising considerable influence upon the day-to-day life of these orders and, in a larger sense, acting as custodians of their traditions.

Aside from their ability to project outwardly the requisite dispositions, spiritual connections, and knowledge, women's ability to wield spiritual authority and power is also contingent upon a number of other variables that operate in conjunction with each other. As was suggested by the example of the *pirzade* women of the Maner Firdausi and the Gudri Shah Chishti orders, these variables include family, class, and generational factors; marital status and maternity; education, particularly in postsecondary institutions; the personality of the woman and her status within the family and/or within the order; the language of the body as it communicates the internalization—or defiance—of prevailing discourses and ideologies about male-female relationships, the proper place and comportment of women in mixed-gender settings, and female sanctity; perceptions of the order by its members and by the surrounding community; and within the inner circles of Sufi orders, communications from *al-ghaib,* usually to the presiding *shaikh,* by which a female disciple's spiritual greatness is acknowledged. Since the character and status of the Maner Firdausis and Gudri Shah Chishtis and perceptions of them among disciples and the surrounding community have much to do with the scope for women to conform to or breach those boundaries that shape their self-expression in the shrine milieu and determine to a large extent the ways in which they are able to participate in Sufi ritual life, some background information on the social locations of these families and the shrines they control is in order to illustrate some of the outward criteria that influence women's ability to perform the work of *piri-muridi.*

## Gender, Status, and Privilege in the Maner Firdausi and Gudri Shah *Silsila*s

The Maner Firdausis' and Gudri Shah Chishtis' membership in what may be considered a social and spiritual elite is reflected in part through the amount and type of wealth held by the order and administered by the presiding *pir* and his extended family. Their current land holdings represent only a fraction of the fortune once possessed by these two lineages;[47] even so, the *silsila*s possess some of the major Sufi institutions in their areas. As direct descendants of the founders of the order in Bihar, the Maner Firdausis lay hereditary claim to the mausoleums of Shaikh Yahya Maneri (father

*Fig. 2.1.* Women at the shrine of Yahya Maneri in Maner Sharif.
Photograph by the author

of Sharaf al-din, d. 1323), Shah Daulat (spiritual descendant of Yahya
Maneri, d. 1608) and to the *khanaqah,* or lodge, where the head of the order
(Shah Sahib) and his family live. The *khanaqah* was founded by Shaikh
Khalil al-din, the oldest son and successor of Shaikh Yahya and brother of
Sharaf al-din. It was once a major regional center for Persian studies and
stands today as the oldest institution of its kind in Bihar.[48] The imposing
mausoleum (*dargah*) of Shah Daulat, built in 1616 by Shah Daulat's disciple Ibrahim Khan, a former governor of Bihar,[49] is today a popular tourist
attraction, while the relatively small, crumbling *dargah* of Shaikh Yahya is
scarcely known outside of Bihar and West Bengal. Nonetheless, according
to the Firdausis, Shaikh Yahya was the greater spiritual master, and for this
reason his mausoleum is locally referred to as the *bari* (large) *dargah,* while
Shah Daulat's is known as the *chhoti* (small) *dargah.* The fact that pilgrims
travel annually from Bihar, Bengal, and, among the Firdausi disciples (a
number of whom reside in the Arabian Gulf States), from the diaspora also
accords a certain amount of prestige to the order and underscores the continued importance of the Firdausis and of the Yahya Maneri *dargah.*

The Gudri Shah Chishti order was founded around 1848 by one Hazrat
Sayyid Malik Muhammad 'Alam, also known as Sa'in ji Baba or Gudri Shah

Baba I (d. 1907), who came to Ajmer from Baghdad at the behest of his *pir,* Hazrat Pir Mustafa. It is said that Sa'in ji Baba became attached to Khwaja Sahib, or Mu'in al-din Chishti (d. 1236), through an Uwaysi *nisbat* (relationship); in other words he became the disciple of Khwaja Sahib through an encounter with the latter in which he was given Khwaja Sahib's blessing.[50] Because of this lack of blood relation to Mu'in al-din Chishti, the Gudri Shahs are considered by the hereditary caretakers of the saint's *dargah* to be of somewhat lesser spiritual status. On the other hand, they have acquired a reputation among local residents, disciples, and associates of the order as people who are concerned with the welfare of the local community (through acts of charity and service to the poor) and trustworthy (since they do not associate with the majority of *khadim log,* and consequently are disconnected from the corruption that plagues the administration of the Mu'in al-din *dargah*).[51] The Gudri Shah *khanaqah* is located beside the Mu'in al-din *dargah;* it was founded by the order's third *pir,* Nawab Sahib (d. 1970), while the physical property was donated by the raja of Dholpur, one of their benefactors. Several generations ago the Gudri Shahs purchased the land and rights to a major shrine in Ajmer, the 'Usmani *chilla.* This shrine, a fifteen-minute walk from the *dargah,* is a multifunctional institution housing relics that belonged to 'Usman Haruni, the spiritual preceptor of Mu'in al-din Chishti; the seclusion chamber (*chilla*) where Mu'in al-din spent much time in meditation; and the graves of the four deceased Gudri Shah *pir*s.[52] The 'Usmani *chilla* is adjacent to the Sufi Saint School, founded by the current *pir* in 1990. The school is an accredited institution that provides education to local children of the lower middle and poorer classes, regardless of religious background, and promotes a message of communal harmony and social uplift.[53] The prestige and success of the order is demonstrated by their growing numbers of *murid*s and visitors to the *khanaqah,* who come from all over the globe, and many of whom are of European, Australian, Canadian, or American origin, but it is also underscored locally by their *Nawabi* background[54] and Sayyid status.

In South Asia Sayyid Muslims are considered to have "foreign" (that is, Persian or Arab) ancestry and to be descended from the Prophet through the progeny of his daughter and his son-in-law, Fatima and 'Ali.[55] Although doctrinally there is no sanction for caste in Islam, in the Subcontinent Muslim social groups may be differentiated from each other in ways that approach castelike distinctions, in part through patterns of endogamous marriage. Most of the *pir*s who are part of the establishment Sufi orders identify themselves as Sayyid, and this is true of the *pir*s and *pir-ma*'s of the Gudri Shah and Firdausi orders. As Sayyids their social prestige tends to be outwardly manifested through economic wealth, a high degree of literacy

*Fig. 2.2.* The Sufi Saint School and 'Usmani *chilla.* Photograph by the author

*Fig. 2.3.* The *chilla gah* of Mu'in al-din Chishti. Photograph by the author

and education, and the respect accorded them (even if only nominally) by those who are their social inferiors. Be that as it may, the forces that have historically enabled Sayyids to maintain their position at the top of the economic scale have largely eroded since Partition.[56]

"True" Sayyids are said to possess an inner quality known as *sharafat,* or "noble character," that manifests itself in an individual's bearing, demonstration of fairness and equanimity in dealing with others, and adherence to the Shari'a. Those individuals who have acquired a reputation for having both the qualities and the social status of a Sayyid are sometimes regarded as the recipients of divine favor. It is no coincidence that many of the famous Sufi masters of centuries past are described in hagiography as belonging to the Sayyid classes.[57] In the Sufi context, the translation of social status into spiritual power is often informed by notions of descent—notions bearing both spiritual and consanguineous referents. Spiritual descent from a Sufi master through ceremonies of investiture transmit not only the authority to pass on the teachings of the master and the order he represents, but also something called *bij,* or seed, which is akin to a kind of spiritual power manifest in the person of the saint. It is sometimes used synonymously with the term *barakat,* a charismatic power that resides in holy people and sacred objects, though unlike *barakat* the transmission of *bij* is highly selective.[58] When the transmission of *bij* occurs through a double process of investiture, its recipient is considered to be proximate to God and his saints in a way that ordinary people, and even other saints, can never be. One component of this double process is the confirmation of transmission of *bij* through with ritual acts of exchange that link the recipient to a chain of spiritual succession beginning with the Prophet Muhammad and ending with the outgoing *pir.* The other component is transmission through the bloodline (a spontaneous act that is said to occur at the death of the former *pir*), where the bloodline also stretches back to the Prophet Muhammad.[59] It is through their connections, then, with a Sufi *shaikh* and with the Prophet Muhammad's bloodline that Sayyid *pirs* are able to provide a link between pilgrim and saint and, ultimately, Allah. This link is manifest in the performance of ritual acts such as prayer, through which the power inherent in the individual and passed down via the Sufi saints from which that individual is descended is transmitted to others.

Marriage and spiritual links with her husband and father, and blood links with her father and son, have conveyed a privileged form of authority upon the *pir-ma* of the Gudri Shah Chishti order, while the Maner Shah Sahib's wife benefits from similar spiritual and blood links. These links enable them to practice *piri-muridi* in ways that are characterized by them as within the bounds of accepted social practice for women of their social

and spiritual standing, and as a matter of practical necessity. Although neither the Gudri Shah *pir-ma* nor the Firdausi *pir-ma* has been formally invested with the insignia of spiritual descent that marks *pir* status, their close association with the *pir*s of their lineage has provided the kind of understanding of Sufi ways that the most intimate disciples strive to obtain from their masters. One important component of the disciple's training involves spending as much time as possible in the *suhbat,* or "company" of his or her master and fellow disciples.[60] There are inner and outer aspects of *suhbat* that produce transformations in the seeker: in one sense, by observing and imitating the *pir*'s outward actions, a disciple acquires the intimate knowledge of God that a perfected *pir* is said to possess.[61] Another aspect of *suhbat* involves the cultivation of mystical states, often through ritual activities such as prayer, meditation, and listening to devotional music.[62] A Sufi *pir* may also instruct disciples through methods of silence that are aimed at erasing distinctions among them, taming their *nafs,* or "lower soul," and protecting them from dangers and temptations during their journeys along the path to God. While the *pir-ma*'s training may not approximate those of her father's or husband's disciples—it remains unclear to what extent these men developed methods of instruction tailored to the needs of their female relatives in the way that they did for their disciples—their close relationship with the *pir* marks their training as different from that of people who come seeking the *pir*'s guidance. Nevertheless, because of the predilection of each of these women for the mystical life,[63] and the fact that each enjoyed a level of access to the presiding *pir* that even their closest disciples did not, each *pir-ma* is believed to have reaped the rewards of the *pir*'s company. These factors have translated into their moral and spiritual development as seekers of God and their practical training in the methods Sufi *pir*s use to aid their followers.

Wealth, social status, and spiritual status all accord the female members of the *pir*'s family a privileged rank that both enables them to circumvent some of the restrictions that bind their less wealthy or socially prominent, upwardly mobile sisters and sometimes restricts their ability to challenge prevailing social ideals about what "honorable" Muslim women do and do not do, especially in the presence of men who are unrelated to them. Yet for the women of these families, the advantages of ownership of the shrines are profound as far as their ability to exercise influence and authority as spiritual guides is concerned. Family-owned shrines encapsulate characteristics of "domestic" and "nondomestic" space and of the "private" and the "public." In so doing they expose the inadequacy of these categories as tools of analysis for this particular study, since within the interstices of these denotations lie scope for women to participate in ritual ceremonies and events in

ways they do not or cannot at other shrines. A closer look at the activities of *pirzade* women in these spaces can help to reveal discrepancies between the ideal and real behavior of women in the shrine setting.

### *Piri-Muridi* and Women's Participation in Sufi Ritual Life

The Gudri Shahs' approach to the place of women within Islam, Sufism, and the ritual life of the order contrasts sharply with the ethos of the Maner Firdausis, although in both cases participation in or exclusion from ritual events and ceremonies conveys in very similar ways how sex segregation may prevent women from taking on the role of *pir* or enable them to do so. Although the Gudri Shah *pirzade* women do not attend the larger festivals and ceremonies at the Mu'in al-din *dargah,* they do attend events at the family-owned 'Usmani *chilla,* where they often sit separate from other guests but not completely hidden from them. Moreover they enjoy close relationships with some of the long-term male *murid*s and do not seclude themselves from them or from other male visitors to the *khanaqah.* The *pirzade* women of the Firdausi order also do not visit the Maner *dargah* of Yahya Maneri during the times of large festivals, much less the mausoleum of Sharaf al-din Maneri in Bihar Sharif, but they do visit the Maner shrines on ordinary days and have visited the Bihar Sharif *dargah* in the past. Instead the Shah Sahib attends the public ceremonies at these and other shrines in Bihar and Bengal as a representative of the order. While in both cases *parda* observance was cited as explanation of the *pirzade* women's exclusion from such events, in neither case does *parda* always prevent women from interacting with unrelated ( *ghair mahram*) men, particularly if these men are disciples of the *pir* or supplicants seeking his aid or advice. Among the Gudri Shah women, *parda* practices tend to be less stringent within the confines of the *khanaqah,* while the Maner Firdausi women maintain *parda* in ways that are as strict within the *khanaqah* as in the world outside. In both cases *pirzade* women are able to do the work of *piri-muridi* in ways that compliment, rather than challenge, the role of the *pir.* In some circumstances the roles of *pir* and *pirzade* women are separate and distinct. In others the roles appear to be somewhat parallel, while in others still the *pirzade* women are able to "stand in" for the *pir* in his absence.

Some of the ways in which *pirzade* women participate in or refrain from communal assemblies and ceremonies can expose how their work is mapped out as a separate but integral sphere of influence in the life of an order. The daughters of the Shah Sahib help with the performance of most ritual ceremonies and activities, whether they occur in the *khanaqah* or in other shrines owned by the order. In the celebration of the Prophet Muhammad's

birthday (*milad al-nabi*), which I was invited to attend in Maner during the summer of 1998, one of the most important ceremonies is the *ziyarat,* or display of relics said to have belonged to the Prophet. As the Shah Sahib seated himself in the middle of a large crowd of women gathered in the *khanaqah,* his daughters gathered close to him and, at his direction, sang poems of praise (*na't, salaam*) extolling the virtues of the Messenger of God. With the exception of the *pir*'s presence, this ceremony is open only to women, while the men observe their own elsewhere in the *khanaqah,* with the Shah Sahib presiding over that one as well. Yet the *pirzade* women's roles behind the scenes are not solely—or even primarily—as subsidiaries of the Shah Sahib or executors of his instructions. They also advise the Shah Sahib about the details of carrying out this celebration. Knowledge about the specifics of ritual observances is passed down orally, and for many generations the women of the family have preserved this information in great detail. Their advice on matters of etiquette and ritual procedure is regarded within the order as a key part of the proper functioning and execution of particular rituals, as germane to the upkeep of *silsila* tradition, and essential in reinforcing the teachings of the Shah Sahib and the other prominent *shaikh*s of the order. Such attitudes toward the role of *pirzade* women are shared by the Gudri Shah order. While in both cases the women of the *pir*'s immediate family are regarded as the organizers of ritual ceremonies and the custodians of ritual knowledge, I cannot say with certainty that such practices are widespread among other Sufi orders.

The Gudri Shah *pirzade* women practice a much less strict form of *parda* than is the case with the women in Maner. Although the order has seen an opening up of attitudes toward women's participation in ritual life, the Gudri Shah *pirzade* women cite *parda* and social propriety as the primary reasons behind their decisions to stay away from most communal ritual activities.[64] During the time of the third Gudri Shah *pir,* Nawab Sahib (1924–70), disciples from Canada began to join, and several entered into his close circle of associates. The women among them also began to participate in ritual events from which most of the order's female disciples had avoided. It was during the fourth *pir*'s tenure, however, that the number of disciples from the West, and from middle-class Hindu families in India, increased substantially. Not only did Americans, Europeans, Canadians, Australians, and Muslim and Hindu women from middle-class family backgrounds become initiated as disciples, but the female *murid*s among them began to participate in ritual events—such as musical assemblies (*mahfil-i sama'*) and poetry readings (*musha'ira*) in the Mu'in al-din Chishti mausoleum, the 'Usmani *chilla,* and the *khanaqah*—that had previously been attended exclusively by men. This apparently does not cause

strains between the *pirzade* women and the female disciples of the order, although the *pirzade* look with a mix of amusement and curiosity upon the female disciples' desire to participate in ceremonies that will be attended by large numbers of men. However, the participation of the youngest *pirzada*, now a wife and mother in her twenties, in ceremonies that her mother and older sisters still avoid, may signal generational changes in their attitudes toward *parda* and the boundaries of social propriety as these apply to *pirzade*. The fifth Gudri Shah Baba's marriage in 2001 to a highly educated woman whose sisters also participate in mixed-gender assemblies has further contributed to the numbers of female *murid*s and associates of the order.

As guides and counselors, *pirzade* women may play roles in the orders that parallel those played by the *pir* himself, but this does not always suggest the reproduction (whether conscious or unconscious) of those roles and their symbolic meanings. Rather, as Jane I. Smith has suggested, women's religion is organizationally complex in ways that blur the distinctions between "formal" and "informal" or "public" and "private" as being the specific domains of men or women.[65] Similarities between the practice of men and women in the realm of *piri-muridi* have much to do with shared perceptions of the nature and obligations of spiritual guidance and a common orientation toward the sources of authority from which these perceptions are derived.[66]

It is also likely that, overall, male and female spheres of influence in the realm of *piri-muridi* have become less distinct as a consequence of the "democratization" of religious authority in South Asian Islam from the late nineteenth century onward, as Yoginder Sikand has deftly argued.[67] In effect the participation of women from Sufi families in more prominent (and perhaps visible) ways in the ritual life of the order may signal the order's ability to adapt to changing times and the criteria by which Sufi groups are judged on the stage of public opinion, particularly to patrons that find strict gender segregation practices unappealing.

Three ways in which male and female spheres of influence appear to parallel each other are in the guidance of the spiritual and moral development of fellow *silsila* members, the conveyance of knowledge about the traditions of the order, and the ritual exchange of insignia. In cases where the association between guide and seeker is a fairly close one, a female *murid* may seek out or be directed to the *suhbat* of the senior *pirzade* women (the *pir-ma* and her daughters) as sources of spiritual authority. This is particularly the case in the Firdausi order. For women who come into the order on a permanent (as daughters-in-law) or conditional (as disciples) basis, the Firdausi *pirzade* women hold a privileged position, just as Shah Sahib and his sons do in the eyes of male disciples. As daughters-in-law marry

into the family, it is chiefly the *pir-ma* as highest-ranking *pirzada* who teaches them the proper performance of rituals, ceremonies, and events and introduces them to the traditions of the *silsila,* while the daughters of the Shah Sahib and *pir-ma* (who will eventually marry and move outside of the home) play a secondary role in this regard. Since incoming daughters-in-law are expected to maintain a considerable degree of reserve in interacting with males in the family, the Firdausi Shah Sahib is limited in the amount of training he may provide the wives of his sons. In light of these restrictions upon male-female interaction, the Firdausi *pirzade* women's relationships with their sisters-in-law may come to share some of the aspects seen in the rapport between the Shah Sahib's sons and new or favored disciples, while the *pir-ma*'s association with the daughter-in-law who will take her place takes on aspects of the relationship between the Shah Sahib and the son who will presumably succeed him.[68] One such aspect is revealed in the ritual exchange of insignia. The Shah Sahib passes on to his successor knowledge of Sufi teachings and mystical insights, which are also embodied in objects—pieces of clothing, jewelry, and other items—that are imbued with the *barakat* of every Shah Sahib who possessed them. Similarly the transmission of spiritual knowledge and the insignia of her position is accomplished by the handing down of information and material goods from *pir-ma* to daughter-in-law, although this exchange does not appear to carry the same "spiritual" weight as the exchanges that take place between a *shaikh* and his successor.

In other cases *pirzade* women may serve as "substitutes" for the *pir,* usually in his absence. Despite their strict observance of *parda,* the Firdausi *pirzade* women's duties as counselors or guides are not necessarily restricted to their interactions with other women. In fact *pirzade* women can employ a variety of strategies that enable them to interact with unrelated men while still observing *parda.* One of these strategies is the use of a mediator. In her husband's absence, the Shah Sahib's wife remains in the women's quarters at the Maner *khanaqah,* unseen by men outside the family but able to correspond with them using a go-between such as a servant or child, through whom she conveys messages, advice, or objects such as amulets (*ta'wiz*). Since the Shah Sahib travels frequently to Bengal and other parts of Bihar in order to visit *murid*s and participate as a guest of honor in ceremonies, ritual events, and festivals at other Sufi shrines, the task of guiding or tending to the needs of disciples and clients often falls to the *pirzade* women. Although the Shah Sahib and several *pirzade* men insist that women can only counsel female disciples, in light of the fact that the Firdausi *pirzade* women do indeed interact with both men and women of the order, it is likely that they provide guidance to some male disciples,

particularly if the latter have been members of the order for a number of years.

Although the Gudri Shah *pir-ma* is rarely obliged to stand in for the *pir,* her son, there are instances when she is called upon to perform a particular task that he is unable or unwilling to do. Here one may discern separate spheres of influence that are not particularly "gendered" but rather speak to the capabilities and preferences of the parties involved. Early one morning during the 1997 *'urs* for Mu'in al-din Chishti, one of the young male guests staying at the *khanaqah* began to manifest signs of possession. As a woman of menstruating age,[69] I was not allowed to witness what was happening, but several of the male disciples recounted the events to me immediately afterward. The possessed man had begun screaming suddenly, spoke in an unfamiliar voice, convulsed, and thrashed about so violently that five men had difficulty subduing him. It was the *pir-ma* who was quickly summoned to his room, although the *pir* himself was present in the *khanaqah,* and it was she who read Qur'anic prayers over him to subdue the spirit. After her recitation he fell into a deep sleep that lasted until late the next day. Although afterward there were allegations among several of the *murid*s that the possession had been staged by the young man to attract attention to himself, what is important to note is that it was the *pir-ma* who was called to defuse the situation. I later asked the *pir,* the *pirzade* women, and several of the *murid*s why this was the case. All replied that she had always been the one to handle such matters and had the requisite training and experience for doing so. At the time the exorcism was happening, the *pir* was engaged with several pressing matters related to the *'urs,* and he later told me that his mother helped him out by taking care of these kinds of "details." It would be a misunderstanding to dismiss this remark as a subtle comment on the relative importance of his role vis-à-vis that of the *pir-ma;* rather what is important to consider is how the *pir* understands the nature of the *pir-ma's* authority, both in relation to his own and on its own merits. In taking up the question of how women are able to exercise and wield authority as de facto *pir*s within the complex hierarchies found in institutional Sufism generally, and in the *pir-murid* relationship specifically, it is helpful to think of female spiritual authority as degrees that are reflected in three kinds of roles, investigated below. Each of these roles in turn reflects hierarchical, schematic notions of spiritual authority within institutional Sufism, the practical aspects of *piri-muridi* as carried out according to rank, and the notion that each role carries different meanings for the men and women who play them.

First, within the world of institutional Sufism as I encountered it in the biographical and didactic literature produced by Sufi masters and their

followers, women had in rare cases been acknowledged as *shaikhs, pir*s, and *sajjada nishin*s. Their appointment as such often coincided with an absence of suitable male candidates. In a few cases, they gained renown as *shaikhs* because of the depth of their knowledge of the inner and outer meanings of Islamic doctrine and practice but were never formally recognized as such, even though the most illustrious contemporary Sufis praised their spiritual prowess. Second, according to the Chishti, Naqshbandi, and Firdausi Sufis interviewed for this study, women could exercise spiritual authority as *khalifa*s, or delegates, appointed by their *pir*. Third, as ethnographic and anthropological studies have demonstrated, some women who are considered saintly or spiritually powerful operate as de facto *pir*s. They tend to work in limited, local settings, to have tenuous or nonexistent links with institutional Sufism, and to engage primarily in loose, associational relationships of service and exchange with clients seeking their aid.

In all three roles, women's ability to exercise spiritual authority in the Sufi milieu is conditioned by concepts of sainthood that draw from (Sufi) literary, broader sociocultural, and locally configured frames of reference. As noted above these concepts, treated at length in the hagiographic literature of Sufism, do not merely describe a saint—they provide a blueprint for achieving and recognizing spiritual prowess. In classical Sufi thought, reflected in such ideas as friendship with God (understood to entail mutual obligations), sainthood is linked to the idea of a spiritual power that is manifest in part as insight into the inner meanings of sacred texts, ritual practices, or ordinary experiences and expressed as the fully realized purification of the soul. The fountainhead of this power is intense, reciprocal love for God and his elect. In a 1988 work that investigates relationships between Islamic and extra-Islamic codes for behavior, Katherine Ewing observed that the idea of sanctity in Islam is colored by a hierarchical understanding in which social and moral authority are ceded to those who are closest to the center, that is, God and the Prophet Muhammad.[70] Sainthood is also tied to culturally specific notions of virtue. As demonstrated in John S. Hawley's edited volume, *Saints and Virtues,* saintly virtue may be conceived in ways that are both deductive and inductive: the facets of virtue highlighted in stories of saints often predate the saint, while saints' stories themselves provide blueprints for virtuous lives.[71] This is no less true for the female saints whose stories are recorded in Sufi literature or memorialized orally within the orders. Among the Chishti, Naqshbandi, and Firdausi Sufis I interviewed, didactic messages derived from the lives of pious and saintly women emphasize these figures' outward conformity to what is accepted among them as duties incumbent upon all Muslim women, particularly the observance of *parda* with its emphasis on veiling and modest

behavior, the performance of obligatory prayers (*namaz, salat*), and the emulation of the examples provided by the Prophet Muhammad's wives and daughters. While such acts and observances are articulated by them as being "normatively" Islamic, the particular manner in which they are carried out, as well as memorialized, speak equally to culturally specific perceptions of their proper performance.

### Succession and Leadership: Woman as *Shaikh, Pir,* and *Sajjada Nishin*

In the Sufi master-disciple relationship, the concept of spiritual guide reflects a spectrum of designations related to the idea of preceptorship. A successor to the head of a Sufi order is called *sajjada nishin,* the "one who kneels" on the prayer carpet of the previous *shaikh,* but the term is fairly synonymous with *shaikh* and *pir* (notwithstanding various nuances to these two terms). These designations are distinguished in part by the nature of the authority granted by a spiritual preceptor and in part by the responsibilities that go with the position. For instance *khadim* Manzar ul-Haque, who serves at the mausoleum of Sharaf al-din Maneri in Bihar Sharif, described the *sajjada nishin* as one who has been given a "trusteeship" by his predecessor. In Sufi circles it is widely believed that the *sajjada nishin* has inherited something of the spiritual power of his predecessor (such as *karamat,* miracle-working power). This power is conveyed by the act of investiture, as seen, for instance, in the ceremony of *bai'at,* or alternatively through the blood, from parent to offspring. Both textual and oral evidence suggest that very few women have become *sajjada nishin*s in any formal sense. One notable exception on record can be found in 'Abd al-Ghaffar Ansari's biography of the sixteenth-century Shattari saint Shahbaz Muhammad Devari sum Bhagalpuri. In the saint's *nasab nama,* or genealogical tree of spiritual descent, one Musammat Bibi Nusrat Marhuma is listed as the thirty-second *sajjada nishin* of the Shahbaziyya *astana,* or shrine, of Mulachak (a quarter of the town of Bhagalpur).[72] The biography is strangely silent about the identity of this woman and the circumstances of her succession; the son-in-law of the current Shah Sahib of Maner, who kindly relayed information about this source to me, explained that Bibi Nusrat Marhuma was the wife of the *sajjada nishin* who had preceded her, formally acknowledged as his successor in the absence of a suitable alternate. As rare as these accounts are, they do suggest that the practical necessity of continuing a spiritual lineage has enabled some women to breach the boundaries that otherwise prevent them from assuming formal roles of authority in what are traditionally male spheres of influence. In such a case, though, where evidence is forthcoming, one wonders whether or not

other women in the Shahbaziyya lineage might someday head the order, using the precedent set by Bibi Nusrat Marhuma as justification of their authority.

The possibility of *pir* status for women within contemporary institutional forms of Sufism may be explained as a matter of choice—in the sense that the terminology associated with the role of *pir* allows for a considerable amount of flexibility in interpretation. Shamim al-din Munammi, a Naqshbandi *pirzada* who is related through marriage to the current Shah Sahib of Bihar, explained that there are two kinds of *pir*s. First there are those who become so through formal master-disciple relationships established through an oath of allegiance (*bai'at*) and who are given sanction (*ijazat*) to guide and counsel others on the Sufi path. The second are those who have developed a close relationship with God through constant prayer, observance of the law, and purification of their minds and souls. While according to him, women may not become the first kind, they can and do achieve recognition as the second kind.[73] In the case of the second, the term *pir* is applied informally, usually by widespread consensus, rather than through any formal, ritually executed act of recognition. Also, informally, the terms *pir* and *shaikh* (or their female equivalents, *pirain/pirani* or *shaikha*) are used to refer to a female spiritual guide who is married to a *shaikh,* as in the example provided by Joyce Flueckiger.[74] Previous studies on female *shaikh*s and *pir*s suggest that these titles connote different things for women than for men, though in effect women *pir*s and *shaikh*s do many of the same things that their male counterparts do.

## Woman as Spiritual Delegate (*Khalifa*)

During the formative period of institutional Sufism, *khalifa*s served as the representatives of their *shaikh*s and engaged in the work of expanding the orders. Their role remains by its very nature subordinate to and in the shadow of the *pir,* as was hinted at by a *khadim* at the mausoleum of Sharaf al-din Maneri:

> Whenever one makes [*khalifa*s], it [can be] one or ten [that one makes], understand? Like now I am so-and-so's *murid.* Other people are *murid*s. Two hundred people are *murid*s. From out of two hundred villages, four, ten, twenty, one hundred, fifty will become *khalifa*s, [but only] ten will do the work [that is associated with spiritual guidance]. To do the work of *piri-muridi* is like getting a ticket to power. You understand? People (that is, spiritual guides) give the *khalifa* a ticket to power. But very few people do spiritual work. The *pir* has this responsibility,

that these [are people] who [will] take lessons from me. Will I be able to carry on this system correctly or not, will I be able to give lessons correctly or not? This lesson will be a spiritual lesson. It is not some *"bazari"* lesson. So not everyone will do this. [Some people] may take advice [from *khalifas*], but many people do not do this [spiritual] work. Who is real? [Those] who are not greedy, who fear God, that is, who fear Allah, will quickly get *khilafat*. But they will make very few *murids* of other people.[75]

It is perhaps for this reason that the investiture of women as *khalifas* has been accepted within many of the establishment Indian Sufi orders. The *shaikh* ceremonially appoints his disciple as *khalifa* by giving him or her a document, *khilafat,* signed by both parties. The bestowal of *khilafat* is an acknowledgment of the disciple's spiritual standing, dedication and devotion to the *shaikh,* and personal accomplishments. It also authorizes the *khalifa* to make disciples and rests upon the presumption that the *khalifa* will endeavor to spread the teachings of the *shaikh*[76] rather than promote his or her own.

As previously noted in this chapter, the denial of women *khalifas'* authority to make *murids* is related at least partly to nomenclature. When asked to elaborate on a *khalifa's* relationship with those who seek her spiritual guidance, the Naqshbandi *pirzada* Shamim al-din Munammi conceded that a woman *khalifa* could recognize others as being equipped to assume a role of guidance. However, he pointed out that there were no actual (that is, formal) mechanisms by which a woman *khalifa* could act upon such recognition; further her recognition of others might be accepted, but there would be no acknowledgment of her act by representative members of an order as a unit. Hinting at the notion of precedent as a key source of information about circumstances under which a woman *khalifa* might actually give recognition to others who merited it, he explained: "My great-grandfather [who was the *khalifa* of his *pir*] did not make anyone a *murid*. And he said, 'You go and become some *pir*'s *murid*. You come to me again and I will teach you. I will give you education. I will teach you Sufism. But I will not make *murids*.' But he had forty-eight *khalifas*. . . . Women can also do this kind of thing, it is no big deal. She can have *khalifas*, but not *murids*."[77]

According to the *khadim* Manzar ul-Haque, a *khalifa* may choose whether or not to carry on the work of the *pir* but is not obliged to do so. Because of the moral obligations that come with guiding others on the Sufi path, many who are recognized by their preceptors as *khalifas* choose not to enroll disciples. Many prefer to counsel others as a matter of course but do

not want the responsibility that comes with formally assuming the position of spiritual guide. While the position of *khalifa* is open to women, the nature of the *khalifa*'s role does not oblige him or her to sustain close personal ties with those who come seeking guidance, as in the case of a *pir*, who is expected to maintain an intimate relationship with his closest *murid*s.

The attitudes of the Firdausis and the Naqshbandi *pirzada*, on one hand, and the Gudri Shahs, on the other, represent two sides of a debate over whether women should appoint their own *murid*s. For the Firdausis and Naqshbandis, it is socially unacceptable; initiating one's own disciples is the preserve of *pir*s, and since women should not become *pir*s in the first place, there is no question of their having disciples. Despite this prevailing view among them, they nevertheless allow for the principle of guidance by grafting the concept of guide-pupil onto that of *piri-muridi*. By contrast the Gudri Shah Sufis of Ajmer did not consider the issue of women *khalifa*s making disciples to be problematic. This is likely because the precedent is well established among them. Hazrat Bela Bai, the disciple of the first Gudri Shah *pir*, Sa'in ji Baba (d. 1907), was formally recognized as the *khalifa* of her *pir* and ceremonially made many of her own disciples.

### Dubious Spiritual Authority: *Bazari tabib,* the Marketplace Doctor

What evidence suggests—and what this book seeks to demonstrate—is that the scope for women to wield authority as *pir*s increases with the movement outward from "standard" or "classical" definitions of *piri-muridi*. However, this movement away from the "center"—ranging from institutional to locally acknowledged forms of "*be-shar*" Sufism ("outside the pale of Shari'a," such as represented by the Malamati or Qalandari *silsila*s, the figure of the *majzub,* or the types of self-styled *pir*s or *faqir*s noted with disdain by establishment Sufis, *'ulama',* and European observers alike)—has long been a controversial aspect of Sufi praxis, in part because it has meant that prevailing social norms, including gender identities and relationships, are ignored or inverted.[78] In India today many Sufis of the establishment orders make a distinction between "true," or *sahih,* and "marketplace," or *bazari,* Sufism. This distinction serves in part to help Sufis of the establishment orders separate themselves from what they see as the "un-Islamic" and objectionable side of devotion to *pir*s. In contrast to the traditions they see themselves representing, the Sufis of the Chishti, Firdausi, and Naqshbandi orders I interviewed tended to characterize *bazari* Sufism as a "corrupt" form of *piri-muridi* that places more importance on cash transactions than spiritual guidance; in other words, *bazari* Sufis chiefly provide services for paying customers. The idea of the *bazar* figured in the discourses

of my Sufi interviewees as a "public" setting where anything can happen. Although the term *bazar* denotes "marketplace," *bazari* Sufis may be found working out of their homes. It is the *idea* of the *bazar* as an uncontrolled arena of activity, rather than the semantic value of the word, that figured into my subjects' explanations of the phenomenon and into their characterizations of the *bazar* as a place that is unsuited and undesirable for the work of true *piri-muridi*. The crux of the *pir-murid* relationship, as they articulate it, is that the *pir* or *shaikh* represents a succession of authorities entrusted with the spiritual and moral perfection of disciples. As part of a chain of spiritual command handed down by formally regulated means, the true *pir*'s power is both subject to and representative of the authority of previous *pirs* of the order. *Bazari* Sufis, I was told, do not conform to this model of authority, and because of this they are in no position to offer guidance to others. Perhaps not surprisingly, many of the women who are widely considered *pirs* today are denounced by Sufis of the establishment orders as *bazari*.

The distinction between "true" and "false" Sufis became intensified in the reformist milieu of nineteenth- and twentieth-century India, and persists today. One *khadim* at the Bihar Sharif mausoleum associated the proliferation of the "marketplace doctor" (*bazari tabib*) with a decline in Sufism and a distortion of the true purpose of *piri-muridi*, the spiritual development of the disciple:

> In this day and age, one mostly sees the *maulwi* [and] *maulana*, most of the time they are doing business. Therefore, all these things have become very dirty, [these people] have spoiled it. . . . Most of the time, ninety-eight percent [of these people] will want to make a business [of their skill in writing *ta'wiz*].
>
> *Piri-muridi* is like this: a *pir* will not want to highlight his own [personal] meaning. A disciple is like this: each one will test the other. Like this: you are a *pir*. I want to become a disciple. I will scrutinize you well beforehand. I will test you. I will understand . . . and you also must understand this—you are the *pir*—that I will make this one my disciple. Will I be able to execute whatever lesson I give [my disciple] or not? That is true, sound [*pakka*]. But this *bazari* phenomenon [of making *murids*] has no meaning.[79]

Among Sufis there exists a hierarchy of spiritual authority and, in the eyes of Sufis of the establishment orders, authenticity. Those who can claim (and document) spiritual and/or blood descent from *shaikhs* of the establishment orders are considered representative of sanctioned traditions. Those whose links to the orders are tenuous, who operate without adequate

spiritual training, without having mastered the discipline of even the low-est, animal self (*nafs al-ammara*) and who have not obtained express per-mission from a *pir* of the establishment orders to perform the work of *piri-muridi* are characterized by establishment Sufis as imposters. In truth there are many kinds of religious specialists who perform counseling and healing services for clients and patrons. Some of these specialists come from the ranks of the scholars of the Islamic sciences (s. *'alim*/pl. *'ulama'*). Although the *'ulama'* have often been portrayed as antagonistic to Sufism and the "extra-Islamic" practices associated with *pir*s and shrines, many of them combine the roles of religious scholar and *pir.* The rank of *'alim* is the-oretically open to women, and in such a capacity women can perform the kinds of counseling and teaching services that go with this position. The terms *maulana* and *maulwi* refer primarily to degrees of specialization in the Islamic sciences and are formally awarded by the board of a *madrasa* upon completion of a series of exams. However, these terms have acquired addi-tional meanings in many parts of the Subcontinent; they can also connote individuals who are equipped to perform practical, spiritual (*ruhani*), or healing services for paying clients. Judy Pugh explains that "Maulawis pro-vide counseling services which constitute an important source of aid and advice for an array of situations from illness and family conflict to prob-lems involving livelihood, education, court cases, and many other con-cerns. Maulawis may sometimes use divination in their counseling sessions in order to clarify a client's circumstances, identify causes, offer advice, prescribe remedies, and predict future outcomes."[80]

In Sufi circles there is controversy about the function of an *'alim* as a spiritual doctor (*ruhani tabib*). This controversy stems from the perception that the nature of the *'alim*'s practice as such is often motivated by financial concerns. These religious specialists are often portrayed as pandering to the ignorance and superstition of the uneducated masses, in the name of profit.

I related details of the healing practice of Amma, a female *pir* in Hydera-bad who was the subject of a study by Joyce Flueckiger. Almost all of those I spoke with in Ajmer and Bihar characterized this woman as a *maulana,* implying the uncertain nature of her authority to engage in the work of *piri-muridi.* To the contrary, Flueckiger identifies two important sources of authority that enabled her subject to be recognized and sought out as a *pir:* "Amma's access to a *professional* healing practice is first dependent upon her husband's ritual/religious position as a mursid and her designation as piranima and then upon her own literacy in the Arabic script."[81]

Although the details of Amma and her husband's Sufi affiliations were not provided in this early portrait of the *pirani,* I later found out from the author that Amma and her husband, now both deceased, identified with

the Qadiri and Chishti orders.[82] Amma, more so than her husband, was
well versed in Qur'an interpretation, particularly the inner meanings of
verses, such as *ayat al-kursi,* that are widely used in rituals of healing and
protection. Yet in my interviewees' opinions, Amma's healing practice represents the kind of devotional Islam that does not fall within the pale of
establishment, institutional Sufism. This attitude was shared by many of
the Muslims with whom Flueckiger spoke during and after her research,
although most confessed that they had had some experience in their immediate or extended family with the type of healing services Amma performed.[83] Amma's healing practice also had to confront opposition from
within her family. While her son-in-law disapproved because of her gender, the reasons behind the objection of her *pir*—the one who taught her the
skills she uses in her healing practice—were not so clear. In Amma's opinion it was her success that angered him.[84] It is possible that Amma's *pir* had
not given her permission (*'ijazat*) to begin a healing practice, or perhaps
that her training was in some sense incomplete, but this is difficult to determine with any certainty. Flueckiger mentions that Amma referred once or
twice to a book—*Chin aur Bangal ka jadu*—that explains treatments for a
variety of ailments involving the use of certain ritual tools (such as prayers,
geometric diagrams, and amulets of various kinds).[85] My subjects in Ajmer
and Bihar suggested on several occasions that the making of *ta'wiz* was
something that could not be learned from such books; rather these kinds of
publications were geared toward practitioners of *bazari* Sufism. This does
not mean that making *ta'wiz* is an activity forbidden to women, as the
Gudri Shah *pir-ma* explained: "The kind of work a women can do is stipu-
lated by her *pir,* who may bestow (*bakhsh*) upon her permission to do some
kind of work or another. If the *pir* gives his sanction, she can do whatever
work he commands. And as for these who merely give *ta'wiz* by looking in
books, their *ta'wiz* have no effect. What the *pir* commands will have an
effect."[86]

Most practitioners of *bazari* Sufism had, according to many of those I
interviewed, merely culled notes from a Sufi *pir* and worked without his
permission. Even worse, others merely studied the widely published books
on magic and spells and thus came to know about making *ta'wiz*. Real,
powerful *ta'wiz,* according to my interviewees, came from a combination
of the teachings and blessings of one's *pir* and divine grace, received by
direct transmission from God. The largely negative reactions that descriptions of Amma's healing practice evoked among my interviewees (noted
also by Flueckiger during the course of her research on Amma) mirrored
the disdain that most Sufis expressed toward my description of the ritual
specialist Rafat, who appears as the subject of chapter 4 of this work. They

tended to see such practices as evidence of the "marginal" nature of the *bazari tabib,* in contrast to how practitioners themselves describe what they do. As Flueckiger has pointed out, such reactions are in part based on a male-centered, literary-historical model of Sufism that denies the ways in which women's religious practices can work to sustain, and even enhance the reputation of, Sufi orders.[87] Moreover these negative reactions also suggest a concern with *bazari* practitioners posing a very real challenge to classical structures of authority in Sufism.

Despite these differences over what constitutes "proper" practice, the permission (*ijazat*) of the *pir* may give scope to women, as ritual specialists, to operate a healing practice in spite of prevailing public opinion about its propriety. While the importance of sex segregation and *parda* may figure in discourse about a woman's scope to act as spiritual authority, teacher, or counselor in a wider public sense, one must also consider the impact of shifting factors of age, social class, environment, education, and circumstance in determining how social limitations on male-female interaction may inhibit women's expression in the realm of the spiritual. These factors are further investigated in the next chapter, which looks at women's growing participation in Sufi musical assemblies and how Sufis and other commentators have engaged questions about the propriety of women's presence in these mixed-gender spaces.

## · 3 ·

# Singing and Reciting

It is not possible for a woman to perform in public. If a woman were to sing in the *mahfil-i sama'*, the men would not be thinking about the spiritual meanings of the lyrics. Rather, they would be thinking worldly thoughts. The reason for this is because the meanings of those songs are manifold. There is worldly love, love of the *pir* and that of the Prophet Muhammad, and love of God.[1]

Celebration of *'urs '97.*
On the occasion of the celebration of *'Urs* of Hazrat Khwaja Moin Uddin Chishti of India in Nov. '97 at Ajmer . . . [the] *Mehfil-e Rindan* (Women Singer[s] Programme) . . . [was] held as usual by the *'Usman Haruni* Moini Gudri Shahi Khankah, Jhalra, Ajmer (India).[2]

In the late evening on this ninth of Rajab,[3] a handful of close disciples from the Gudri Shah order are busy hanging richly decorated sheets from the courtyard walls of the *khanaqah*. A few men arrive bearing rolls of carpets—some of exquisite Persian design, others plainer, well-worn, and less conspicuous—and spread them on the dirt floor. A few feet away, a young man in a cream-colored tunic and pants (*kurta-pyjama*) and matching embroidered skullcap assembles a sound system on the other side of the doorway leading to this makeshift assembly hall. A local reporter and his cameraman discuss how they will cover this event for the local paper, *Dainik Navjyoti*. At around 10 P.M., Sufis from various orders, several long-time associates of the order that is hosting tonight's event, and other invited guests begin to filter in; they find the Gudri Shahs' fifth and current pir, Inam Hasan, and his closest circle of *murid*s[4] already seated, acknowledging their arrival with a glance or slight nod of the head. Upstairs and away from public view, the *pir*'s mother and sisters walk back and forth, making last-minute preparations. A couple of the *pir*'s sisters appear from time to time overhead and look down upon the proceedings, the hair and mouth of

each one concealed with a long scarf (*dupatta*). The first troupe of musicians enters the assembly and sits down. A few begin to set up their instruments—a harmonium, a *dholak* (drum played at both ends), a pair of *tabla* drums, and a *bulbul tarang,* which is an instrument somewhat similar in appearance to a harpsichord. Others in the group rub their palms together in anticipation. These latter, who will use the synchronous clapping of their hands as accompaniment to the vocals and instruments, survey the room anxiously as guests continue to filter in and settle down around them.

After a few minutes, the *pir* glances at the troupe, and a voice rises from among the *qawwali* musicians. A middle-aged, portly man dressed in a white cotton tunic and pants (*kurta-pyjama*), his shoulder-length hair topped with an embroidered cap, releases a booming, undulating sound. His notes wind up, down, and around the assembly hall and continue in solitude for a couple of minutes. As his voice fades out, the voice of another man fades in, eclipsing the first. Except for the *bulbul tarang* accompanying these initial soloists, the musicians sit silently, gazing alternately at the singers, their instruments, and the audience. After a minute the second soloist concedes the floor to the leader of their *qawwali* troupe, who quickly adjusts her *dupatta* to make sure that her hair is suitably covered, raises a wrinkled hand, catches the end of her fellow musician's note, and lifts it higher, taking it in a new direction. Munni Bai's opening verses signal the rest of the musicians to chime in their accompaniment. The *mahfil-i rindan* (assembly of love songs) has begun.

They have come from as far away as Agra, Nagpur (Maharashtra), Baroda, and Mumbai. Some of tonight's performers are captivatingly beautiful; many are adorned with gold jewelry, rich clothes, and makeup. A couple of the singers throw haughty glances around the room as they perform, glaring sharply at the musicians who inadvertently strike discordant notes. The performers exude confidence in themselves and in the command they hold over their troupes; they make sweeping gestures when moved by a particular verse, their powerful voices carrying far into the night. They sing songs of praise to the Prophet Muhammad and to the Sufi *shaikh*s Mu'in al-din Chishti and 'Usman Haruni,⁵ songs that strive to convey a hint of the possibilities for sublime manifestations of mystical love and longing for the Divine Beloved, for such are the experiences sought by Seekers of God. From the reaction of the audience, it is clear that everyone has been moved by tonight's performance, even as all observe the highest standards of decorum. We handful of female participants in the assembly—a few of the Gudri Shah *murid*s; the *pir*'s youngest sister, a child of sixteen; and me— try not to call too much attention to ourselves: we deliberately sit in the back of the room, move as little as possible, and when rising to gift the

performers with an offering of cash (whether alone or sharing the act of gift giving with other male or female attendees), we sit down again with as little fanfare as possible. Still we can hardly hide the fact of our pleasure that the principal *mahfil-i rindan* performers are of our own gender. The men—even those who had looked askance at the female qawwals as they entered the assembly—are visibly enthralled by the performances. By the end of the sixth and final performance, commanded by the exquisite Salma Tabassum of Nagpur, each of the *qawwali* troupes has been given large sums of money blessed by the *pir,* who by touching the cash to his head each time it is passed to him, removes its negative taint.[6] One man has gone into trance (*hal*), erupting into a whirling frenzy that we, the audience, acknowledge by standing until the *hal* has left him. As the *mahfil-i rindan* comes to a close, the entire room reverberates with excitement, devotional fervor, and pure joy.

## Traditions of Female Devotional Performance in the Indo-Pakistan Subcontinent

Although the *mahfil-i rindan* may appear to be an unusual or special circumstance that is endorsed by a particularly open-minded Sufi order, there are several examples of female traditions of devotional performance in Indo-Pakistan. In Shiʻi Islam, the month of Muharram is marked with performances by *zakira*s, or female reciters of elegies that commemorate the Shiʻi *imam*s and the *ahl-i bait* (members of the Prophet Muhammad's family).[7] There are also what linguist and women's studies scholar Shemeem Burney Abbas has referred to as "female roving traditions,"[8] which are associated with nomadic and seminomadic groups. These traditions comprise music and singing performances held in praise or honor of the saints and include female performances of Sufiana *kalam,* or "the teachings of the Sufis," set to music. Among the performers of the Subcontinent who work in devotional settings one must also mention the Sidis, the Africans of India and Pakistan, who have their own examples of female singers performing in the name of the Sidi saint Bava Gor.[9] The Baul singers of West Bengal and Bangladesh, who gained widespread popularity in the wake of Bengali polymath Rabindranath Tagore's open admiration of them, have long counted female performers among their ranks. Today performances by Baul women may be witnessed in such disparate venues as festivals for saints, community awareness events sponsored by NGOs and state governments, and YouTube videos. Finally women's *mahfil*s have been reported in numerous works of and about Sufism, although there is little evidence to suggest that women performed *qawwali* in these settings.[10]

The objections to female performances one finds among Sufis are objections not merely to female performances of particular genres such as *qawwali*, which has traditionally been seen as "men's territory," but rather to women's performances and participation in mixed-gender assemblies of *mahfil-i sama'*. In many cases women's presence at these *mahfil-i sama'* is prevented or—if tolerated—opposed in principle. These objections reflect long-standing discourses in classical Sufi tradition about the propriety of such performances. Although one may find a variety of objections within the arguments presented against women's performances in mixed-gender assemblies, most focus on the probability of women's presence being a distraction from the primary objective of participation in these assemblies: a focus on cultivating love for the divine. Women's presence is often understood to be a distraction that draws the adept away from divine love and perilously close to worldly attachments. This probability is exacerbated by the fact that one may derive multiple meanings from the poetic content of *sama'* performances, which often conflate mundane and divine love, idol worship and *tawhid* (divine unity).

Some advocates of *sama'* who maintain that women should be permitted to attend *sama' mahfils* have sought to outline the limits of propriety by distinguishing between the act of recitation and the act of singing. The former is widely understood to be Islamically correct, as it includes the slow, measured recitation of the Qur'an (*tawil*) and connotes an atmosphere of performance that is morally and ethically circumspect, while singing implies worldliness, frivolity, and self-aggrandizement. Recitations by women may then be justified with a theological argument: since recitation of the Qur'an is incumbent upon all believers, women's performances may be understood as a religious obligation. In Indonesia, Malaysia, and Egypt, women's recitation of the Qur'an in assemblies convened for such purposes may be seen less as public performance and more in terms of devotional intent, but such performances also intersect with a growing transnational movement of "Islamic Awakening" at whose vanguard women have asserted their right to sit.[11] Similar circumstances have influenced the emergence of female *zakiras*, professional reciters who perform in all-female or in mixed-gender Shi'i *majlis*es during the month of Muharram. The precedent set by Zaynab, the sister of Imam Husain, was a performance of the first elegy to relate the circumstances of the massacre at Karbala; her performance has served as a model for subsequent generations of pious Shi'i women. By the eighteenth century (and likely even earlier), *zakiras* had emerged as the preservers of the history of the Shi'i community and as religious leaders among Shi'i women. Their emergence is traced by Diane D'Souza to several key historical developments, including the

prior existence of a tradition of elegiac poetry, the activities of religious reformers who sought greater public roles for women, and the growth in numbers of educated women.[12] Although the growth in women's public religious performances may be a relatively recent phenomenon, despite the existence of historical precedent for them, they also reflect some of the socioeconomic changes that have made female devotional singing in the Sufi *mahfil* increasingly possible and, for many, increasingly disturbing.

Historically women who were among the classes of professional performers sang and danced for assemblies composed entirely of men (or in all-female assemblies).[13] Most renowned and somewhat romantically remembered among these classes were the courtesans, or *tawa'ifs*. Courtesans sat at the top of the hierarchy of women who were paid to serve as mistresses or lovers to men of means. They were typically educated in various arts, including music and dancing, so that they could provide adequate diversion to the men who patronized them and paid considerable sums for their services—kings, merchants, wealthy men of various classes. Usually courtesans had sexual relationships with these men, although most had very few relationships of this type during their lifetime.[14] They were distinguished from ordinary classes of prostitutes, such as *rakhelis* or *veshyas*, who did not enjoy the same kind of respect, wealth, training, or social status as the *tawa'if*.[15] Until the early 1900s, it was chiefly courtesans who specialized in vocal music, and patrons sought out the most famous among them from afar, paying them to perform in salons or private *mahfils*.[16] Families of means hired them to sing at various functions, particularly weddings, where their songs often made use of lewd, insulting, and even obscene lyrics, particularly directed at the groom and his family, detailing the act of consummation.[17] In eighteenth- and nineteenth-century Awadh, *tawa'ifs* or *domnis* frequently performed for public and private assemblies convened by the Nawabs and by their wealthy subjects. Ethnomusicologist Regula Burckhardt Qureshi has noted that while *tawa'ifs* usually sang for men, *domnis* typically performed for all-female audiences; the women of both of these groups often included religious singing as part of their repertoire.[18] Particularly famous during these times was the courtesan Begam Haidar, who performed elegies in honor of the martyred Shi'i leaders (*imams*) for mixed-gender audiences during Muharram, the month of mourning, in the Lucknawi *nawab* Ghazi al-din Haidar's shrine (*imambara*).[19]

Some of the daughters of renowned male musicians also took up the art of singing and playing instruments, as in the case of Bai Tilokdi, the daughter of Tansen, the famed musician of Emperor Akbar's court. In 1651 a mosque was erected in Ajmer for Bai Tilokdi. It is located today opposite the

police station in the *dargah bazar* near the Mu'in al-din mausoleum. Although Bai Tilokdi appears to have been a musician of some repute, her name is mentioned in very few extant written sources. It is difficult to say whether she was a *tawa'if* or not, even if Bai is a common appellation for women of the courtesan classes. If Prajnanananda's description of the Saraswati Devi who was married to one Mishri Singh, whose descendants formed the main school of *vina* recital and who was the musician daughter of Tansen, refers to this same Bai Tilokdi, then it is likely that she did not fit neatly into the categories of either courtesan or court musician.[20] It is possible that Bai Tilokdi might have performed for private audiences, audiences that may have been all male or all female, that she performed with her famous father, or that she included religious singing as part of her repertoire, as did many of her counterparts.

## Courtesans and *Pirzade* in the Court of Mu'in al-Din: Hierarchy, Physical Space, and Body Language in the *Mahfil* Setting

As the case of Bai Tilokdi suggests, not all popular female performers were courtesans; however, the long-observed association between courtesans and musical performances remains prevalent, inscribing the performances of many noncourtesan female musicians with its imprint and fueling perceptions of female singers who perform publicly as women of questionable moral standing.[21] This association is especially resonant within the setting of the Mu'in ud-din *dargah*. Up until the latter half of the twentieth century, the *dargah bazar* surrounding the tomb of Mu'in al-din Chishti was heavily populated with courtesans. According to the accounts of some civil servants of the British Raj, and as related to me by the Gudri Shah *pir,* his mother, and sisters, *tawa'ifs* used to sing in the Mu'in al-din *dargah* itself, but this is no longer the case. Writing in the early part of the twentieth century, the civil servant Har Bilas Sarda informed his readers that the commingling of male and female musicians in the *dargah sharif* in Ajmer used to take place every evening in the spaces that are still used by *qawwals* today, namely, the two courtyards located immediately south and east of Mu'in al-din Chishti's tomb. Every Thursday evening, he noted, "some" dancing girl "from some part of India" used to come and dedicate performances (*mujra*)[22] to the saint.[23] The *dargah* of Loh Langar Shah in Mangalore was also reputed to employ professional dancing and singing women for pilgrims' entertainment, although it is not entirely clear if these women were *tawa'ifs* or other types of women who sold sexual services.[24] With a tone of disdain, Bishop John Subhan's 1938 work on Sufi saints and shrines noted

that the musical assemblies at many Indian Sufi shrines had degenerated into "secular festivals" that were often attended by professional dancing (*nach*) girls who allegedly performed in honor of the saint.[25] Despite several efforts by factions among the shrine's management to put a stop to the practice—during the colonial period and after—*tawa'if*s and other professional singing and dancing women were still performing at the Mu'in al-din *dargah* during the time of Nawab Sahib, the third Gudri Shah *pir,* who died in Agra in 1970 but had frequented Ajmer from an early point in his spiritual career.[26] The presence of "professional" women in the precincts of the *dargah* was apparently tolerated—even encouraged—by the shrine management. But if this suggests a social and moral degeneration within the milieu of Sufi shrines, the roles that such women could play within, rather than just on the margins of, Sufi circles also indicates the complexities and ambiguities inherent in the relationships between flesh-and-blood Sufis and the ordinary people who sought their company.

Nawab Sahib had always felt disturbed by these kinds of performances, but to the consternation of his disciples, he began to approach the courtesans in the *dargah bazar.* According to accounts given by the Gudri Shah Chishtis, many of these women became his *murid*s, and with his help most of those who did so eventually married and became "respectable" women. Munni Bai, who has been performing *qawwali* at the Gudri Shah *khanaqah* in Ajmer for many years, can still recall the early days of the *mahfil-i rindan* and the opposition it aroused from the *khadim*s and *sajjada nishin*s from the Mu'in al-din *dargah.* I was told by the women of the Gudri Shah *pir*'s family that unlike the courtesans of the *dargah bazar,* Munni Bai never married and remained a *tawa'if* until she became too old to do so anymore. Although she continued to perform at the *mahfil-i rindan* until the late 1990s, she could not support herself on *qawwali* singing alone (in part because of loss of patronage[27] and in part because of the faltering of her voice in old age); when not visiting Ajmer, she resides in Agra, where she sells cheap plastic goods in the open market.[28]

Despite her social location, marginal in comparison to the female *murid*s and the Gudri Shah *pirzade* women, Munni Bai commands respect within this Sufi milieu. When I met her, a week before the *mahfil-i rindan,* she was resting outside of the tomb of Zahur ul-Miyan (Gudri Shah Baba IV), her head uncovered, but her scarf (*dupatta*) nearby. Smiling and friendly, she invited me to come over, sit on her mat, and talk. As we chatted about her life and the hardships she faced living alone in Agra, several men and women paused to ask her permission before entering the tomb, as if she were its caretaker, but she assured me that this was not the case. One of the

men who stopped by seemed to have an openly flirtatious relationship with her; he squeezed and rubbed her legs as she squealed in delight and then insulted him. This behavior, I later noted, contrasted markedly with her body language as I observed it at the *mahfil-i rindan*. Her head was covered respectfully, her body movements were always reserved, and she never displayed anything more than minimal spoken contact with the musicians in her troupe, all of whom were men.

Although the standards of *parda* to which Munni Bai is expected to adhere are much different from those expected of the female *murid*s and of the Gudri Shah *pirzade* women, such modest body language was the requisite norm of behavior among the Gudri Shah Sufis during *qawwali* assemblies. This was true whether they assembled at the Mu'in al-din *dargah,* the 'Usmani *chilla,* or the order's nucleus—the *khanaqah.* Even when visiting *mahfil*s where the code of behavior is obviously lax, the disciples of the Gudri Shah order are enjoined to observe the highest standards of comportment. This is more a learned behavior than an obligation that is imposed on *murid*s and associates of the order. As a *murid* of Nawab Sahib who has developed an enduring and close relationship with the Gudri Shah Chishtis, Munni Bai is treated with affection and regarded with admiration. Although the quality of her voice has deteriorated considerably since her younger days, she receives the outward respect of the members of her troupe as the lead *qawwal.* As one of the longest-standing members of the Gudri Shah *silsila* and a former tenant of Zahur ul-Miyan,[29] she is loved by the closest members of the order and the women of the family. Munni Bai's low social position would, in other circumstances, hamper her from mingling socially with members of the highest social classes, which In'am Hasan's family, as Sayyids, represent;[30] however, her association with the family and the *silsila* mitigates the apparent boundaries of these class divisions. Social and gender hierarchies do emerge in quotidian life, though, through individuals' exclusion from or inclusion in ritual activities, spaces, and events.[31]

The mother and one of the sisters of the current *pir* of the Gudri Shah order explained the ambivalence toward gender divisions in relation to the inability of most women performers to penetrate the closed circles of Sufi collectives: "In many Sufi societies, there is no respect for these women [who sing]. They are not allowed to participate in the activities which take place in the [inner circles of the] Sufi milieu. And in Indian society, these kinds of women are not given any respect. Indian society is very bad [in this sense]. As for Sufis, some of these women may be very great,[32] but they are not allowed into Sufi society."[33]

Social hierarchies and gender divisions are also expressed physically, through the language of the body and its spatial situatedness within the

*mahfil* setting. Although they disagree with any general prescription that would exclude women from participation in Sufi circles, the women of the Gudri Shah *pir*'s family characterize women's participation in the *mahfil-i sama'* as something they find morally dubious. This is not because of any inherent impropriety in the mixing of the sexes, but rather because such mixing demonstrates the influence of customary practices and because the inner intentions of the parties that commingle are not always "pure." As Apa, the mother of the current *pir,* explained,

> It is Hindu customs [*dastur*] which allowed dancing and musical per-
> formance by men and women together. Krishna and Radha danced
> and sang *bhajans* together. This kind of thing is not a part of Islam,
> this [allowing women to sing in mixed company]. It is an accretion
> from Hinduism. Sufi *qawwali* is, in truth, a male thing. The problem,
> in addition, is when the women are made up prettily. It is not a big
> deal for someone like me, dressed in white, plain, and an old woman,
> to mix with the men. But for young women, it is not right that they
> should go in front of men. There are very bad men [out there].[34]

Although the *pirzade* women of the Gudri Shah Chishti order find women's participation (as singers or as audience members) in the *mahfil-i rindan* problematic, there are some occasions on which they also attend musical assemblies. One of these occasions is the death-day anniversary of their father, the fourth Gudri Shah *pir* Zahurul-Hassan Sharib. The musi-cal assembly for Zahur ul-Miyan's *'urs* is held at the hilltop 'Usmani *chilla* shrine, located on the Ana Sagar lake outside the old city. What distin-guishes the *pirzade* women from non-*pirzade* women as participants is the way in which they set themselves apart from others. Indicators of their social and spiritual status become manifest in the way they maintain a spatial distance from others and in the body language they display, partic-ularly with their participation in the act of gift giving (*nazrana dena*). Instead of sitting, as other women participants do, among the members of the assembly (or, as is equally common, behind the men), they congregate in a group that is spatially separate from, but in plain view of, the other participants. Like others they offer cash to the *qawwali* musicians when moved by a particular performance, song, or couplet. However, unlike the rest, the *pirzade* women do not rise to make the offering. Rather they use a child, male relative, or servant as go-between. Similar observations can be made about many of the women attending the large public *sama'* assemblies in the *dargah* of Mu'in al-din Chishti.

The *pirzade* women also attend the birthday celebration (*milad*)[35] for Hazrat 'Ali (the cousin and son-in-law of the Prophet and the fourth

*khalifa* of Islam), which in the first year I attended took place on the thirteenth of Rajab (November 14), 1997. However, unlike in the *mahfil* setting, in the *milad* the *pirzade* women do not maintain a spatial and physical distance from the other participants. The celebration of Hazrat 'Ali's birthday, among the Gudri Shah Sufis at least, tends to be strictly a family affair (in this sense meaning family, disciples, and close associates), which explains the presence of the *pirzade* women. Moreover it is celebrated at the *khanaqah,* which is also a domestic setting, since this is where the *pir* and his family live. More specifically the central part of the celebration, the recitation of prayers and listening to songs of praise to Hazrat 'Ali, takes place in the bedroom that was once used by Nawab Sahib, the third Gudri Shah *pir.* The bedroom is also a place where the current *pir, murid*s, and associates meet frequently to pass the time together in silence or conversation. On the afternoon of the *milad,* we all gathered in this intimate chamber. During part of the ceremony, the *pirzade* women sang songs praising Hazrat 'Ali, while the mother of the *pir* kept time with the *daf,* a flat drum played with the hand or a stick. Toward the end of the *milad,* the women played a tape recording of devotional songs in honor of Hazrat 'Ali while the *pir's* youngest sister performed a dance that she has performed since early childhood, a dance that is both sensual and teasingly seductive. I found myself feeling a bit shocked at her performance, which might have been endearing if a child had been dancing instead of a young girl on the verge of adulthood. I asked the *pir* as well as several of the *murid*s why this sort of behavior was acceptable, while the women of the family would not attend the public ritual events that took place during the *'urs* and looked upon other women's participation in the *mahfil*s with a mixture of humor and disdain.

In fact I learned that family and *silsila* tradition had much to do with the way the *milad* for Hazrat 'Ali was celebrated in the Gudri Shah *khanaqah.* While Zahur ul-Miyan himself did not entirely approve of it (nor did he really approve of the *mahfil-i rindan*), he acquiesced to the traditions of the order. Moreover it seemed apparent that the women enjoyed being able to perform at the *milad.* It gave them a chance to participate in ritual activities in a way that was socially acceptable, because it occurred within the boundaries of the home, among friends and family, rather than among strangers. This being the case, there was nothing for them to fear about how their participation would be viewed by outsiders. In the intimate setting of the *khanaqah*-as-domestic-space, with a limited number of participants who were also considered close friends in attendance, there was no ostensible threat of compromising the high social and spiritual status of the *pirzade* women in the eyes of the wider public.

## Women's Musical Performances and the Socioeconomic Bases of Change

Despite the ambivalence surrounding women's musical performances in the public settings of establishment Sufi shrine milieus, there are a growing number of female *qawwal*s who perform in the *mahfil-i sama'*. For example the Pakistani singers 'Abida Parvin and Reshma enjoy reputations as *qawwali* and Sufiana *kalam*[36] singers par excellence in Pakistan and India and have performed for Sufi *'urs* celebrations as well as for commercial musical venues. 'Abida Parvin in particular is regularly billed in the Indian and Pakistani press as a great "Sufi" singer (as opposed to being merely a singer of "Sufi" music), and many see her as the successor to the inimitable *qawwali* powerhouse Nusrat Fateh 'Ali Khan, who died in 1997.[37] Other female *qawwali* singers of India and Pakistan have also become famous, though less so.[38] Some, such as Nurjahan Begam, who trained in the Agra school (*gharana*) under the celebrated Ustad Khan Sahib 'Abd al-Qadir Khan; Anisa Sabiri of Mumbai and of the famed Sabiri Chishti order, a woman who is internationally renowned as a singer of *ghazal, thumri, dadra, chaiti, hori,* and *qawwali* music; Umm-i Habiba, praised for her a cappella recitations of poems of praise to the Prophet Muhammad (*na't-i rasul*); and Prabha Bharati, a Hindu woman who was sought after in Sufi circles before her recent demise, perform commercially as well as for private venues.[39] Others, such as Shakila Punvi, Shakila Bhopali, Kamini Devi, and Nurjahan Barodawali, perform exclusively in the *mahfil-i sama'* setting. The rise in numbers of female singers who are able to perform in Sufi settings would seem to suggest a growing acceptance of their activities, but this is not necessarily the case. In fact the number of women who perform in intimate settings at establishment shrines remains low, and those who perform *qawwali* at larger, public, or even commercial venues continue to struggle for recognition from their fellow musicians and from others who are intimately connected to the institutions of Sufism. Rather, the growth in numbers of female singers indexes a number of ongoing socioeconomic changes that are affecting Sufis as much as anyone else. These include the growth in popularity of *qawwali* through the professional music and film industries, which have contributed to the popularity of Sufi music, and the involvement of secular institutions in the management of shrines.

Although more female singers of Sufi music may be seen performing at Sufi shrines and commercially, their rise in popularity has also exacerbated existing tensions within Sufi circles between "professional" singing and "devotional" singing. *Pir* Shamim al-din Munammi, a brother-in-law of the current Shah Sahib of the Bihar Sharif Firdausi order,[40] distinguished on several occasions between Sufis and what he referred to as "professional" singers of "Sufistic music." Since singers such as 'Abida Parvin and

Reshma perform commercially and accept cash payment for their performances,[41] he insisted, they cannot properly be called Sufis, though he conceded that they are indeed "followers of Sufism," or disciples of a Sufi guide, loosely speaking.[42] While Qureshi has argued that *qawwali* musicians are typically distinguished from *murid*s who have embarked on the path to God, implying a hierarchy of discipleship, the linkages between professionalism and lack of sincerity on the Sufi path are exacerbated in this era of "Bollywood *qawwali*." Some shrines reportedly refused to allow even the late Nusrat Fateh'Ali Khan and troupes such as the Sabri Brothers to perform at *'urs* festivals, citing the lack of propriety that their performances encourage among the audiences gathered. Ideally participants assemble for the purpose of deriving spiritual benefits from the power of *sama'*, which they are able to do through the mediation of the *pir* who presides over the event.[43] Commercial performances of *qawwali*, by contrast, are often seen in Sufi circles as "secular" performances that provide little more than vulgar spectacle for the masses, who have little sincere interest in or aptitude for the path to God.

The presence of greater numbers of women performers also directly relates to changes in the ways that many shrines are being managed today, as I realized during the course of an interview with the head of the Maner Firdausi order. In that interview I brought up the case of a female singer I had heard about during my first excursion to the region in 1996. Shortly before I arrived that summer, a female *qawwal* had performed during the *'urs* at the High Court *dargah* in Patna, the state capital, for a large crowd of male and female pilgrims. Did not that prove, I asked, that women were increasingly allowed to perform in shrine settings, despite prevailing perceptions among Sufis that they were not? The Shah Sahib's answer surprised and disappointed me. As he explained it, the High Court *dargah* is not under the management of a Sufi order or *pir*, but rather is under public (that is, local government) administration. In an institution thus governed, female *qawwal*s may be called to perform, and these performances are also used to convey a message about "progressive attitudes" toward gender equality. Although, he felt, such a *dargah* is "authentic" (*sahib*), meaning that it is indeed a holy site containing the relics of a deceased Sufi saint, the methods of its administration are not sound, because those in charge do not rely on or include the consensus of a Sufi order. The woman's performance, then, was linked with a "public" setting in which control could not be maintained, one that admitted people of any ilk and was geared toward entertainment rather than the spiritual nourishment of those in attendance. Both *Pir* Shamim al-din Munammi and the Shah Sahib of Maner agreed that under these circumstances hooligans (*badma'ash*) use

the occasion of the *'urs* to harass female attendees, and that since these affairs have degenerated into nothing more than vulgar spectacles, there are no spiritual benefits to be gained from attending the *sama'* perform- ances they sponsor. Although these kinds of statements also reflect the struggles of some Sufis with socioeconomic changes that are transforming the face of Sufism today, they are not merely a reflection of contemporary discourses. On the contrary, debates about *sama'*, and women's presence and performances in musical assemblies, reflect long-standing controver- sies about Sufi praxis. That is not to say that the debates over praxis have themselves remained static and unchanging. Rather, they demonstrate how contemporary arguments about women's participation in these events draw upon classical tropes in Sufism, foundational texts in Islam, and the notion of *silsila* "tradition" in order to articulate—and modify—positions on the topic as contexts and circumstances require.

### Women, *Sama'*, and Performance in Classical Literature: Articulating the Present through the Mirror of the Past

There is a wide range of opinions about the permissibility of *sama'* in the classical literature of Sufism. And although observers of Sufi praxis, in- cluding many Sufis themselves, agree that the Chishtis have historically embraced *sama'* as a path to spiritual illumination while the Naqshbandis and Firdausis have tended to reject it, there is a wide spectrum of attitudes surrounding the merits of *sama'* among the Sufi orders.[44] Within these debates several classical texts of Sufism have also addressed the propriety of women's performances in the *mahfil-i sama'*. In discussing this subject, the Chishti, Firdausi, and Naqsbandi Sufis whose *sama'* and *milad*s I attended frequently cited the views expressed by such eminent adepts as 'Ali ibn 'Usman al-Hujwiri (d. 1071) and al-Ghazali (d. 1111) alongside the views of the prominent Sufi *shaikh*s of their own particular *silsila*s.

'Ali al-Hujwiri drew on an already well-established set of discourses about the proper observance of the *mahfil-i sama'* to enumerate the condi- tions for lawful audition. One of these was Abu Nasr al-Sarraj's (d. 988) *Kitab al-Luma'*, which itself evoked a much older set of discourses on audi- tion, beginning with Hadis reports that the Prophet Muhammad was not entirely opposed to the recitation of poetry and its accompaniment by musical instruments.[45] Indeed a significant number of Sufis whose opinions have come down to us express their views on the permissibility of musical performances in consideration of the particular contexts and circum- stances of that performance. One framework that has guided these opinions is cited by al-Sarraj as originating with the "sober" Sufi al-Junayd (d. 910):

the tripartite dimensions of time (*zaman*), place (*makan*), and company (*ikhwan*). These dimensions are understood by al-Hujwiri thus: "The rules of audition prescribe that it should not be practiced until it comes (of its own accord), and that you must not make a habit of it, but practice it seldom, in order that you may not cease to hold it in reverence. It is necessary that a spiritual director should be present during the performance, and that the place should be cleared of common people, and that the singer should be a respectable person, and that the heart should be emptied of worldly thoughts, and that the disposition should not be inclined to amusement, and that every artificial effort (*takalluf*) should be put aside."[46] Two centuries later Nizam al-din Auliya and Sharaf al-din Maneri, among other *shaikhs*, elaborated upon these dimensions. According to the compiler of the *shaikh*'s discourses, *Fawa'id al-Fu'ad*, Nizam al-din discussed this issue in some detail after having listened to a violent invective against *sama'* by one of its detractors, who had spoken publicly about it and stirred up quarrels among Muslims. The *shaikh* did not approve of the detractor's tone or comments but nevertheless felt that musical assemblies should be subject to restrictions: "There are certain requirements that should be fulfilled before *sama'* is held. And they are: *musmi'* (singer), *masmu'* (that which is recited), *mustami'* (audience), and *alah-i sama'* (musical instruments).... *Musmi'* here means the singer. He should be a full man, neither a boy nor a woman."[47]

According to Sharaf al-din Maneri, "The place should be a hospice of the sheikhs, or some building that is clean and tidy, well ventilated and well lit. The company should consist of friends and dervishes, people endowed with discrimination, and able to converse properly. They should be people who practice austerities. As for the time, it should be when one's heart is completely free of preoccupations."[48]

As the *shaikh* explains, since the ancestors (that is, the Muslims in the time of the Prophet) and the great *shaikhs* who preceded him listened to poetry accompanied by melodies, and since the Prophet himself did not unilaterally condemn the recitation of poetry using musical instruments, music should not in itself be considered unlawful (*haram*). However, he felt, those who have not established control over their lower instincts (*nafs*) should not listen to music. The multivalent meanings of Sufi poetry, which deals with love in its human as well as divine manifestations, was seen as problematic for many writers on the subject. It was presumed that while a spiritually disciplined person could grasp the mystical truths behind the poetry, the ordinary person was likely to focus on the superficial, morally ambiguous content of the music. Moreover, as a reciter of poetry, a woman (or young man) is more liable to become the focus of sexual desire. Quoting the Persian Sufi *shaikh* Ustad Abu 'Ali Daqaq (d. 1015 or 1021), Sharaf al-din

*Fig. 3.1.* The *dargah* complex of Sharaf al-din Maneri

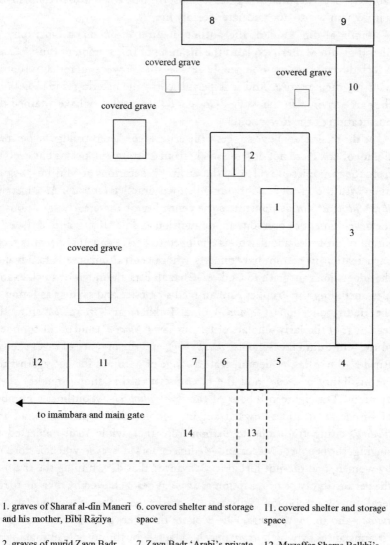

1. graves of Sharaf al-din Maneri and his mother, Bibi Raziya

2. graves of murid Zayn Badr 'Arabi and his mother

3. mosque

4. Islamic primary school (maktab)

5. cells and covered shelters

6. covered shelter and storage space

7. Zayn Badr 'Arabi's private prayer chamber (hujra)

8. cells rented out to pilgrims

9. hospice for mental "patients"

10. tank used for ablutions before prayers

11. covered shelter and storage space

12. Muzaffar Shams Balkhi's private prayer chamber (hujra)

13. covered shelter

14. graveyard

taught that "audition is forbidden to those [people] in whom the base soul (*nafs*) is abiding, and is permitted to the abstemious ones [who have] obtained [success in] their struggles [against the base soul], and to those lovers with whom we do not associate worldly life."⁴⁹

Zamir al-din Ahmad, the author of *Sirat al-Sharaf*, a biography of Sharaf al-din Maneri, explains the meaning of this statement thus: "*Sama'* is forbidden to the common people because their lower soul remains [dominant in] their nature. And it is permitted to the ascetic-minded because they are striving [in the way of God] and [because] they have attained the purification of the lower soul."⁵⁰

As the examples above suggest, the criteria for determining the permissibility of *sama'* did not develop solely from existing Sufi praxis but evolved from the examples provided by the earliest generations of Muslims, beginning with the Prophet Muhammad's own practice (*sunna*). Al-Ghazali's *Ihya' 'ulum al-din* demonstrates the centrality of these early traditions in the development of opinions about audition and its effects, and in the evolution of attitudes about who is equipped to derive spiritual benefits from participation in communal concerts whose central purpose is to advance the adept along the path to God. Al-Ghazali lists a number of stock examples, including the Prophet Muhammad's practice and sayings as found in the Hadis collections (*Sahihan*) of al-Bukhari and Imam Muslim, the teachings of the early scholars of Islamic law ( *fuqaha'*) and of the founders of the four Sunni law schools (*madhahib*), and the practice of sages such as Farid al-din 'Attar, to demonstrate a range of opinions for and against the permissibility of *sama'* and the circumstances that should qualify these opinions. The eighteenth book of the *Ihya' 'ulum al-din* outlines a number of disparate attitudes toward singing among the companions and the *fuqaha'*, citing traditions to demonstrate that while many objected to singing, the people of Mecca and Medina endorsed it, even when performed by women, and did not forbid it. Convinced that determining the truth of the permissibility or proscription of *sama'* is best achieved by turning to the legal sources of opinion (with a focus on the *nass*—that is, the Qur'an and *sunna*—and analogy, or *qiyas*), he explains that there are four steps and seven circumstances by which *sama'* may be adapted for the purpose of making an impression on the heart that brings the believer close to God. The seventh circumstance specifically concerns Sufi *sama'*, which, al-Ghazali says,

> is the listening of him who loves God and has a passion for Him and longs to meet Him so that he cannot look upon a thing but he sees it in Him (Whose perfection is extolled), and no sound strikes upon his ear but he hears it from Him and in Him. So listening to music and singing

in his case is an arouser of his longing and a strengthener of his passion and his love and an inflamer of the tinderbox of his heart, and brings forth from it States (*ahwal*) consisting of Revelations (*mukashafat*) and Caressings, description of which cannot be comprehended,—he who has tasted them knows them, and he rejects them whose sense is blunt so that he cannot taste them.[51]

Yet there are circumstances under which *sama'* becomes a hindrance and a danger to the adept, and these include the singing performances of women. Thus one of the "accidents" by which *sama'* becomes unlawful is

that the producer of the poetry or music be a woman *upon whom to look is not lawful and from listening to whom temptation is dreaded;* included with her is also the beardless youth whose temptation is dreaded. This is unlawful on account of what it in it of the fear of temptation, and it is not on account of the singing. . . . Thus the arousing of temptation is the rule which ought to be followed, and the unlawfulness should be limited to that. This, in my opinion, is the more probable view and the nearer analogy (to the issue of the lawfulness of looking upon a marriageable woman), and it strengthened by the tradition of the two girls who sang in the house of A'isha, since it is known that the Prophet was wont to listen to their voices and did not guard himself; temptation in this case was not to be feared and therefore he did not guard himself. So then, this varies with the circumstances of the woman and the circumstances of the man in being young or old. . . . And hearing (*al-sama'*) may invite to looking and drawing near which is unlawful; so that, too, varies with individuals.[52]

Finally al-Ghazali concludes that *sama'* itself is lawful and wholly within the pale of Islamic Shari'a.[53] As the text above suggests, the question of women singing is less about the classification of a woman's voice as being forbidden to a man whom she may theoretically marry than about the manner in which her voice may serve as a vehicle for arousing profane lust rather than longing for Allah in the heart of the believer. Thus the onus of responsibility for being aroused to temptation ultimately lies with the participants rather than the performer. Participants in the *sama'* are enjoined to cultivate the proper conditions within themselves to ensure that the *sama'* has the desired effect: enabling the production of a kind of effervescence (*ghalayan*) within the listener through the disciplining of the self, the conquest of the base instincts, and the cultivation of a temperament that allows one to hear the spiritual meaning as opposed to the material sound of the *sama'*.

There was a general concurrence among the *shaikh*s of this early period with al-Ghazali's views that *sama'* was inappropriate for beginners and common people, women and boys.[54] Yet even during the early period in which the Sufi orders emerged, a few among them seem to have regularly allowed female musicians to perform in or attend the *mahfil-i sama'*. According to al-Munjibi's *Risala al-sama' wa'l-raqs,* the injunction that young boys or women must not sing in a *mahfil-i sama'* was seldom followed.[55] With the expansion of the orders and the growth of shrines, views on *sama'* were qualified by the ways in which Sufi poetry, literature, and music drew greater numbers of ordinary people toward Sufism and its idioms of expression. Despite his reservations about whether the benefits of *sama'* outweighed its dangers for ordinary people, and citing al-Ghazali, Sharaf al-din Maneri concedes that *sama'* could be beneficial for those whose hearts were preoccupied with both God and worldly thoughts if, through *sama'*, preoccupation with God grew from preoccupation with worldly thoughts.[56] Further, he admits that a woman's voice can be a vehicle for mystical illumination:

> It can happen that there is one and the same couplet, but each one who hears it understands it in a different way, according to his own condition and outlook. For example, a slave girl, while filling a pitcher at the river bank in Baghdad, was singing this couplet:
>
>> Undoubtedly the Master of the Heavens is pure;
>> But lovers are caught up in grief and difficulties!
>
> One man fell into a trance, exclaiming, "You are right!" Another also fell into an ecstasy, muttering, "You are wrong!" Both of them were correct! The one who said she was correct had his attention fixed on all the grief and effort of a lover [of God]; while the one who disagreed with her saw only the spirit, contentment, and union with the Friend that is found in love. Sometimes it happens that the mere sound of the words, without even understanding their meaning, is enough to send them into a trance.[57]

These statements illustrate the importance of the inner disposition of the one who is engaged in listening to *sama'*, as 'Ali al-Hujwiri noted: "Its lawfulness depends on circumstances and cannot be asserted absolutely: if audition produces a lawful effect on the mind, then it is lawful; it is unlawful if the effect is unlawful, and permissible if the effect is permissible . . . right audition consists in hearing everything as it is in quality and predicament. The reason why men are seduced and their passions excited by musical instruments is that they hear unreally: if their audition corresponded

with the reality, they would escape from all evil consequences."[58] The mean-ing of correspondence is further illustrated by Nizam al-din discussing how Shaikh Shihab al-din Suhrawardi never listened to *sama'*: "Shaykh Shihab ad-din summoned some musicians and arranged for a musical gathering. Then he himself retired to a corner where he engaged in obedi-ence to God and remembrance (*dhikr*) of Him. Shaykh Awhad Kirmani and the other participants in the musical assembly became absorbed in the music. The next morning one of the khanaqah servants came to Shakykh Shihab ad-din—may God have mercy upon him—and said: 'There was a musical gathering here last night, and every moment that group was afraid they might be bothering you.' 'Was there music?' asked Shaykh Shihab ad-din. 'Yes!' exclaimed the servant. 'I was not aware of it,' replied the Shaykh."[59]

Nizam al-din uses this narrative to illustrate how it was possible to hear but not hear, that is to say, to use the occasion of *sama'* to become so totally focused upon one's spiritual discipline that the material quality of the music is completely drowned out by the effect that it produces: in this case total absorption in God.

The Sufis of the Firdausi and Gudri Shah Chishti orders draw upon the discourses of these preeminent *shaikh*s to explain their own positions on *sama'* and on the permissibility of women's participation and/or perform-ances in the *mahfil-i sama'*. These discourses, particularly those of eminent *shaikh*s included within the lineages of each of these orders, were under-stood to form part of what was referred to as "*silsila* tradition." Yet in each case there appeared to be a disconnect between the views of these ancestors (*buzurgan-i din*), which weighed against women's performances and par-ticipation, and those of the living Sufis of these two orders. With the excep-tion of the Gudri Shah *pir,* his mother, and "inner circle" *murid*s, the prevalent view of members of the Chishti and Firdausi orders interviewed for this study was that women should not participate, let alone perform, in mixed-gender *sama'* assemblies. What does this suggest about the ways in which women have been able to overcome these ostensible restrictions within the space of the *mahfil*?

As studies in praxis theory have suggested, ritual performances can pro-duce ambiguities in identity, which may be reflected in actions that appear to "go against the grain," or in counterhegemonic discourses about a collec-tivity or collective identification.[60] When these performances are informed or shaped by discourses that are themselves ambivalent, founded as they are upon ideas of spiritual awakening that ultimately deny the importance of gendered identity, then characterizing them in oppositional terms becomes problematic. Spiritual awakening is in turn mediated by the modalities of

occasion, place, and person, and these modalities, as seen in the pronouncements of 'Ali al-Hujwiri, al-Ghazali, Sharaf al-din Maneri, and Nizam al-din Auliya, are at once framed by foundational themes in Islam (particularly Prophetic *sunna*), and early Sufi literature (since these have the power to serve as a cohesive force in the idea of "*silsila* tradition"), and inherently able—even prone—to transcend this framework in ways that reflect the importance of context. This interplay is apparent in how the Sufis of the Gudri Shah Chishti and Firdausi orders explained the meanings and application of the dimensions of place (*makan*), occasion (*zaman*), and company (*ikhwan*) in their own practice.

As the examples below suggest, the idea of place (*makan*), as articulated by many Sufis today, transcends the directive that *sama'* is more appropriate to a Sufi shrine; beyond this general rule, the perceived importance of a Sufi shrine or the spaces within it (in the case of larger shrine complexes) is directly related to a woman's prospects for attendance or performance in the *mahfil-i sama'*. Generally a woman's ability to attend or perform in these assemblies tends to be more restricted at the large *dargah*s that are administered by *pirzade*, associated with a particularly revered saint, and patronized by pilgrims on a statewide, regional, pan-Indian, or international level. However, there are important qualifications to this general rule. Despite the admission of the general public into the spaces of such shrines, women and children are prevented from entering the *dargah's* main assembly hall (*mahfil khana*) during the *'urs* of Mu'in al-din Chishti, when a nightly *mahfil-i sama'* takes place.[61] In the smaller, locally renowned *dargah*s, female singers seem to have more scope for performing (*hazari dena*)[62] in the name and honor of the saint before a mixed audience, as an act of devotion and thanksgiving. Vidya Rao, a celebrated singer from Delhi known for her performances of *thumri*, agreed with this general observation. Keenly interested in Sufism, Vidya once traveled to a large and well-known *dargah* in Bareilly, UP, in the hopes of being allowed to perform in the name of the saint buried therein. The shrine's *pir* promptly refused her request, but not because of her Hindu identity. When she informed him that she had performed on other occasions at less famous shrines, he explained that it was fine for a woman to sing at a small *dargah* but absolutely unacceptable that she should be allowed to do so at a large, important one.[63]

Similarly discourses on *zaman*, or occasion, both incorporated and transcended classical ideas about whether *sama'* should be performed seldom or frequently, for celebratory times or for the sole purpose of deepening spiritual awareness. While the Chishtis of Ajmer hold *sama'* assemblies daily, the Maner and Bihar Sharif Firdausis do so only annually, on the occasion of Sharaf al-din's death-day anniversary celebration, and without the use

*Fig. 3.2.* Women outside the *mahfil khana* in the *dargah* of Mu'in al-din Chishti. Photograph by the author

*Fig. 3.3.* View from above the tomb of Mu'in al-din Chishti. Photograph by the author

of musical instruments. In each case participation in the musical assembly is conceived as a way of inspiring mystical experience (*hal*), fostering nearness to God, or nurturing the love of the *shaikh* in the hearts of participants, and it serves to nourish the spiritual development of the individual. Yet the question of whether the *mahfil* was to be a private or public ceremony emerged more frequently in my conversations with Sufi *shaikh*s and their disciples as a defining criterion for determining the permissibility of women's attendance or performances at these events. As these conversations suggested, the question of occasion often elided with the question of place, and with the question of the authority of the *pir* who presides over the occasion.

Generally public *mahfil*s are held in the open spaces at a *dargah*. Private *mahfil*s may be staged in a chamber or semiclosed space within a *dargah* or in a Sufi *khanaqah*.[64] These kinds of assemblies are generally off-limits to those who are uninitiated or not closely associated with the order. However, since they are presided over by a single *pir*, who represents the highest authority in the assembly, it is up to him to decide who will or will not be excluded. If he agrees or sanctions it, women may be admitted as performers or audience participants. This was the case in the Gudri Shah order. Although the subject of women singing in the *mahfil-i rindan* has not been without controversy in this order, the authority of the *pir*—specifically the third *pir*, Nawab Sahib, who instituted the tradition of the *mahfil-i rindan*—was invoked to explain how women could be allowed to perform in the *mahfil-i sama'* setting. Similarly, the presence of women at a poetry assembly (*musha'ira*) in a space that is generally off-limits to them—the assembly hall (*mahfil khana*) in the Mu'in al-din *dargah* during the *'urs* festival for the saint—was explained as a permission given by the authority of the *pir*s of the Gudri Shah order. Since it was the Gudri Shahs who traditionally arranged the poetry assembly during the festival, the head of their order, and not the shrine's hereditary functionaries, possessed the ultimate authority to decide whether or not women could be admitted into this assembly.

While most of the Sufis I spoke with presented arguments from Islam (as a system of values) and the traditions of their order as evidence for or against women's participation as audience members or as singers in a public *mahfil*, these arguments also drew on local customs, perceptions, and social mores that promulgate an ideal of behavior in which female modesty, propriety, and segregation of the sexes figures as the ideal social arrangement. These ideals are supported by evidence within the classical written sources of Sufism, which overwhelmingly evince a marked opposition to women's presence at the *mahfil-i sama'*, for reasons briefly outlined in this

chapter. Doubtless, these sources—the Qur'an, Hadis, and the teachings of past Sufi masters—have a considerable influence on the opinions of Sufis today, if only as indicators of an ideal. What, however, of the unclear and ambiguous passages these same sources contain, which can also be used to support a case for the permissibility of women's performance in the devotional setting? Sometimes this ambiguity is overlooked or de-emphasized in order to promote an ideal of femininity in which "respectability" is measured by the exclusion of women from what are viewed as traditionally male spheres of influence. Such exclusion is promulgated—and outwardly perceived—as the norm. However, as this chapter has demonstrated, there are exceptions to the general rule of gender segregation in the *mahfil-i sama'* setting. Although the Gudri Shah *pirzade* women believe that women should not attend musical assemblies where the audience is of mixed gender, they themselves attend such assemblies on specific occasions and in particular places. Moreover they are subject—and subject themselves—to restrictions that enable them to convey messages about the propriety of the event and their presence within. These restrictions are manifest in where the women sit, their body language, and in the way they participate in ritual performances such as reciting and singing (*hazari dena*) or gift giving (*nazrana dena*). Thus while the *pirzade* women themselves may internalize and project dominant discourses about the propriety of women in the *mahfil* setting, their presence and participation in it effectively challenge these very discourses. The more time I spent among them, the more it seemed to me that the *pirzade* women were not unaware of this fact.

Beyond the practical and sociological implications of these actions, the framing of the performative event suggests an ideal trajectory for the purification (and ultimately perfection) of souls that may act as an additional enabling mechanism for women's participation in the *mahfil* setting: the importance of the outward reality (Shari'a) must be acknowledged and comprehended as an initial step along the path; progress is made possible through the guidance of the *shaikh* and the examples provided by the pious ancestors, or *buzurgan-i din*. At a higher stage in the refinement of the individual soul, a glimpse of ultimate truth, or *haqiqa*, comes within reach, culminating in the experience of *wajd*, or ecstasy, that the performance is intended to elicit. In a "successful" performance, then, the liminal space that is established by the careful observance of such preconditions creates a precious moment of selflessness, where gender becomes irrelevant.

# · 4 ·

# The Work of Petitioning

Women who are in a state of physical or mental illness go there (to the smaller shrines). They may sing in a state of anxiety and abandon. . . .

Common people, general people, especially ladies cannot sing in a *dargah*. It is prohibited in front of the men. . . .

But [these days] there are all kinds of people, all kind of opinions. Women may be given permission to sing in the smaller shrines.[1]

### Petitioning the Saints in Bihar Sharif

I first came to Bihar on July 4, 1996, determined to find out more about the existence of shrines erected solely for women in this state. With the help of a colleague, Dan Madigan, a young Jesuit priest working on his Ph.D. at Columbia University, I was able to get in touch with Father Paul Jackson, himself a Jesuit priest whose work on the Sufi shrines of Bihar fascinated me, particularly for his description of the shrine of Bibi Kamalo, the maternal aunt of the fourteenth-century Firdausi *shaikh* Sharaf al-din Maneri. Father Jackson lived at the St. Xavier School in Patna, worked closely with the Muslim community in the surrounding areas, had translated the one hundred letters of Sharaf al-din, and was well liked and highly respected by the Firdausi Sufis of Bihar Sharif and Maner. With his help and kind willingness to introduce me to the Firdausi Sufis, I set out to discover more about the phenomenon of women *pir*s. On July 4, Father Jackson, my husband, Jeff, and I set out by car to visit the Shah Sahib of Bihar Sharif, a town located about forty kilometers southeast of Patna. Despite being the district headquarters of Nalanda, which boasts the oldest university in the world, in addition to a number of Buddhist monasteries, Bihar Sharif was quite a depressed locale, disappointing for a place that housed the Firdausi Islamic school (*madrasa*), which until the first half of the twentieth century was reputed to be one of the best *dini madaris* in the region.

Passing through a squalid neighborhood, we were delighted to see that the area surrounding the Firdausi Sufi *khanaqah* was, by contrast, tranquil, clean, and pleasant. As we crossed under the archway leading to a compound that houses, among other things, the *khanaqah*, the *madrasa*, a sacred building commemorating the Shi'i imams (*imambara*), and a private prayer chamber (*hujra gah*) used by Sharaf al-din Maneri, we could distinctly hear the sound of singing coming from the inside the *hujra gah*. Father Jackson explained to us that the *hujra gah* contains a cell that has been plastered over and enhanced by the addition of a two-level structure. The structure consists of two adjoining cells, a raised, roofed, but otherwise unenclosed prayer hall, a small metal gate leading to a sad and neglected-looking courtyard, and just beyond that a larger gate bearing an inscription of its identity as the *hujra gah* of Sharaf al-din Maneri. Originally it consisted of one simple cell that Makhdum Sahib used when he returned to the area after many years spent wandering, meditating, and living in the hills in Rajgir, a town popular with Buddhist tourists that is a thirty-minute drive from here. Today the *hujra gah* is used by the family of the current Shah Sahib of the Firdausi order, and by local women, for prayer. As we neared the building, the sounds of singing became clearer—the voice was that of a woman. Curiosity pulled me forward, and Father Jackson suggested that I go inside the cell and sit down, while he and Jeff waited outside. Covering my head with my *dupatta* as a sign of modesty and respect for this sacred space, I passed through the first, then the second gate of the *hujra gah*, noting the covered, elevated prayer hall situated next to the cell in which Sharaf al-din prayed. Inside the niches of these prayer spaces someone had stacked several copies of the Qur'an—some clothbound, some bare—and the bound, individual Qur'anic chapters called *sifarat*. Crouching down low, I entered the cell and sat down near the entrance. What I saw intrigued and amazed me.

To my right sat a woman dressed in a beautiful, expensive-looking red sari embroidered with gold thread work. She glanced sadly at me but said nothing. With one hand she clutched a bar of the small, locked gate that separates the two cells. Tied to this gate were numerous bits of cloth and string, which visitors had left as reminders of the vows they had made in the name of the saint. To my left sat the singing woman, much darker in complexion than the first, dressed in a plain, maroon sari that was tattered, dirty, and disheveled. She sang with abandon, gesticulating freely with her arms and hands, her unbound hair framing her face, shoulders, and upper arms. She did not seem to notice my presence. I tried to make sense of what I was seeing by listening to the words of the woman's song but could only

make out a few verses, which she repeated several times. In these verses she asked Allah for the gift of a child. After sitting a while, I rose and left, disappointed that I had been unable to speak with the women sitting in the *hujra*. Father Jackson took Jeff and me to visit with the Shah Sahib, a most gracious host in whose *khanaqah* we passed a couple of hours, along with a large crowd of local women and a few men who had come seeking his help. As we returned to our hired taxi, we could hear the woman in the *hujra*, still singing as loudly and as fervently as before. Father Jackson explained to me as we passed the cell that she was a woman who petitioned God and the saint on behalf of other women; such a practice was not uncommon at this shrine.

On February 22, 1999, I returned, alone, to Bihar Sharif with the intention of trying one more time to meet the type of female ritual specialist[2] I had heard so much about but was unable to find. My previous attempts had been unsuccessful, and to my surprise and disappointment, everyone I questioned in Bihar Sharif—the women who visit the *hujra gah* to pray, read the Qur'an, or present their own petitions (which often occurs in the context of making a vow); the servants at Sharaf al-din's *dargah;* the members of the Firdausi *pir*'s family (*pirzade*); the disciples of the Firdausi order (*murid*s); and local residents—knew about these kinds of ritual specialists but had no idea how common they were in Bihar, let alone India. Furthermore they were not comfortable talking about them. A few among those I consulted, including the current Shah Sahib (who succeeded his father shortly after my first excursion to Bihar in 1996), advised me to stay away from these kinds of people, because they were troubled and unpredictable. But I was determined to find what seemed to be a crucial bit of information for a study of the role of women in Sufi circles today.

A young father from Pushpa Vidyalay, the Catholic seminary where I was staying about a mile away, accompanied me to the shrine, worried that I was traveling there alone. As we passed through the shrine's first two gates, I realized that a woman was sitting inside the cell, praying. She was quite dirty, with a torn purple shawl thrown over her shoulders, underneath which she wore a purple sweater over a yellow tunic and royal blue trousers. Her shoes, deposited outside the second gate leading to the *hujra gah,* were worn out blue and white plastic sandals. Her hair was partially matted and slightly bleached by the sun. Her teeth protruded significantly, and she seemed to have some advanced form of gum disease. Her eyes were bloodshot and large and sometimes riveted on you, sometimes seemed to be looking straight through you. She appeared to be somewhere between thirty-five and forty years old, although she could have been much

younger. Hard living and chronic health problems cause the poor to age much more quickly than nature intended. Some might say she looked like a madwoman. As I turned to the father to ask him not to enter, the woman asked us both to come inside. We did, but my escort left soon after, seeing that I was settled down and safe. The woman immediately asked me what I had come for, and I told her to pray, which was not untrue, since I had established the practice of spending some time in the *hujra* to offer the *fatiha* prayer (the opening verse of the Qur'an) and the Lord's Prayer before visiting the Firdausi *khanaqah*. Her Urdu was articulate and colored with a Bihari accent. She did not speak with me in Maggahi, the local dialect, as did many of the other village women I had encountered in Bihar Sharif, although this may simply have been because I told her I had come to Bihar from Delhi.

I told her I had heard about women who, being perceived by others as especially close to God, prayed for and presented petitions on behalf of other people. I asked her if she could do this, and she immediately said yes, then inquired whether I had brought any money with me. I handed over fifty rupees, but she said it would be better if I had one hundred, so I gave her another fifty. Reassuring me (I must have looked apprehensive), she explained that the money would be used to carry out the work of petitioning on my behalf. What this meant exactly I never found out, but she told me that she would give it to a man in her village to procure amulets (*ta'wiz*) for me. She showed me some of the ritual paraphernalia she had brought with her that day—scented oils, a small, clay lamp (*chiragh*), incense (*agarbatti*), and several *ta'wiz* printed on pieces of paper—and explained that she was doing this same type of work for another client (a man), and that I had nothing to fear. I left it at that and told her the subject of my petition: recently a very lucrative opportunity had opened up for my husband and me to teach middle school in Saudi Arabia. She assured me that I would get what I wanted.

The woman, who initially told me her name was "Shahida," said that by the end of the week she would write me two *ta'wiz*, for which I was to pay her two hundred rupees. I was to wear one of the *ta'wiz* on my right arm, and the other she told me to give to my husband to wear. She instructed me to meet her again at the shrine the next day with another one hundred rupees, for which she would offer prayers to the saints on my behalf. The day after tomorrow I was to bring her two hundred rupees for the *ta'wiz*.

This first day, "Shahida" had me write out my husband's and my names, as well as the address of Sharib House in Ajmer, where the man I consider my spiritual guide resides. She looked at the words I had written in Urdu and read them back to me slowly and with some difficulty, but ultimately

satisfied, she took the paper and wrapped it around the money I had given her. Then she began to recite prayers in Urdu on my behalf—a simple statement of my problem and request. Handing me a piece of string she had retrieved from the gate leading to the *hujra*'s innermost chamber, she instructed me to recite whatever prayer I knew, since I did not know at the time how to recite the *durud,* which is a prayer to bring blessings upon the Prophet Muhammad. When my prayer is answered, she instructed me, I should return to the *hujra,* remove the string, and throw it into the inner chamber (which always remains locked). When I asked her why, she told me that *buzurgan din* inhabited the inner cell, and that was why it remained locked. *Buzurgan din* (or in grammatically correct Urdu, *buzurgan-i din*) is a term that was used by "Shahida" and many others to refer to the *"pahunche hue log"* (literally "the people who have arrived," that is, spiritually advanced people) or deceased *pir*s whose intercession is sought out by believers. Interestingly the Shah Sahib of Bihar Sharif had a very different explanation for why the chamber remained inaccessible. In 1998 he told me that he had begun to keep the gate bolted and padlocked to prevent the women who frequented the shrine from sleeping in there all night, as they had been in the habit of doing. I neglected to mention this to "Shahida," thinking it was an unimportant detail and likely irrelevant to her.

Procuring a second string from the gate, "Shahida" told me to recite the first verse of the Qur'an, the *fatiha.* At the end of the week, I was to buy a bottle of good *'itr,* or scented oil (and she admonished me to spend no less than ten rupees for it), and distribute it along the threshold of the innermost chamber of the cell. She then led me upstairs to the prayer hall and had me tie the second string to a clothbound copy of the Qur'an, which she referred to as the *qalam sharif.* I had never heard this phrase before, and she did not explain its exact meaning, but it seems to point to an important association among the pen, or *qalam;* the act of writing, which is especially relevant to the task of producing amulets; and the Qur'an, the scriptures of Islam, from which many important prayers are derived.[3] She also said that at the end of the week, I should take the scented oil and spread it down the line of cloth-covered books sitting inside one of the niches in this prayer hall, vertically down the *mihrab,* or niche indicating the direction of Mecca, then down the line of cloth-covered books to the right of the *mihrab.*

We spent the entire morning and some of the afternoon sitting inside the *hujra gah,* praying together that our respective petitions be granted. For herself she requested a husband, in-laws, and the return of property that had recently been stolen. Most of her prayers seemed impromptu to my ears, but she repeated these words several times:

O Allah, please be so kind as to accept my prayer
In the name of God please be so kind as to fulfill my goal:
May a husband be granted to me.
And please be so kind as to return my belongings to me.
Send me my belongings.
Allah most high you are my only support;
There is no other support;
We have no other support.

She said that the man she wished to marry—a *khadim* at a small mausoleum located in Paharpura—had demanded a dowry of thirty thousand rupees from her. Strangely enough, she did not request the money for her dowry from the saint, although I did hear her request many other things, gifts that are given to the newly betrothed, such as kitchenware, appliances, clothing, and a Hero Honda scooter. Addressing Allah, she explained what she had already done to encourage a favorable response: "Agarbati jala diya . . ." (I have lit some incense).

Added to these prayers was a curse directed at the ones who had wronged her:

Please make blood flow from their noses and mouths.
I will recite the *milad sharif* + and the Qur'an.
Please pray, Hazrat, that I get my belongings back.
In the glory of God most high;
In your glory may I get my belongings.
Allah, send my troubles far away.

Later, by way of explanation, one of the sisters of the Gudri Shah *pir* in Ajmer would repeat part of this curse when I struggled to recall it from memory. Unfortunately I have been unable to find out any further information about it.

After five hours of prayer, conversation, and reciting petitions, I left "Shahida" and the *hujra gah* in a state of exhaustion but thrilled that the information I had been seeking for so long had finally come to light. The next few days would provide insight into how the framework of ritual petitioning at this shrine incorporated elements of foundational Islam and local perceptions of spiritual authority. I would also learn more about how attitudes toward the female ritual specialists at the *hujra gah* of Sharaf al-din Maneri were as much a commentary on social and class divisions as an expression of fear or uncertainty about the "madness" of women such as "Shahida."

*Fig. 4.1.* The mausoleum of Sharaf al-din Maneri within the *dargah* complex.
Photograph by the author

### Ecstatics or Profits?

The following day I arrived, a little late, to our meeting. "Shahida" was not inside the *hujra gah,* so I headed to the Firdausi *khanaqah* to pay my respects, only to find that the Shah Sahib was out of town for the next few weeks. As I returned I met "Shahida" on the road. She wore the same dirty shawl as yesterday but had changed into a burnt orange tunic and pants, which were filthy nevertheless. She looked like she had not brushed her teeth or combed her hair in ages. She was babbling to herself and did not notice me at all until I grabbed her shoulders and looked her straight in the eye. She excitedly clasped my shoulders, and we made our way to the cell together.

That day I learned more about "Shahida." She has three brothers and three sisters, none of whom comes to this shrine. The three brothers support her financially, since their parents have died and she has never been married. The sisters are married and have moved to villages not far from where she lives. She seems to work here alone, though she mentioned several times that she performs her "work" in conjunction with her "Dada Jan," which I initially took literally to mean her paternal grandfather. When I asked repeatedly if he was a *pir* or religious scholar (*maulwi* or *maulana*), she told me that he was a spiritually advanced (*pahunche hue*) person who told her what to write on the amulets she gives to her clients. I

decided not to ask her why, if she is writing these *ta'wiz,* they always seem to be machine-printed: the *ta'wiz* she showed me the previous day was marked with verses of the Qur'an and the names of the "*panj-i pak,*" or "five pure ones": the Prophet Muhammad, 'Ali, Fatima, Hasan, and Husain,⁵ as well as several of the names of Allah that are used in mystical formulas. I held my tongue when she increased the price of the *ta'wiz* I would receive from two hundred to three hundred rupees, explaining that the extra one hundred rupees would be used for the ink and the printing. But I could not help recalling at that moment the warnings of many people I have spoken to over the years, who told stories about some *pir*s and *maulana*s who demand large, often exorbitant, sums of money from their clientele for the purchase of prayers, amulets, and other healing implements. One friend of ours in Patna, a Christian mechanic who earned only 1,000 rupees a month, was told by the *pir* he visits that he would have to pay 1,500 rupees for a single *ta'wiz* in order to get his missing wife to return home. Still I could not help feeling intrigued by this woman and grateful to have met her. And the fact that she had been willing to spend the morning and half of the afternoon of the preceding two days sitting with me in a cell, reciting prayers and requests, made me think that her motives might not be just monetary.

### The Ritual Process: Forms, Significations, and Exchanges

On the third day I learned more about the "Dada Jan" to whom "Shahida" had been referring. She told me that he is a *buzurg*—in other words a deceased Sufi saint, from whom she receives "inspiration." Several times she suddenly interrupted the conversation between us in order to place her head on the ground in front of the gate leading to the cell's innermost chamber. She lay there for some time and then resumed our conversation with instructions for me. I also learned that "Shahida's" real name is Rafat, which she confirmed by using it in her petition to the saints and to God. Although she said that she is reciting *na't,* her recitations seem to contain elements of several other poetic forms I have encountered, namely *hamd, manqabat,* and the informal way of presenting one's troubles (*musibat pesh karna*), which tends to start out quietly and crescendo to a wailing, moaning peak. This last form of prayer is common among the women who visit the *hujra gah* to pray or perform vows. It seems to be improvised for the most part, though not entirely thrown together at random. Like other women I have seen at the *hujra gah,* Rafat uses royal imagery in her prayers, identifying us as lowly supplicants appealing to the king's munificence and paternalism.⁶

> O my Khwaja Sahib,
> O my great *pir,*
> The beloved slaves of God,
> O send away the troubles of the[se two] people of the Messenger's
>   [the Prophet Muhammad's] community.
> O Messenger of God,
> We have come into the royal court to beg [you].
> Fill our sacks, father (*baba*).
> And we have come, great king, into your royal court
> To beg.
> We are begging for our husbands,
> Please grant us both our requests, father (*baba*).

The requests became more specific toward the end of her recitation:

> O messenger of God, give your drink of unity.
> From your door give to Rafat,
> And give to Kelly.[7]
> She is asking for employment for her husband,
> And I am asking that my [future] husband contract marriage
>   [with me].
> The king's messenger is returning for us by the royal highway.

What distinguishes Rafat's petitions from the others I have heard is that sometimes she alternates between speaking in the voices of the petitioner and the one being petitioned:

> Fill our sacks, Khwaja!
> Fill our sacks, Khwaja!
> We have come into your royal court, Khwaja!
> Dada Jan, please fill our sacks,
> Dada Jan, please fill our sacks . . .
>
> Of course I will give to you, daughter,
> You have come to my royal court to beg.
> How could I not give to you?
> O messenger of God, both girls are mine [under my protection].

As was the case with the other women I have spent time with in the Maneri *hujra gah,* Rafat's tone and mood became chillingly intense the longer she recited. At the end of each recitation it seemed as if she would burst into tears. The sound of her wailing and moaning prayers stayed inside my head long after I left the shrine for the shelter of Pushpa Vidyalay.

The ritual acts we performed were consistent with what I have seen when pilgrims complete a vow or have a petition fulfilled. The long-term conclusion to this ritual, as stated by Rafat, is that when my husband and I get jobs, and I have had a son (this latter having been an initial request of mine, which I quickly dropped, but she did not), I am to return to the *hujra gah* and give her two thousand rupees, as well as feed her a number of sweetmeats. Most important I have to make an offering of incense, rose water, and scented oil to Makhdum Sahib Sharafuddin Maneri at his *dargah* and pray the *fatiha* there.

On the third day I received two *ta'wiz* from her, as well as instructions about how to wear them, and paid Rafat the three hundred rupees I had promised. As I suspected they would, the demands for cash continued. She asked me to bring three hundred rupees more the following day for the final ritual implements (a small, clay lamp and a third *ta'wiz*), but I balked (not without some theatrics), and she lowered the request to two hundred, which she insisted upon.

The next day's session suggested that ritual agents such as Rafat are willing to modify the work to be done according to what their clients can afford. On that day I told her I could only give her fifty rupees, whereupon she tried to convince me to take a loan if I could not procure more money. In any case she took the money I had given her and explained that she would use it to buy some scented oil and *kewra* water, which would be used in conjunction with her work on my behalf. Since I did not bring all the money she had requested, she agreed to forego the application of scented oil to the lintel leading to the innermost chamber of the *hujra* cell but insisted that I bring two hundred rupees the following day.

Aside from these kinds of "adaptations," it seemed to me that there had been a great deal of improvisation involved with this ritual petitioning. She asked if I would go to Sher Shah's tomb[8] but quickly changed her mind about it. At other times she told me I would have to stay in the *hujra* cell from early morning until early evening, while in fact our sessions usually began at 9:00 or 9:30 A.M. and rarely lasted beyond 2:00 P.M. Besides this, Rafat had begun to incorporate the names of two Sufi *shaikh*s I mentioned during the course of our conversations, names that she probably would not have used had I not brought them up: Khwaja Sahib (Khwaja Mu'in al-din Chishti) and Sharda Pir Sahib (this is the phrase she uses to refer to the current *pir* of the Gudri Shah order, who lives in Sharib House in Ajmer). Moreover her inclusion of the names of multiple spiritual sources in her petition—Dada Jan (which, as I found out today, actually refers to Yahya Maneri, the father of Sharaf al-din), Dadi Jan (Bibi Raziya, the

mother of Sharaf al-din), and Sharfa Bihari (a local designation for Sharaf al-din)—is something I had not heard before.[9] She even called upon the names of Bibi Kamalo, the maternal aunt of Makhdum Sahib and a famous saint in her own right who lies buried in a shrine in Jahanabad district, and Pir Jagjot, Makhdum Sahib's maternal grandfather.

> Bibi Kamalo, Bibi Daulat,
> We have come Bibi Kamalo, we have come, Bibi Daulat,
>
> Bibi Kamalo, Pir Jagjot Shahab al-din, may God have mercy
>   upon them,
>
> We have come, grandfather (Nana Jan) . . .
> O Khwaja baba, fill our sacks
> Fill our sacks, Khwaja baba, great king of India
> O Prophet, fill our sacks, fill our sacks

What seemed strangest to me is that included in some of her appeals to the saints was the name of Harun al-Rashid (d. 809 C.E.), who is none other than that famed 'Abbasid caliph of the Arabian Nights tales, the Righteous Ruler of eighth- to ninth-century Baghdad. And still the names she chose to include in her prayers and appeals were not necessarily random. She emphasized those spiritual influences that I have shown—by mentioning them to her—to have meaning in my life, namely, Mu'in al-din Chishti and Inam Hasan, the current *pir* of the Gudri Shah order. And her petitions are mainly directed toward five Sufis who are relevant in a local context, namely the saint in whose prayer chamber we are performing this ritual and four others who are closely linked to him by ties of kinship. These five saints of the Firdausi and Suhrawardi orders—Yahya Maneri, Bibi Raziya, Sharaf al-din Maneri, Bibi Kamalo, and Pir Jagjot—are among the most widely and well known in the area. Such associations have apparently been observed by others as well; for instance, in her book on *qawwali* music in India and Pakistan, the ethnomusicologist Regula Burckhardt Qureshi maintains that *qawwali* poems that focus on a local saint tend to display a variety of associational links. Poems in which these links are central address figures of the Sufi hierarchy, including God and the Prophet Muhammad and sometimes living *shaikh*s as well.[10]

After Rafat finished praying to the saints, presenting her prayers in the form of song, she recited a spoken petition, which I was asked to repeat after her, both of us placing our right hands[11] on the gate leading to the innermost cell. The spoken petitions usually lasted ten to fifteen minutes or so and stated our requests in several different ways. Afterward Rafat extracted dried flowers from the garlands draped over this gate and gave me a handful to take home. Sometimes she took a handful for herself, sometimes not, but it

was always the case that our petitions were presented jointly and closed with the taking of flowers from the cell gate. Although I had initially questioned her identity as a ritual agent who works on behalf of clients, I began to believe that she did enjoy some authority in these matters in the eyes of some of the local residents. I had seen her help others with their prayers after finding out why they had come to the shrine. No one seemed to protest her interference, and indeed some visiting women even sought her assistance.

Where Rafat learned the practice of petitioning saints and distributing *ta'wiz* remains an open question, although I have some ideas. She alternately claimed that her training came straight from the deceased *"pir"* Sher Shah (the sixteenth-century Afghan ruler Sher Shah Suri) and from "Dada Jan" (Yahya Maneri). I suspect that some of her knowledge, at least, came from a more recently departed source. On the first day we met, Rafat told me that she was a disciple (*murid*) of the former Shah Sahib—the now-deceased *pir* who I met through Father Jackson during my first trip to Bihar almost three years prior. Rafat spoke fondly of him, which is not at all surprising: the former Shah Sahib seemed to have a special rapport with the local women who visited him, one that his son and successor had not yet demonstrated. I believe that as the former Shah Sahib's *murid,* Rafat gained some kind of knowledge of the process of prescribing *ta'wiz* and lighting lamps in supplication to *buzurgan-i din,* though considering the number of nominal disciples the Shah Sahib had and the strong cultural bias against the mixing of the sexes here, even where this involves a *pir* and his female disciples, it is equally as likely that she did not receive much, if any, formal guidance or training from him.

I am less certain about her writing abilities, since the *ta'wiz* she gave me were not handwritten. In truth I thought that she only had a tenuous grasp of reading and writing. She claimed to have studied up to the second or fourth standard (her claim varied), though I had no way of knowing for sure. She had never written anything in my presence, and when she read what I wrote (at her dictation), she made many errors. When I asked if she ever came to the *hujra gah* to read the Qur'an, as I had seen so many other women do, she said yes, and added that in the next day's session we would read the Qur'an together. It was clear that to a great extent, her responses to my queries were conditioned by what she thought I wanted to hear, and that these rituals were conducted with that in mind as well.

## The Final Day's Work

On February 26 I came to the *hujra gah* to meet Rafat for the last time, having decided not to bring the full amount of money she had requested. I brought one hundred rupees instead of two hundred and presented the

money to her, explaining that it was all that I could get. Although she begged, cajoled, and schemed to try and find a way for me to get another one hundred rupees "loan" (explaining that it was Dada Jan's "order" that I bring two hundred rupees to get the work done properly), she finally relented after much wailing and excuse-making on my part, and I received the ritual implements she had promised to give me: a third *ta'wiz* for a son, and the *chiragh*, which I was told to keep burning in my house all night. The third *ta'wiz* looks exactly like the other two, which, I thought at the time, did not say much for the quality of Rafat's work.

I began to believe, though, that she could read a bit better than I originally thought. She could obviously read Urdu, despite the poor state of her reading skills. On that last day she obviously read what I had written (even correcting a couple of things). Unless she has an extremely keen memory, I do not see how she could have been merely memorizing what I had written, since I filled three or four pieces of paper with writing.

I also had to reassess my initial suspicions about her motive being mostly profit: it seems that what Rafat told me is true—the "work" can be done even if people cannot afford to pay fully for it, although I doubt that anything would be done for a person who did not give any offering (*nazrana*) at all, whether in the form of cash or goods. I brought up this issue with Rafat once again that day, asking what happens when a person could not afford to pay for her services. At first she indicated that she did not do work for someone who paid absolutely nothing, but then modified her statement, saying that if people could not pay, their work is done very slowly (that is, they would not get results very quickly). By contrast the work of those who can pay her fees (which are always determined, according to her, by "Dada Jan's" order, received by inspiration from the unseen world) is accomplished much more quickly and efficiently.

That last day's prayers resembled those we had been offering up already, except that they were shorter. What was different that day is that we spent a lot of time writing out the petitions we had been making all week. Below I reconstruct from memory, to the best of my ability, what I wrote on a slip of paper at Rafat's dictation. It is translated here into English.

> Peace be upon you, Dada Jan
> Jeff     Kelly
> May Jeff find employment may Kelly find employment
> Gulzar Muhammad Azad Muhammad[12]
> May all [of us], brothers, sisters remain happy
> And friends [whose friendship will] flourish
> Sharib House

> Khwaja Sahib Gharib Nawaz (Mu'in al-din Chishti)
> Behind the *dargah*[13]
> May Rafat contract marriage with Sonu
> And may [we be given] 2,005 *bighas* of land[14]
> May blood flow from the noses and mouths of those
>     who have stolen [from me], Shamim and Tara,
> And [may they] drop Rafat's belongings in [her] courtyard.

When I had finished writing these requests (there were several more as well), Rafat took one piece of paper, folded it into a small square, and threw it into the innermost chamber in the *hujra* cell. The other she folded and took for herself. I also wrote a third slip for her, a short request for her marriage to Sonu and the return of her stolen goods, which she folded and placed with the second slip of paper, saying she would take them to Sher Shah.[15]

One written request Rafat told me to keep summarizes the main focus of my petition and the obligations it would incur, should my request be granted:

> Peace be upon you, Dada Jan
>     For Jeff and Kelly two boys, their names are Gulzar Muhammad and Azad Muhammad, and a girl, Shahina Parvin.[16] They will remain very fortunate (that is, have good luck). The mother and father [of these children] will get [good] jobs. Jeff will remain very, very happy [thanks to your] prayers. God most high willing. Then give coconut, rasgullah, pista and a golden lamp to Rafat, [your] friend.

### Ambivalence and Disassociation in Rituals of Petitioning

The ritual of petitioning the saints, as performed by Rafat on our behalf, contained several key features that emphasize the importance of the recited (*pesh karna, sunana*), written, and spoken word. Rafat began by reciting my request, calling upon the intervention of the most prominent saints of the area, although prefacing many of these recitations with the name of God (Allah) or the Prophet Muhammad: Dada Jan (Yahya Maneri), Dadi Jan (Bibi Raziya), Sharfah Bihari (Sharaf al-din Maneri); the Sufi *shaikh*s who—she surmised—figure most prominently in my life, namely Khwaja Sahib (Mu'in al-din Chishti) and Sharda Pir Sahib (Inam Hasan); and finally other figures who, to my knowledge, are not commonly associated with Sufism, namely the sixteenth-century Afghan ruler Sher Shah and the 'Abbasid caliph Harun al-Rashid. Afterward her recitations were followed by spoken requests that simply stated the matters at hand but required my active participation, at her direction. Finally Rafat pointed out the necessity

of writing out the requests on paper and depositing them inside the *hujra* cell (in the chamber where she believes the saints reside) or in the mausoleum of Sher Shah, which seemed of considerable importance to her work as a ritual agent. Besides the immediate requests, some parts of the ritual conformed to what seems to be standard practice for all supplicants at the shrines in my survey. It was necessary, for instance, that the ritual be conducted inside the *hujra* itself, although others have told me that the women who do the work of petitioning can do so in any sacred place that is imbued with spiritual power (*barakat*) of the saints, such as the mausoleums where their earthly remains lie.[17]

The importance of following certain procedures in the work of petitioning underscored the centrality of Islamic symbols, many of which serve to emphasize the "authentic" (*sahih*) character of the ritual. A charge that has been leveled against devotion to the saints, and indeed against some of the more "heterodox" Sufi orders, is that they do not emphasize the primacy of Allah and the importance of key Islamic symbols—for instance Qur'anic prayers—in their practices and rituals. Perhaps in response to the occurrence of de facto worship of *pir*s living and deceased, many *pir*s today insist that one should not attribute any of the miracles that might occur through the medium of the Sufi *pir* or saint to that person him- or herself; rather one should recognize that all power comes from God and acknowledge that recognition verbally. Although it is difficult to determine to what extent this advice is followed by the disciple of a *pir* or ordinary pilgrims to a Sufi shrine, among the *pir*s and Sufi families I have had access to, there is a marked emphasis upon the fundamentals of Islam—most significantly the importance of following the law (Shari'a) and belief in the supremacy of a single, unique God. Rafat's practice of addressing Allah before the beginning of some of her recitations, as well as her use of the names of God (among others) in the *ta'wiz* she distributed, suggests the importance of acknowledging the sources of the spiritual power that believers tap into. In the case of this ritual of petitioning, the sources are manifold. Although it would be difficult to argue that Rafat always conceded the primacy of Allah or even the Prophet Muhammad in her litany of recitations, the fact that she often included these two names indicates that she was at least aware of their importance in the work of petitioning. Regardless of the prayer or petition being presented, she always prefaced her words with an address to a powerful source such as God (for instance by reciting the *bismillah*, namely "in the name of God, the merciful, the Compassionate"), the Prophet Muhammad, or one of the saints who, it is believed, can provide a direct link to God, such as Yahya Maneri.[18] What was more evident was that her use of Hadith and Qur'anic prayers (*durud, fatiha*) before and (some-

times) after presenting the petitions highlighted the importance of these symbols of authentic (*sahih*) practice in "Islamic" reckoning.[19]

As for the requests themselves, there are four kinds associated with the work of petitioning I witnessed in Bihar Sharif, which reflect both transcendent Islamic and local cultural practices: first, formulaic requests are widely used in Islamic practice, whether in the Sufi shrine setting or elsewhere—*fatiha* prayers, the *bismillah,* and a *durud,* which precede the statement of the petition and succeed the fulfillment of the supplicant's request. The *fatiha* is the first verse of the Qur'an, but it may also be read in the name of one or more saints. Read as such, it is considered a blessing transferred to the saint or saints in whose name it is read. The *bismillah* is an invocation that is used in many contexts, especially at the beginning of any project. It establishes that the prayer is being recited in the name of God. The *durud* calls blessings upon the Prophet Muhammad and his family. These prayers are systematically used in a variety of ritual contexts, particularly those involving the praise, commemoration, or celebration of significant events in the lives of the saints of Islam.

Second are requests that the petitioner sings (as in *qawwali*) or recites (as in prayer or petition). These include prayers and poems of praise to the Prophet Muhammad (*na't, salaam*), to God (*hamd*), and to the saints (*manqabat*), which others I interviewed in Bihar indicated was standard and correct practice for women in Rafat's position. When speaking with people about the women who do the work of petitioning in the *hujra gah,* I often used the word *sing,* but many of those I spoke with distinguished between singing and reciting. A few did use the term *sing* (*gana*) but seemed to be doing so only because I had brought up the term first. Several women in Bihar Sharif insisted that the proper terms to describe what the women did were *offer, present,* or *recite* (*pesh karna, sunana*). One woman explained her distinction between the acts of singing and reciting by saying that singing in a Sufi shrine (especially by a woman) was morally unacceptable. This attitude reflects the ambivalence with which music is viewed by some Muslims. Even among some Sufis—such as the Bihar Sharif and Maner Firdausis—music and singing are viewed with suspicion. Although *qawwali* singing is important in the Chishti order and others, the Firdausis of Bihar do not sponsor *qawwali* events outside of the death-day anniversary celebrations of the saints. I am told by some of the Firdausi Sufis that even when permitted to sing, *qawwali* singers are forbidden to use musical instruments.

Third are spoken requests that state the request simply, soberly, and coherently. In this case both petitioner and requester recite, with the former guiding the latter. These may be short or lengthy, lasting up to twenty minutes in my experience.

Last is the informal way of stating one's case, which is repetitive and rhythmic. It begins in a steady tone and reaches a crescendo of wailing and crying. The servants of Sharaf al-din's *dargah* and the family of the Bihar Sharif Shah Sahib strongly disapprove of this form of prayer, which I have witnessed only among the women who visit Sharaf al-din's *hujra gah*. Once I did see a woman wail at the *dargah,* but only briefly, as one of the servants of the shrine quickly put an end to it. Locally people refer to this kind of petitioning as *apni musibat pesh karna* (presenting one's troubles), and many also believe that the women who come to the shrine to do this are sick in body and mind.

Some practices—taking sacred substances (*tabarruk*) from the shrine, usually flowers or sweets, the burning of lamps (*chiragh*) during and after the period of petitioning, and the use of *kewra* water, incense, and scented oils, which are said to please the saints and "sweeten" their disposition toward the requester—seem to be standard rituals in the process of petitioning a Sufi saint. Other practices depend on the individuals involved. Some female ritual agents are said not to take money for their services, but I have come to believe that some kind of offering (*nazrana*) is usually given to the agent. In the "work" Rafat did on my behalf, the contract between ritual agent and requester was negotiated by payments of cash and sealed by the requester's promise to pay the agent an additional sum in cash, food, and goods upon fulfillment of the petition, while the agreement between requester and Sufi saint is sealed by an offering of thanksgiving prayers, a donation to the saint's final resting place, an offering of *fatiha* prayers in the name of one or more saints, and the removal of the string or piece of cloth that has served as a reminder of the requester's petition.

## Hierarchies of Practice in Light of Islamic Shari'a

Most of the people I spoke with about the female ritual agents at the Maneri *hujra gah*[20] characterize these women as operating outside of the "official" channels of negotiation between "source"—that is the servant of the shrine or the *pir*—and supplicant. They also judge their actions by how they conform or do not conform to prevailing social views about the "correct" place of women in society vis-à-vis men. In particular what emerged from my conversations with others about ritual agents such as Rafat was the importance of *parda* and sex segregation, female subordination to male authority (spiritual and otherwise), class distinctions, and ritual expressions of devotion to the divine that are mediated through "official" channels within the Sufi order or lineage and that do not contravene the "proper" boundaries of social etiquette. Her association with the "folk" and esoteric elements of

devotion to saints undoubtedly influenced responses to Rafat's ritual activities among my interviewees, including the (Maner and Bihar Sharif) Firdausi and Gudri Shah Sufis and local residents of Bihar Sharif who regularly visit the *khanaqah, dargah,* or *hujra* shrines, yet these responses also exposed certain ambiguities about the subject of women ecstatics as ritual agents. In the eyes of my male Firdausi Sufi interviewees, Rafat fell unequivocally into the camp of *bazari,* but the women of the Firdausi order seemed to have more ambivalent attitudes toward her.

While condemning the ritual agent's actions as "against Islam," "forbidden," ineffective, or indicative of a lack of social respectability, many women (including the women of the Shah Sahib's family) were also willing to acknowledge that the women who do the work of petitioning at the Maneri *hujra gah* fulfill a need for people who may have (or perceive themselves as having) no other viable (or desirable) recourse. In a place such as Bihar, widely considered a "backward state"—a place where corruption, caste-based violence, and poverty tend to be more acute than in other states—people from the lowest social strata are extremely reluctant to go through "official" channels in order to solve their problems. Indeed dealing with official channels is often seen by the poor in Bihar (as elsewhere) as an invitation to trouble. Instead they often rely on what is locally referred to as a "source," or *zariya* (sometimes the English term is used, sometimes the Urdu)—in other words an agent of higher social or spiritual rank and influence than themselves—for help.

A source may be sought out for various reasons—to intercede with local, state government, or police authorities or to present a petition to a Sufi *shaikh, pir,* or God. In rituals of petition and prayer, using a source can entail, even within a particular type of activity, operating on several levels.[21] In order to solicit the aid of a powerful spiritual source such as Allah, the Prophet Muhammad, or Sharaf al-din Maneri, believers may enlist the services of a *pir* who is attached to a Sufi shrine or the head of a Sufi order, the disciple of a *pir* who has been designated a "successor" (*khalifa*), or one who is otherwise related to a Sufi *shaikh* by spiritual or blood descent.[22] In the cases of many of the women who frequent Sharaf al-din's *hujra gah* in Bihar Sharif, however, this course of action is not always seen as desirable. While the functionaries and hereditary families attached to the Firdausi Sufi shrines are widely perceived as being sympathetic toward men and women of any social standing, they are viewed by some women with a mixture of apprehension and misgiving. This especially seems to be the case with the new Shah Sahib, a young, highly educated man; his predecessor, though less educated, seemed to enjoy a special rapport with the many women who came seeking his aid. Some of the women I interviewed quite

frankly stated their doubts about the sincerity and intentions of the *kha-dims, pirzade,* and Shah Sahib. Others had more faith in the efficacy of the prayers of the petitioning women (and perhaps felt more comfortable sharing their problems with another woman, especially one who did not come from the elite classes). A few women simply used every possible avenue to ensure that their prayers would be heard and fulfilled. They sought out the aid and guidance of the Shah Sahib and *khadim*s but also performed prayers and vows on their own at Sharaf al-din's prayer cell.

The presence of female ritual specialists at the Maneri *hujra gah* poses a challenge to the "official" means of negotiation between saint and supplicant in two ways. By acknowledging a female petitioner as a more effective (or equally effective) source than the *pir* or *khadim*, one in effect challenges the spiritual authority of the latter. By giving *nazrana* to an "alternative" female ritual agent instead of to the *pir* or *khadim,* a supplicant essentially deprives these latter two of an important—and in the case of the servants of Sharaf al-din's *dargah,* their sole—means of livelihood. It is no wonder then that the actions of ritual agents who compete with the authority of those who "officially" mediate between the realms of the spiritual and the mundane tend to be viewed as suspect by the latter.[23]

How do local depictions of women such as Rafat reflect overarching ideals about femininity (particularly Islamic) and spiritual authority? Most of those I spoke with immediately described these women as the kind of people who do not come from "respectable" families; in academic parlance one could say that these women exist on the margins of society. In the gazetteers, census reports, surveys, and Orientalist accounts produced in nineteenth- and early-twentieth-century India, women who serve as ritual agents at the shrines of Muslim saints—for instance by becoming conduits of the power of deceased saints—are depicted as belonging to the lower classes. Their "work" is reported as occurring most often at shrines of saints of dubious reputation (such as Shaikh Saddu of Amroha) or shrines that are said to attract chiefly pilgrims of the lower classes and castes (such as the shrine of Ghazi Miyan in Bahraich). These kinds of women do not seem to operate at the shrines for major saints of the establishment Sufi orders, shrines that have a long-held tradition of hereditary authority and spiritual succession.[24] In all of the cases I witnessed or was told about, the women who visited Sharaf al-din's *hujra gah*—as supplicants or as ritual agents—were described as poor, illiterate or semiliterate, and emotionally or mentally "unstable" or "mad" (that is, deranged). According to the *pirzade* men and *khadim*s of Bihar Sharif, the women's actions undermine accepted standards of Sufi practice and contribute to the dubious reputation Sufism has acquired over the last few centuries. By persisting in

"ignorance," "superstition," "evil" ( *jadu,* or black magic),[25] and other activities that are expressly "forbidden" in Islam (such as worshipping anyone or anything other than God), they demean the "true" (*sahib*) spirit of Sufism. Overwhelmingly my male interviewees expressed their disdain for these kinds of activities in terms that emphasized the importance of "correct" social etiquette:

> Those people [who] say their mad, insane words, those people keep on with their singing.[26]

> Whatever voices are [reciting], one should speak as properly as one can (*achha se accha*) for God's love.[27]

> They should not do this. No woman who comes here should cry like that for help. They should speak silently from the heart (*dil se*) or they should ask quietly.[28]

In general the people I spoke with described the women who came to the *hujra gah* seeking the aid of the saints as wailing their troubles aloud because they were sick, mentally troubled, or facing difficult circumstances in their lives.[29]

> The people who are sick go there ... [they are] sick in their minds, not in their bodies.[30]

> Whether man or woman, people should not cry out like that. If there is mental trouble [they] will cry out like that, or if there is some [mental or physical] sickness. Or if they are a beggar (*bhikh mangne wala*), like the beggars you see in the street asking for money.[31]

> These women who sing may be sick, or mad. These kind of people do come into the shrines to sing. They sing in a state of anxiety (*pareshani*) or abandon (*bekhudi;* being unaware of one's actions).[32]

Some of these women are described as being under the influence of dubious forces from the unseen world: "The situation [with] the women who are singing in the *hujra* is that spirits ( *jinn*) and so on are with them, like the influence of an evil spirit that people can't see."[33] Others were said to perform the work of petitioning solely for profit: "In this day and age, these people mostly make a business of writing and selling *ta'wiz.* These kinds of things have really spoiled the [reputation of ] Sufis. Ninety-eight percent of the people [doing this kind of activity] will only make a business of their skill."[34]

Yet this last speaker also indicated that there were acceptable circumstances under which a woman could perform ritual services for another. In

his household the women organized all-female gatherings, assemblies in which they recited *na't*, poems of praise to the Prophet Muhammad and which were arranged with his help or by the women themselves. On some of these occasions, "If they need to, they will ask someone [a woman who is considered to have exceptional spiritual power] to come and pray [in our house] during the time of prayer (*namaz*)."[35] Certain standards of deportment had to be maintained, however. "There is *na't*, women sing this. There is *parda* for women. Not *parda* of the face [meaning not the kind of *parda* that requires women to cover their faces]. There is *parda* of the voice [meaning that women should not raise their voices aloud]."[36] Several local women agreed wholeheartedly with his final point: "A woman should not speak loudly in front of the men. It is prohibited in Islam."[37]

These last speakers also conceded that some of the women who performed the work of petitioning for others did so mainly for altruistic motives: "Some [of them] sing in God's name. They sing on behalf of others and present prayers to God, saying, 'God, accept [my] prayers.' These women must have faith. . . . [They do not demand money; rather] they do it out of their own [sense of ] joy. People [may] give them an offering [*nazrana*], or they make an offering to the *dargah*."[38]

## Women, Ritual Agency, and Divine Madness

The ambivalence with which some women spoke of the female pilgrims at the *hujra gah* reflects general attitudes toward "ecstatic" forms of devotion. While the idea of spiritual ecstasy is acknowledged as very real, such an idea has a complex relationship with the spiritual ecstatic as a living being. The women who frequent the *hujrah gah* are not locally described as spiritual ecstatics as such, but insofar as the terms used to describe them bear some resemblance to attitudes I encountered about the "true" ecstatic—the *mastani, divanavar, majzub*, or Qalandar—it is possible to come to some conclusions about why local residents could view women such as Rafat as an object of both scorn and sympathy. First, like the "spontaneous" ecstatic—the individual in whom the experience of the divine is direct and not conditioned by a regimen of spiritual discipline and ascetic practices[39]—Rafat is prone to sudden states in which she appears to be divorced from ordinary reality. In the ritual setting of the *hujra gah*, these states are indeed conditioned by ritual practice (though not exclusively so), and through the repetition of prayers for extended periods of time, which culminates in a wailing and moaning pitch. Although less structured and more improvised than, for instance, the Sufi practice of the repetition of names of God (*zikr*), which itself can induce the experience of a spiritual state (*hal*), the

informal ways in which women at the Maneri *hujra gah* "present their troubles" (*apni musibat pesh karna*) share some elements of *zikr* performance. Yet unlike other women I have encountered in shrines and Sufi lodges, Rafat is prone to these states outside of the ritual setting. Whenever I was with her outside of the *hujra gah,* she was often volatile at one moment, yelling at people in the street for no reason, talking to herself or to others unseen by me, and in the next moment perfectly calm and collected as she explained what I was to do for the following session. One day we rode by cycle *riksha* into the market after having spent most of the day in the shrine. I was equally embarrassed, worried, and amused as she began yelling as loudly as she could at people in the street, and from the look on our driver's face, so was he. Yet when we alighted from the *riksha* at one shop that sold the ritual implements I would need, she was calm and collected again and explained very coherently and confidently what items I should buy, as the shopkeeper—who had been gazing at us with an alarmed expression as we rode up to his shop—rushed to display the items she referred to. Elsewhere in the market people backed away from Rafat when she came too close, but when she confronted them directly, calmly, they engaged her in conversation, though somewhat uncomfortably, it seemed.

It is difficult to distinguish, as one *pirzada* man in Patna told me, between ordinary madness and divine madness. The ecstatic may appear to some as a madman, while others will see him as a holy man. If such a person acquires a reputation for miracles, he or she is apt to be considered "holy," or at least in direct communication with the other world (*al-ghaib*). This is equally true for the wailing women at the *hujra gah* of Sharaf al-din Maneri. People more often than not characterized these women as mentally disturbed, although the motives for such characterizations varied among those I spoke with. When it came to the question of ritual agents such as Rafat, however, such characterizations were colored by an attitude of disdain. While most of the men I spoke with—*pir*s and *khadims* in Bihar Sharif and Patna—were unequivocal in their opposition to the kind of "work" performed by female ritual agents, some of the women (local residents, women of the *pir*'s family) were more sympathetic. This is not surprising. Women often expressed their dissatisfaction with the status quo, even as they insisted upon a model of social relations that emphasized the importance of modest behavior for women and women's separation from and subordination to men. For instance one woman I spoke with, "Dadiji," a "respectable" upper-middle-class, older widow, stressed the need for maintaining *parda*—while complaining that she could not even go to the market alone for fear of what people would say. Later that day, when I asked her if she believed there could be a "Rabi'a" today (Rabi'a al-'Adawiyya, the

ninth-century female saint of Basra), she responded that women like that did exist today, adding the complaint that there was a general tendency to speak ill of such women, to accuse them of being "weak" when, in truth, they were quite "strong" (in their faith and devotion to God).

If local women could view petitioners at the Maneri *hujra gah* with some ambivalence, the attitudes of the men I spoke with about these women were more unequivocally oppositional in tone. The disdain with which the Shah Sahib and the servants at Sharaf al-din's *dargah* viewed female ritual agents at the *hujra gah* must be considered in light of the competition and challenge to authority posed by the female ritual agent. Her authority—unmediated by the "official" structures of command within the Firdausi order—undercuts the claims of the Firdausi establishment to control of ritual life and brings into relief the debate about women's "proper place" in the Sufi setting. Simply put, women such as Rafat—with her disdain for established hierarchies of spiritual status and power, her disregard for the ideal modes of social relationships in which women are subordinate to men's authority, and her volatile, unpredictable moods—do not play by the rules. That Rafat was conscious of the challenge she posed to such rules was underscored by her response to my question of whether or not she would continue to do the work of petitioning after she got married. She would, she insisted. When I asked her what she would do if her husband forbade her to come to the shrine anymore, she insisted that she would come anyway, even if she had to defy him to do so.

The dichotomy between men's and women's attitudes toward female ritual agents is not as stark as I have perhaps represented it here. At the level of the symbolic, the female ecstatic can occupy several different subject positions simultaneously in the opinions of local residents. On one hand, female ecstatics were generally described as "close" to God, "mad," or "mentally disturbed" (and thus not wholly responsible for their actions), which emphasizes how they stand outside the ordinary boundaries of human social order and meaning. On the other, they are conceived as representative of the excesses and corruption that have crept into Sufism, in part because they are conceived as making "a business" of the writing and selling of amulets and in part because they operate outside (and in competition with) "official" structures of spiritual authority. Yet, with the poverty and desperation that plague many in Bihar and with the reluctance of some among the poor to go through these structures, the women who operate as ritual agents are also seen by some as fulfilling a need in a community where relief services are either nonexistent or inefficient.

While most people I spoke with did not entirely approve of the activities of the women who do the work of petitioning in the Maneri *hujra gah,* some

of them tried to explain how, despite prohibitions in Islam and the disdain of the *pirzade* and *khadims*, women such as Rafat could engage in the type of work that they did. Unanimously my interviewees characterized the female ritual agents as existing and operating outside of the "proper" (*sahih, nishchit*) boundaries of social and ritual relationships. These terms are used in conjunction with both transcendent Islamic and local cultural referents that are not easily separated in analysis. The ideals of *parda,* the segregation of the sexes, and female subordination to male authority all come into play in discourse; yet none of these can be called exclusively Islamic referents: they are also shaped by particularities of context and the social location of actors. Thus interpretations of the meaning of *parda* often incorporate specifically Islamic referents—such as the veiling of the Prophet's wives and daughters, although *parda* practice in the setting of Bihar Sharif among lower-, middle-, and upper-middle-class women differs greatly from *parda* as practiced by women of these social groups in Patna. And for the upper middle classes, as I have shown in an earlier chapter on *piri-muridi, parda* practices can be somewhat flexible even among the women of a single family, dependent upon external factors of place, time, and setting, as well as internal factors of age, spiritual status, and personality. As for women who are perceived as being prone to fits of madness or unmediated experiences of spiritual ecstasy, the necessity of maintaining *parda* is mitigated by their position as people who exist outside the boundaries of the "normal" social order. Because these women are "mentally troubled," "unstable," "mad," "sick," or "possessed" by otherworldly forces such as *jinn,* they cannot reasonably be expected to abide by social norms. This "outsideness" is both a justification for their behavior and a reason for viewing them with some suspicion. They circumvent the channels of traditional spiritual authority as represented by *pirs* and *khadims,* operating instead on their own (or in conjunction with them, although unbeknownst to "official" authority). They compete with others who depend for their living upon pilgrims' donations and offerings (*nazrana*). Most important, their methods of dealing with spiritual sources such as the saints are unconditioned, spontaneous, uncontrolled, and loosely structured. It is precisely because they operate on the margins of Sufi society that they are able to operate as they do.

### Ritual Practice as a Reflection of Social Location

Some of the people I spoke with in Bihar indicated that the social position of women such as Rafat plays a decisive part in their ability to work on behalf of male and female clients without serious threat of social ostracism. The

pressure to conform to locally accepted standards of social "respectability" is, generally speaking, somewhat less acute for the marginalized poor, although those who are upwardly mobile tend publicly to adopt signs (and local standards) of respectability, such as having women observe *parda* and wear the *burqa'*, a long garment that covers everything but the hands and feet.[40] While a woman from the Sayyid or *shaikh* classes tends to be faced with an enormous amount of social pressure to uphold the dignity of her social station by, for instance, wearing the *burqa'* or at least concealing her head and shoulders with a small covering (*dupatta*) or a large one (*chadar*) when going out, traveling with a male escort, or distancing herself from lower-class people, women of the lowest classes are generally able to move about more freely (because of the necessity of working, for instance, or because they do not observe a strict form of *parda*) and tend to face less rigid restrictions upon male-female interaction in their daily lives.[41] What is distinctive about the petitioning women I encountered, and what distinguishes them most obviously from other women pilgrims, is that most of them came from the lowest levels of society. Clothing, deportment, speech, place of residence (*muhalla*), and nomenclature can all serve as important indicators of identity. Most important, these indicators can identify social position and caste (or castelike) groups, such that an observer can often reasonably surmise to which social stratum, caste, or religious community an individual belongs.

While caste among Indian Muslims does not have the same religious foundation as it does for Hindus, the Muslim community in India has nevertheless retained some castelike features, most notably in marriage practices. Many sociological studies of Indian Muslims define caste identity by occupation or birth, although there is no definitive consensus on the identity and place of certain groups. In my own fieldwork, the subject of Muslim caste came up frequently in conversation, particularly with those belonging to the highest groups on the social scale: Sayyids and *shaikh*s. Sayyids, who claim descent from the Prophet Muhammad's family, and *shaikh*s, whom some scholars have described as claiming descent from the clans of the first three spiritual-temporal leaders (*khalifa*s) of Islam (although it is widely believed that these two castelike designations have been fabricated by some upwardly mobile individuals and families), may intermarry freely without risk of social stigma.[42] Most of the *pirzade* and *khadim*s connected to the Sufi shrines I have visited in North India come from these groups. The middle groups have been identified with a great deal of latitude by scholars. While Mohsen Saeidi Madani lists a number of group names—Mirza, Khan, Quraishi—that are disputed by others, there is a consensus among scholars as well as my sources in India about the names

of middle-caste groups such as Pathan and Ansari.[43] While the names of many of the upper-caste and a few of the middle-caste groups among Indian Muslims are connected to birth and descent (real or claimed), most of the middle-caste and "low-caste" groups among Muslims are defined in terms of occupation: weavers (*julaha*), washermen (*havari* or *dhobi*), vegetable sellers (*rayin*), sweepers (*bhangi, halalkhor, chuhra*), singers (*mirasin*), barbers (*na'i* or *hajjam*), and tailors (*darzi*). Some of these groups have Hindu and Muslim divisions, while others, including butchers (*qassab, qurashi*) and washers of the dead (*ghassal*) are now entirely Muslim in some states (such as Bihar).[44] Some features of the castelike distinctions found among Muslims approximate those of Hindu caste groups, which contributes to the distinctiveness of various Muslim communities. For instance Madani identifies localities and mosques that differ on the basis of caste among Muslims. In Ranchi, Bihar, mosques are identified as a vegetable sellers' mosque, a butchers' mosque, dyers' (*rangsaz*) mosque, and so on, while neighborhoods also maintain invisible boundaries between higher and lower castes. Moreover professional guilds can also enforce social differentiation on the basis of occupation.[45]

F. R. Faridi and M. M. Siddiqi have identified ritual factors as indicators of caste identity among Muslims, pointing out that low-caste Muslims can be identified by the practice of Hindu customs. The Mapillas of Malabar, for example, are described by the authors as "highly superstitious" practitioners of "tomb worship and black magic."[46] Similarly Katherine Ewing's study of Pakistani *pir*s suggests that distinctions between "white" magic (*nuri 'ilm*) and "black" magic (*kala 'ilm*) (the one perceived to derive from God and from the spiritual power of the Sufi *pir,* the other perceived as manipulating other spiritual forces present in the world) can carry class, community, and caste referents: "Th[e] relationship between black knowledge and the Christian community is seen in the formulation of one Christian *pir: 'Nuri 'ilm* can only be used to satisfy the needs [of ] clean people. For unclean people, the *pir* will use *kala 'ilm.'* When he was asked who unclean people are, he replied: 'people who eat pork,' in other words, non-Muslims, i.e. Christians."[47]

In other cases Ewing notes, the dichotomy between *nuri 'ilm* and *kala 'ilm* as referents of "white" and "black," "clean" and "unclean," Muslim and non-Muslim is blurred, particularly when the practitioner of both is a *jadugar* (a Hindi term that is sometimes translated as "practitioner of black magic" or "sorcerer" but has no exact correspondence to either term) or a *malang,* one belonging to those classes of *pir*s and ascetics who stand outside (and sometimes in opposition to) the establishment Sufi orders.[48] However, this is not to suggest that the practice of both white and black magic is not

found in establishment Sufism. Desiderio Pinto's study at the mausoleum of the Chishti *shaikh* Nizam al-din Auliya in Delhi shows that *pir*s of the establishment orders may bring harm upon another person under unusual circumstances: "Another woman walked into the *pir*'s office on another occasion. The *pir* gave her a *ta'wiz* that he had prepared beforehand, which he told her to bury in a graveyard. She had to bang it while reciting the name of her husband, who was living with another woman and giving her endless trouble. He said, 'If you want, I can bring about his death. I do not generally do this kind of work for anyone. But for you I would. Give the order and it will be done.'"[49]

Although she is not a *malang* or *jadugar*, the kind of "work" done by Rafat is viewed by others as suspect, although the spiritual sources upon which she calls are themselves not suspect. However, her willingness to pronounce curses against her enemies (the ones who had stolen her belongings) was seen by some as indicative of her "outsideness" in relation to Sufism of the establishment orders. In the opinions of the women of the *pir*'s family in Ajmer, those who practiced *jadu* or harmful magic in any form could not be trusted; such people represented the unpredictable, fear-inspiring "other." The servants of the shrine at Sharaf al-din Maneri's *dargah* in Bihar Sharif shared similar views about the female ritual specialists who worked at the Maneri *hujra gah*. Such women were, in their opinion, of the same ilk as the women who came to the *dargah* to practice *jadu*. Their characterizations also added religious and class dimensions to such practices; according to these *khadims*, the women who came to the mausoleum with the intent of acquiring power for harmful magic were Hindus or women from "bad" (that is, poor or unobservant Muslim) families. Indeed, within many mainstream Sufi circles, there is a marked disdain for "dubious" practices such as harmful magic, particularly where they are associated with the Hindu "other" or Sufi "outsider"—such as the false (*naqli*) *pir* or those antinomian figures who openly flout the laws of Islam, for example the Qalandar or *malang*[50]—or with those my subjects deemed "ignorant" and "superstitious," who were inevitably from the lowest social groups.

It is difficult to tell how representative Rafat is, in part because of a lack of evidence for the existence of more women like her—women who perform ritual services for others. Although the most apparent details of Rafat's situation that I could provide to others—her physical appearance, external behavior, and relationship with the Firdausi Sufis (as the *murid* of the former *pir*)—often prompted them to talk about her in terms used to describe the ecstatics (*divanavar, majzub,* Qalandar) who exist on the margins of establishment Sufism, in truth she does not fit neatly into any of these categories. Yet like these marginal figures, Rafat is able to move

around relatively freely, and she is not bound by ties to husband or children. As the disciple of a Sufi *pir,* she may indeed be perceived as having some authority in spiritual matters by those who come to her for aid. Because she is a "free agent," she has more scope to act as a ritual agent on behalf of others, but it is also for this reason that she is relegated to the outer edges of Sufi society. Her methods too—particularly her style of wailing and moaning loudly while engaged in prayer—also place her outside the mainstream of Sufi practice. As Parry notes, in mourning rituals in Banaras expressions of grief are "structured" by gender;[51] similarly expressions of emotion before the saints of Islam differ among men and women at the Maneri *hujra gah.* In the setting of the establishment orders, men weep, shout, or rip their clothes when spiritual states (*hal*) descend upon them. Such behavior occurs within the ritual setting and is monitored by others present, particularly those who are close to the *pir.* By contrast the intense displays of emotion that I witnessed among women petitioners at the *hujra gah* are controlled by the women themselves. Although I do not wish to imply that such a woman is not experiencing a type of spiritual state, as I have understood it the wailing and moaning is more indicative of a particular "style" of prayer than a spontaneous "state."

Like the female ritual agents at the Maneri *hujra gah,* the hereditary functionaries attached to Sufi shrines act as mediators between spiritual source and client. However, these latter do so according to carefully prescribed models of negotiation. They do not (least of all publicly) engage in the type of behavior (wailing, crying, moaning loudly and plaintively) that someone such as Rafat is willing to enact on clients' behalf.[52] And while a *pir* or *khadim* may pray to (or in the name of) a deceased Sufi saint on behalf of clients, he tends to do so as a matter of course. In other words ordinary clients' names may be included in a litany of prayers the *pir* or *khadim* recites as part of his quotidian "work" of helping clients and disciples attain what they desire or need. Alternately individual clients or disciples may be prayed for individually. *Khadims* and *pirs* help clients in many other ways too: they prescribe amulets and prayer formulas; they expel demons from the possessed by reciting prayers and/or "beating" and coaxing the entity out of the individual (this method of exorcism is not exclusive to Islamic practice);[53] *pirs* can release the spiritual power they inherently possess (by virtue of having inherited the "throne," *gaddi,* or "seed," *bij,* of their spiritual predecessors) by such ritual acts as blowing their breath into jars filled with water (which is believed to then become imbued with *barakat* and which the client may drink to cure any number of ailments) or directly on to the client; they counsel clients, intervene with local authorities, and donate money and goods or arrange for services to be performed for clients

who are in financial need. Moreover, by virtue of the fact that these "official" ritual agents often deal with a large number of clients, their services tend to be fairly standardized and thinly spread.

By contrast a ritual agent such as Rafat is both willing and able to give her clients special attention. Her emotional displays in the *hujra gah* fulfill clients' images, expectations, and experiences of spiritual power being manifested. Desiderio Pinto mentions such expectations among the clients of the *pirzade* and *khadims* at the Nizam al-din *dargah* in Delhi. One of the *khadims* explained to Father Pinto that

> sometimes we have to make a big *tamasha* [demonstration] to convenience the client. We may surround him with lighted joss sticks. Then we call out the *jinn*. The *jinn* has to leave him because of what we are reciting. Suppose people have brought me a woman troubled by a *jinn*. If I just tell them that the *jinn* has left her, they will not believe me. So, we light a lamp, act as if we are catching the *jinn* with our hands and flinging him into the fire. Then we tell them that the *jinn* has been burnt and will not trouble her again.[54] It is most important that they are convinced. If they doubt, nothing can be done to help them. The work is done without all this *tamasha*—but the *tamasha* is necessary to convince people.[55]

Rafat's fervent displays of devotion, accompanied by her willingness to spend many hours a day doing work for a single client, contribute to her appeal as a ritual specialist. Because she outwardly manifests the characteristics of a person who has one foot in the world of ordinary reality and one in the unseen world, or *al-ghaib*, others perceive that she is indeed able to commune with otherworldly (*ghair dunya*) forces. Her appeal as a ritual agent also has much to do with her personality, her learning, and others' perceptions of her "work." Because she is not shy or demure and is willing to offer her services (even when unasked) to potential clients as well as to the other pilgrims who visit the Maneri *hujra gah*, she is able to assert her authority as a person with some knowledge of the procedures involved with petitioning a spiritual source, reciting prayers, and performing a number of other ritual acts associated with *buzurgan-i din*. She is also able to provide *ta'wiz* and other ritual implements for clients and seems to be well versed in formulaic and Qur'anic prayers (*fatiha, durud, bismillah*), the devotional poetry used in the work of petitioning (*na't, hamd, manqabat*) and informal modes of prayer (*apni musibat pesh karna*). Her use of such symbols as Islamic prayers, her acquaintance with Qur'anic formulas (such as *ayat al-kursi*, used in healing practices), and her familiarity with

symbols that are well known among Muslim believers are intended to signal to others that her skills are authentic (*sahih*) and efficacious. Ultimately
others' acceptance of her abilities is determined by the efficacy of her rituals—as one *pirzada* man told me, referring to how a woman is considered a
saint, "people believe when they see results!"[56] Still, Rafat's references to
Islamic symbols of authority and authenticity are tied in with her status as
a disciple of the former head (Shah Sahib) of the Firdausi Sufi order. These
combined factors, coupled with the setting in which Rafat operates—a setting of which the public at large is virtually unaware, a place that has been
claimed by local women as a devotional space of their own, which does not
come under the constant scrutiny of a hereditary functionary—enable
Rafat to continue petitioning on behalf of clients. In light of the current
Shah Sahib's opposition to the actions of the local women who frequent the
*hujra gah* (as manifested in his decision to keep the gate to the inner chamber locked at all times), however, how long she will be able to do so remains
an open question.

# Conclusion

*Reconsidering Women's*
*Experiences at the Intersection*
*of Discourse and Practice*

The primary objective of this book, to investigate the discrepancies between prescriptions for and descriptions of women's activities in the world of Sufi shrines, is not intended to convey a facile dichotomy of authority and challenge to that authority. Rather than assume a fundamental tension between two apparent opposites, discourse and practice, I highlight the coexistence of these two as shifting "modes" of expression that are informed by, help constitute, and ultimately transform each other. My sense of discourse considers Michel Foucault's concept of the relationship between discourse and "discursive subgroups,"[1] the former a unitive mechanism seeking to analyze, name, form, and otherwise explain its object, the latter a series of "dispersions" representing points of diffusion rather than points of contradiction, although they may appear to give rise to mutually exclusive understandings.[2] However, this does not lead me to reconfigure narratives of (self-)identification as fragmentary, unstable, and incoherent. Rather, as I have argued in chapters 2, 3, and 4—on the changing terms of discourse on women, spiritual authority, and participation in ritual activities at Sufi shrines in Ajmer, Bihar Sharif, and Maner—praxis draws upon predominant discourses of selfhood and action, at least insofar as it is understood to be a strategic mechanism with the power to transform and be transformed by discursive resignifications of the meanings of "propriety," the "authentic" Sufi, and the "good, virtuous" Muslim woman. If this premise is accepted, then it would follow that practice may shift and disperse in response to sociocultural processes in ways similar to those in which prevailing discourses shift and transform in light of similar processes. Yet I also hold that, while the individual actor has the ability to draw self-reflexively upon a repertoire of embodied and discursive significations in order to conform to

changing significations of propriety, piety, gender, and (spiritual) power, he or she is also constrained by structuring forces and mechanisms (discursive, institutional, and otherwise). Thus social actors are able to adapt individual "performances" in the shrine setting to their own evolving sense of the symbolic capital these significations hold, how the capital is held, and in what configurations, but their ability to do so is limited by the symbolic and material conditions that enable those performances and by the forces (or circumstances) that threaten to disrupt or destabilize them.

Prevailing discourses about women's participation in communal ritual events revolve around particular (or context-specific) articulations of gender, social, class, and spiritual identity as well as the notion of precedent, or "*silsila* tradition," all of which operate discursively to exclude women from public ritual life. Arguments for this exclusion of women emphasized the importance of maintaining segregation of the sexes as a requisite of Islamic Shari'a. Discourses about sex segregation were often subsumed under the rubric of *parda* observance, although as I have demonstrated earlier and will illustrate below, the idea of what constitutes *parda* observance is not singular by any means. Indeed changes in *parda* observance among Muslim women have occurred in response to several factors, including personal preference (the exercise of which has been facilitated by the widespread loosening of *parda* among Muslim women of the upper and middle classes, greatly diminishing the stigma against those who do not practice it), women's increased visibility in the workplace and in institutions of higher education, and the spread of education and literacy (which has, at the very least, enabled many women to understand what the sources of Islam say about their rights and duties and indeed may act as a counterweight against more rigid discourses about Islamically correct gender roles and relationships, particularly among those who have lived in the Arabian Gulf for a period of time).

Sex segregation was a particular concern of the *pirzade* women of all three orders. The *pirzade* linked the importance of such segregation to their status as members of the highest social class (Sayyid) and representatives of a prominent spiritual lineage. The practice of *parda* varied among these women, ranging from dress codes (the wearing of head and body coverings such as the *burqa', chadar,* and *dupatta*) to physical absence from social situations in which men unrelated to them were present, to a series of avoidance behaviors and gestures of modesty (such as sitting separately from the men in ritual events they did attend or censoring themselves when a senior male relative was present).

In its discursive significations, *parda*-as-ideal stood in contrast to practical considerations. For instance I found *parda* observance to be less rigid

among the younger *pirzade* women in general, particularly if they were attending (or had attended) college or if they worked outside of the home. These considerations notwithstanding, all the *pirzade* women I interviewed insisted that *parda* was necessary for them. Such arguments emphasized the insistence in Islam on *parda* for Muslim women as a medium of "social normativity."[3] However, the *pirzade* women also acknowledged that today *parda* observance had loosened among most middle- and upper-class Muslim women—by choice as well as from necessity—and in light of that fact, acknowledged that they did not always maintain the kind of separation from men that Islam had prescribed for members of their community. Nevertheless they frequently distinguished between themselves as *parda* observant and women who made no attempts to live up to the ideal of *parda*. While the *pirzade* women in my study admitted the precariousness of their own *parda* observance, they often cited the necessity of maintaining *parda* as an explanation for why they did not attend communal ritual events. In the one instance I did witness, wherein the Gudri Shah *pirzade* women attended the 'urs celebration for their father (a celebration attended by members of both sexes) at the 'Usman Haruni *chilla,* the women maintained what I refer to as *symbolic parda* by remaining physically separate from the rest of the guests, though in full view. In so doing they were able to maintain their social and spiritual status in their own eyes and in the eyes of the members of the assembly. Thus *parda* observance—signaled as much by the intention (*niyyat*) behind it as by its outer manifestations and performative dimensions—could serve as both a marker of high social status and an ideal of Shari'a-observant Muslim women's behavior.

Explanations of the exclusion of women from communal ritual events referred to the notion of precedent ("tradition," the teachings of Sufi *shaikh*s, the example of the saints and exalted figures of Islam) as a reason for the denial of such participation to women. Such an idea could also operate as justification for the inclusion of women, however. In particular the traditions of the order (or rather what were cited as such by those I spoke with) as well as the authority of Sufi masters prominent within figured significantly as primary (or at least key) points of reference for both the Firdausi and Gudri Shah Sufis.

For the Gudri Shahs, both men and women cited the examples of the last two *pir*s of the order as setting a precedent.[4] For the Maner and Bihar Sharif Firdausis, two branches of the Firdausi order that do not seem to have produced *pir*s of late who enjoy the same kind of stature within the *silsila* as the third and fourth Gudri Shah *pir*s do for that order,[5] the writings of the thirteenth-century Firdausi *shaikh* Sharaf al-din Maneri on the subject of women in the musical assembly served as a key explanation for

why women were not allowed to attend musical assemblies. Since Sharaf al-din himself opposed women's presence in the assembly, it was reasoned, it is improper to allow women to attend even today. Such opposition on the part of the *shaikh* was cited by the *khadim*s in Bihar Sharif as well as the *pirzade* men and women of Bihar Sharif and Maner as part of Firdausi tradition. The *shaikh*'s opinion on this matter was thus projected in discourse as the model for current practices and attitudes concerning the interaction of men and women in the ritual setting. Linking the *shaikh*'s teaching on women and music with current practice in effect sought to establish a relation of continuity with Firdausi "tradition." These linkages serve as "structuring" mechanisms that establish a "normative" (and thus legitimating) rubric for current practices. In other cases the parameters of this rubric extended to ideas of a "true" (*sahih*) Islam heavily reliant upon the examples of the Prophet (*sunna*) and his family (*ahl-i bait*); the contrast between what constituted *sahih* as opposed to "false" (*ghair mazhab*) Sufi practice; and the Shari'a, which I have translated earlier as "Islamic law" but which in discourse referred to a rather more expansive sense of moral-ethical behavior and attitudes in which references to the legalistic aspects of Shari'a did not play an obvious part.

In the arena of practice as I witnessed it, an arena that does not lend itself easily to classification (or to control, the further one moves out from the *pirzade, khadims,* and central *dargah*), discourses seeking to identify a "normative" rubric shifted meanings of what constituted the ideal (or what could be construed as "correct" practice) according to the context in which practice took place. Moreover the idea of tradition as explanation for current practices often revealed itself to be quite inadequate, not only because of the heterogeneous nature of the field of practice, but also because of the inherent precariousness of the very notion of tradition.

The *shaikh*'s teachings about women and the musical assembly could serve as a model for subsequent generations of Firdausis precisely because the *shaikh* so intended them to be and because of the care with which Sharaf al-din treated the subject in his letters.[6] His teaching did not cover all questions that later generations would have to confront, however, and this being the case, the Firdausis' discourses about current practices not treated in Sharaf al-din's writing relied upon various modes of reasoning (or none at all), some of which reflected changing conditions of discussion and reflection on these practices. One case in point is women's participation in the Prophet Muhammad's birthday celebration (*milad al-nabi*). One of the brothers-in-law of the Shah Sahib of Bihar Sharif explained, when I asked him why women could not hold their own all-female assemblies in honor of the Prophet's birthday, that there was no precedent for this practice. By

contrast neither he nor the Firdausi Sufis used this line of reasoning to explain why women could participate in all-female *milad*s that were not related to this particular commemorative event. One possible explanation is that the institutionalization of all-female *milad*s has come about in response to women's ability and desire to stage them. Such ability and desire on the part of women reflects social and economic changes that have modified gender relationships, particularly in the past thirty to fifty years. (I highlight this span of time as one during which one may cite, in particular, the rise of the middle class and what several friends in South Asia have referred to as "middle-class values.") Greater access to the texts of tradition (including, but not limited to, the Qur'an and Hadis); frequent travel by *pir*s, in effect leaving the women of the household in charge in their absence; the spread of education and literacy among the upper and middle classes (which adds to women's confidence in their ability to take on greater responsibilities); and changes in gender relationships (exemplified in part by changing *parda* practices) have all contributed to increasing the scope for women to exercise greater agency both within and outside of the domestic setting.

In one example I witnessed in the women's quarters at the *khanaqah* in Maner, the *pirzade* women made most of the arrangements for the event (for both men and women), and women were the singer-reciters, but the event was spearheaded by a male authority figure—the Shah Sahib of Maner. The Shah Sahib's presence was likely intended to create a parallel structure between the *milad* for women and the same event for an all-male audience that observed the *milad* in another part of the *khanaqah*. Perhaps such parallel staging conferred upon the all-women *milad* a similar ritual status as the all-male event. Another possibility is that the climax of the *milad*—the display of the Prophet's relics—necessitated the Shah Sahib's presence as head of the order (a position he represents at all major Sufi ritual events that the Maner Firdausis sponsor or attend). In this event women actively participated as organizers (the *pirzade* women) and singer-reciters (the *pirzade* women and devotees), yet their actions were not completely autonomous, as the Shah Sahib prompted the selection of poems to be recited.

One factor that should be taken into consideration in the articulation of discourses about practice is the type of event being referred to. Compelling evidence for women's autonomous activity in the ordinary *milad* setting was offered by one of the sisters of the Shah Sahib of Bihar Sharif, who explained that women could arrange their own *milad*s if they so desired. Such *milad*s tended to be "ordinary" *milad*s because the focus was not on the Prophet per se but on one or more important saintly figures, and because

these *milad*s were not obligatory for the occasion of the Prophet's birthday. Linguistically the status of these two types of *milad*s is represented by the "*sharif*" designation appended to the Prophet's *milad,* which is known as the *milad sharif* in contrast to the simple, or ordinary, *milad.* The term *sharif* conveys reverence, holiness, and greatness. The *dargah* in Ajmer, for instance, is known as the *dargah sharif* in contrast to other *dargah*s in the area, conveying the notion of a hierarchical relationship among the Sufi sacred centers of Ajmer. The Shah Sahib's sister indicated that these kind of ordinary *milad*s—sometimes impromptu, sometimes planned far in advance—were typically arranged and presided over entirely by women, without the necessary presence of a male authority.[7] At no time did any of my Firdausi subjects' explanations of why women were permitted to stage their own *milad*s refer explicitly to "tradition" as explanation, although as I will show, one very specific notion of tradition did play a part in the apparent social acceptability of such events. What did seem to be the case, nonetheless, was that the staging of all-female *milad*s conformed to my subjects' ideas about the necessity of gender segregation or the observance of *parda.*

All-female *milad*s are permissible for the women of the Maner and Bihar Sharif Firdausi orders, I surmise, precisely because they allowed the *pirzade* women and the female disciples of the order to maintain *parda* by shielding their activities from the eyes of men unrelated to them. One other possibility—again highlighting the range of applications of the idea of tradition—was revealed to me during the course of a conversation with the daughters and a son-in-law of the Maner Shah Sahib about all-female *milad*s. What emerged from this conversation was that a more recent idea of tradition has evolved from the practice of senior women in the family passing down oral knowledge about the order and the proper performance of rituals to their daughters and daughters-in-law. This was referred to as a "verbal tradition" (in English) by the Shah Sahib's son-in-law. He explained that it is primarily the Shah Sahib's wife (as senior female) who is responsible for handing down this tradition. Interestingly the Maner *pirzade* juxtaposed this sense of "verbal tradition" with what they referred to as "*khanaqah* tradition" (an ambiguous phrase that seems to refer both to the immediate family and to the tradition of the Maner branch of the Firdausi order). *Khanaqah* tradition was characterized as placing due emphasis upon the notion of the "equality" (in a spiritual sense) of men and women. Such a notion was cited by the Shah Sahib's son-in-law as the reason why women played such an important role in the Maner Firdausi order as custodians and disseminators of information and ritual knowledge. Thus the idea of tradition as explanation for the staging of all-female

*milad*s recognizes several points of reference: the importance of *parda* observance (here emphasizing the physical separation of the sexes); the notion of the spiritual equality of men and women (this idea is found widely in works on Sufism that deal with the question of women); and what, in the absence of literary evidence, I have tentatively surmised to be a relatively recent practice in the Maner Firdausi order, of women assuming the role of custodians of tradition, whereby they assume responsibility for maintaining, arranging, and overseeing ritual events and for passing such knowledge down to their daughters and daughters-in-law.

In the Gudri Shah order of Chishti Sufis, the authority of tradition also operates as a key reference point for practice, but what was emphasized by the Gudri Shahs (much more so than in the case of the two Firdausi orders) were the precedents set by recent *pir*s of the order, namely the third and fourth Gudri Shah *pir*s, Nawab Sahib and Zahur ul-Miyan. As did the Firdausi Sufis, the Gudri Shahs affirmed that generally women were not allowed to participate fully in the ritual life of Sufi orders. However, unlike the Firdausis, the majority of Gudri Shahs I spoke with tended to attribute such exclusion to other Sufi orders rather than their own. There was one exception to this general statement. Notably it was the Gudri Shah *pirzade* women who alone insisted that women were not allowed to attend musical assemblies. Subsequent conversations with the *pirzade* women on this topic, however, revealed that the precedents established by Nawab Sahib and Zahur ul-Miyan also operated as justification for the contemporary presence of women *murid*s and associates in such gatherings.

In two examples, one provided by the Gudri Shah *pirzade* women and the other provided by the current *pir* of the order, certain kinds of women had indeed attended what were formerly all-male assemblies. These women were in effect "marginalized" women—in other words they moved in some manner outside the category of ordinary women. Perceptions of such women as being somehow "outside the norm" figured into the *pirzade*'s explanations of why what was acceptable for these women was not acceptable for ordinary women. In the first example, Inam Hasan's mother and two of his sisters told the story of a woman, Ghariban Bibi, known affectionately as Khala ("Aunt"), who was closely associated with Nawab Sahib (although she apparently was not initiated into the order). This woman was described to me as a *majzub,* one of those types of "enraptured" mystics said to be constantly absorbed in the thought of God.[8] Such mystics represent a sort of antinomian element in the world of the Sufis, since *majzub*s have acquired a reputation for extreme forms of behavior and for breaking rules (much like one other such antinomian element in the Sufi pantheon, the Qalandar). As the Gudri Shah women related, there

was a *mahfil-i sama'* being held in a lodge in Agra, which women were not permitted to attend. Khala put on a long coat (*shervani*) and disguised herself as a man in order to enter the assembly. Undetected, she was not content to settle down just anywhere but sat next to Nawab Sahib in the very front of the *mahfil*. At some point during the program, a young participant recognized her, threw her out into the street, and began to beat her severely. At that instant all the lights in the lodge went out, and its flag fell from the roof to the pavement below. When Nawab Sahib realized what was happening, he became furious and exclaimed that Khala was a "very big" saint and should not be treated so badly. After the *mahfil,* Nawab Sahib abandoned the lodge, claiming that it had been ruined and that *mahfils* could never be held there again. The young man who had thrown Khala out of the assembly and beaten her died a few days later under unexplained circumstances. As related by the Gudri Shah *pirzade* women, not only did this incident underscore the ways in which the "rules" did not apply to extraordinary women such as Khala, but it also set off a chain of events that helped to change the parameters for other women's participation in these kinds of privately sponsored assemblies.

The incident involving Khala has become a part of *silsila* history, although any straightforward reading of this incident as justification for current attitudes toward women participating in musical assemblies sponsored by the Gudri Shah Sufis is problematic. In effect Khala's behavior does not function as a model for all women in the Gudri Shah order. Rather it serves as an explanation of how one exceptional woman in the history of the order breached the constraints that prevented ordinary women from participating in communal ritual events.[9] The story of Khala was related as an example of the spiritual insight of Nawab Sahib (for recognizing Khala's sainthood when others of his circle did not) and the order's acceptance of and reverence for such extraordinary individuals, regardless of gender. It is Nawab Sahib, not Khala, whose actions were ultimately responsible for paving the way for women's greater participation in ritual life in this order.

The second example I wish to highlight, prefaced by Inam Hasan himself, is the precedent established by Nawab Sahib (following the incident with Khala) of inviting women to come sing in a special musical assembly he dubbed the *mahfil-i rindan* (translated in the Gudri Shah *'urs* program guide as "assembly of love songs"). Some of the women who performed in the inaugural program, as I mentioned in chapter 3, were initially courtesans. As courtesans they represented women of a marginalized status: marginalized because (despite the fame and personal wealth some of them enjoyed) courtesans carried the stigma of being social outcastes of a sort.

Some of the other female *qawwali* singers in the assembly were not courtesans, but the attitudes of non Gudri Shah Sufis toward them remained overwhelmingly negative. In the history of the Gudri Shah *silsila,* the disdain with which the *mahfil-i rindan* singers were treated by their detractors emerged in the story of how their presence in the assembly provoked violence against Nawab Sahib on the part of rival Sufi groups, particularly the functionaries associated with the Mu'in al-din *dargah* in Ajmer and their followers.

Nawab Sahib's institution of the *mahfil-i rindan* contributed to many changes in the makeup of the order and shaped certain aspects of its identity. It identified the order as one that was open to women's inclusion—not only as participants but also as performers—in the type of events from which most orders excluded them. Discourse about the *pir'*s establishment of the *mahfil-i rindan* served to signal both the progressive thinking of the master and his willingness to go against the tide of opinion to initiate changes in the order.

Unlike the story of Khala, discourse about the establishment of this ritual figures into current practice as a precedent-setting example and, as such, is used by Inam Hasan as well as (male and female) disciples to support the presence of women in the musical assemblies sponsored by the order. While the story of Khala figures as an important part of the history of the women in the *silsila,* it was in no way referenced by the Gudri Shahs I spoke with as *silsila* "tradition." Instead it represented one among a number of significant events in the life of the order, incidents that in their telling served to highlight the example of the Sufi master, to contextualize his attitude toward women's participation in events from which they had previously been excluded, and to enhance the order's appeal (particularly to me, as a woman and a researcher of women's activities). Such motivation for telling these stories was more evident in the attitudes of the *pir* and his mother than in those of the sisters of the *pir.* With the telling of the institutionalization and continued observance of the *mahfil-i rindan,* discourse about the history of the order shifted, for it was not only history but *silsila* tradition that was highlighted as an explanation for women's activities. The tradition of this *mahfil* was initiated at a time when other changes were occurring in the areas of male/female relationships and the movement of women into areas considered traditionally "male." These changes were very significant for the female disciples of the order, for they allowed them greater scope to participate in activities from which they had previously been excluded.

The idea of tradition as I encountered it in three Sufi orders can project a number of overarching sources of authority: Islam and Shari'a as umbrella

categories, the tradition represented by the teaching of *shaikh*s prominent within the order, and the traditions of the order wherein the notion of tradition can reflect meanings that are both general (the Firdausi and Chishti orders as a whole) and specific (the Gudri Shah order or the Maner Firdausi order), the latter of which was often portrayed as synonymous with *khanaqah* or *silsila* tradition. Ironically it is within the specific designation that I found the widest possibilities for diffusion of the idea of authority as an explanation for current practice. What this diffusion suggests is that in "lived religion," discourse as explanation, classification, and reasoning is one among many strategically chosen perspectives that can work to define, underscore, or assert moral and spiritual authority. However, I believe that strategy—which suggests intentionality—is not always at the heart of the disjunction among discourses about the place of women in the milieu of Sufi shrines. Rather such disjunction also suggests an ambivalence that points to conflicting understandings of discourses of exclusion and inclusion.[10] I take the attitudes of the *pirzade* women of the Gudri Shah order as illustrative examples, for it is within this order that I found the most obvious ambivalence among women vis-à-vis the question of their participation in ritual life. While in one instance the *pirzade* women could express disdain for the increasing numbers of female disciples willing to "mix" indiscriminately with men in the ritual setting, in another they treated female disciples' interest in being a part of Sufi society with humor. It was as though they viewed such women as "wanting to behave like men" (my phrase, based on their innuendoes), while they themselves placed great importance upon the kinds of things their brother regarded as unimportant: makeup, fine clothes, jewelry, and getting married (at that time the *pir* had no interest in marrying, while his sisters were eager to find him a wife). In fact he often criticized them for their lack of interest in the life of the order. Several times he confided to me and others present that his sisters complained too much about having to help with the arrangement and organization of ritual events and lamented the failure of his efforts to persuade them to "experience the world" (his phrase)—which I understood to mean that he wished they would take more of an interest in the world around them (the social milieu of Sufis) and the wider world (he kept encouraging them to travel, which they were reluctant to do). Nevertheless even the *pirzade* women took pride in their father as a man inclined toward progressive attitudes about women in the life of the order.

The Gudri Shah *pirzade* women expressed ambivalence about "Sufi society's" attitude toward women. While they insisted that women should not mix with men in the ritual setting, they also expressed the opinion that men were "bad" because (in general) they did not accept women into Sufi

society, even though some women were "very big" saints (their phrase). This statement came in the wake of their narration of the story of Khala entering the musical assembly. Perhaps the most obvious instance of their ambivalence came in the disjunction between their insistence that they did not attend musical assemblies and their presence in the assembly held on the occasion of their father's death-day anniversary (*'urs*). In their self-imposed exclusion from most communal ritual events and their presence at their father's *'urs,* the articulation of their own identities appeared as an ideal vantage point from which I could assess how they were able to reconcile such an ostensible conflict of interests. On one hand their separation marked them as being of a "higher order," conscious of their need to appear "respectable." On the other hand, their presence at the *'urs* for their father identified them as members of a saintly lineage, as dutiful daughters respectful of their father's memory, and as important family members who possessed the know-how to assist in the execution of such an event. At the same time, they were able to remain physically and psychologically distant from men they did not know, thus conveying their status as *parda*-observant women.

As an indication of how current practice can modify the unitive discourse of exclusion, one must consider the increased (and increasing) visibility of women in the public sphere, their apparent desire to participate in events from which they have typically been excluded, and their willingness to intrude into these events. One example of the latter that I witnessed occurred at the great assembly hall at the *dargah* in Ajmer during the celebration of Mu'in al-din Chishti's *'urs.* A number of women who had been listening from the outside brazenly walked into the hall, some apparently frustrated by the poor visibility the "women's view" afforded, others under the pretense of looking for male relatives. The chaos of the event and the size of the crowd facilitated their entry, although they were all systematically turned out by men in charge of monitoring the assembly (Sufi attendants, not the police who are hired by the *dargah* administration to provide security).

The changing composition of the disciples and followers of the Firdausi orders in Bihar Sharif and Maner—in particular the predominance of women as pilgrims to Sufi shrines, as disciples, and as uninitiated clients of the *pir*—suggests that what one *khadim* in Bihar Sharif stated is a growing trend. He said that women gathered around the edges of the musical assembly during the *'urs* for Sharaf al-din, and that the *khadim*s of the shrine were unwilling (or more likely unable) to make them leave, although they did take care to make sure that such women remained, as it were, on the margins of such gatherings. My interview with the Maner Shah Sahib

revealed that the functionaries attached to shrines had less control over women's entry into the assembly than the *khadim* at Bihar Sharif had stated and that overall, women's entry into such gatherings was increasing. The Maner Shah Sahib highlighted the difficulties involved in attempting to reconcile the authority of precedent (here in the form of Sharaf al-din's teachings) with the reality of current practices. He explained that although Sharaf al-din had written that women should not be present in the musical assembly, in practice (*fi'l hal*), some *khanaqah*s had made arrangements for women in the form of special places (which I have referred to elsewhere as "gendered" or "female" space) such as separate halls or designated areas within the assembly hall. In the case of assemblies held in an open area, women stand on the periphery of the gathering (in some cases they actually sit inside the gathering, he noted), and no one prevents them from doing so. This admission on the Shah Sahib's part concurred with the information I received from his daughters and son-in-law. However, the tension between such practices and authoritative discourse was revealed in the Maner Shah Sahib's insistence that even though women today did sit inside or on the edges of the assembly, such participation was not proper (*sahih*). This tension reveals the contradictions engendered by social relationships and opportunities for women, as well as modified expectations for women's behavior, particularly as they are conceived of as subjects threatening the status quo.[11]

I turn now to the subject of discourse about women and spiritual authority and juxtapose this with my observations about how women are able to assume the roles of ritual specialist and of (what I refer to as) de facto *pir*s. Here I highlight the factors I mentioned earlier—ideas of Islam (as essentialized category), "true" versus "false" Sufism, and the Shari'a—as examples of mechanisms used by my subjects to establish a legitimizing rubric by which current practices among women could be explained as conforming to (or contradicting) an ideal of Muslim femininity. What emerged in my interviews and observations was that for both men and women, the process of interpreting the roles and actions of women as spiritual authorities (or saints) was particularly complex and as varied as the criteria elaborated by my subjects for sainthood in itself. The ambivalence with which the subject of women as spiritual authorities was treated by my interviewees underscored the ways in which female sainthood as a concept was closely linked with my subjects' own conflicting views about women's increased agency, authority, and visibility in the public milieu.

I would first like to mention briefly the problems I encountered in assessing the role of women as spiritual authorities, for this inevitably reveals a lacuna in my research. I found that the subject of women as spiritual

authorities in their own right afforded few actual examples for observation, and as a result my assessments of this arena are limited, in contrast
to my evidence for women's participation in ritual events at the shrines in
my survey. Yet the very discourses I encountered about the subject of
women as spiritual authorities revealed the parameters of such authority to
be wider than I had at first surmised. I had been looking for evidence of
women as *pirs*, which few people were willing or able to discuss in much
detail, let alone admit the possibility that a woman could become a *pir*. It
was in two arenas that I eventually found evidence for women as spiritual
guides (which I connect to the notion of the de facto *pir*). The first, in
the world of the *pirzade* women and the milieu of shrines affiliated with
the establishment Sufi orders, alerted me to the fact that spiritually gifted
women—the exceptional among the *pir*'s disciples, but more notably
(because there exists wider scope for it), the female relatives of the *pir*—are
able to perform many of the tasks that are typically performed by a *pir*. The
second pointed to two very different worlds. On one end of the spectrum
exist the near-obscure, private spaces—which I have referred to as "auxiliary" shrines. On the other is that most public of spaces, the marketplace
(*bazar*).[12] In both these places, I found the greatest scope for women to act
autonomously as spiritual guides, although their actions were opposed by
most of the *pirs*, *pirzade,* and *khadim*s I interviewed. Not surprisingly, the
discourses of the majority of my interviewees (including the individuals
just mentioned and local "sharif" Muslims who knew about such women)
portrayed the activities of such women as "un-Islamic" or in contradiction
to the Islamic Shari'a. The *pirs* and *khadim*s in Bihar (where I encountered
one woman I referred to as a "ritual specialist") disparaged the actions of
such women by referring to them as marketplace doctors (*bazari tabib*) in
contrast to themselves as doctors of the spirit (*ruhani tabib*), implying a
dichotomy between "true" and "false" Sufism. I will highlight contradictions in their attitudes toward such women shortly. First, however, I turn
to the more general tone of discourses I encountered about women and
*piri-muridi.*

The opinions of the majority of my subjects, regardless of gender, class,
or social standing, was that women could not become *pirs* but could do the
work of *piri-muridi*. While the former implied autonomy and unambiguous
authority, the latter implied agency and an authority that is subordinate,
complementary, and conditional in relation to male authority. The latter
was linked to Shari'a standards for Muslim women, while the former was
characterized as being "against the Shari'a." What kinds of activities did
*piri-muridi* encompass, and how did these compare with the work of a *pir*?
In chapter 2 I assessed the ways in which women's activities operated in

conjunction with the ritual and spiritual duties of the *pir* or offered a sub-
stitute in his absence. Women assisted in initiation ceremonies (*bai'at*) prescribed and distributed amulets, performed prayers on behalf of others,
counseled disciples and clients of the *pir,* conveyed knowledge about the
traditions of the order (particularly to their daughters and daughters-in-
law), and in one instance handled a case of possession even while the *pir*
was present. These kinds of activities were represented by my subjects,
regardless of gender, as being both necessary and expedient (because of the
*pir's* large clientele and because frequent travel made it impossible for him
always to be physically present for his followers). My subjects in Bihar also
explained that in cases where the concern for sex segregation was pro-
nounced, women could serve as the conveyers of ritual implements (such
as *ta'wiz*), prescriptions, and the *pir's* advice to women clients who practiced particularly strict forms of *parda.*

At times *pir*s, *pirzade,* and *khadim*s explained that "women were the
helpmates of men" and thus reasoned that women could engage in this type
of "work." As helpmates to the *pir,* women's activities were depicted as
being in conformity with Islam and with *parda* practices. (These two categories were often linked by my subjects with phrases such as "In Islam
there is *parda*" or "*Parda* is necessary for Muslim women.") I have already
discussed how *parda* practices can shift according to context. In ways similar to those I have outlined in this chapter and earlier, regarding the *pirzade*
women's participation in communal ritual events (see especially chapters
2 and 3), women's activities as de facto *pir*s can be made to conform (in discourse as well as in practice) to various conceptions about what constitutes
*parda* practice.

Aside from ascriptions of birth, marriage, and discipleship, both men
and women identified another category in which women could operate
legitimately as spiritual guides (for men and women): the woman-as-saint
(*waliya*). The *pir*s, *pirzade,* and *khadim*s I interviewed in Ajmer and Bihar
often cited examples of women from Muslim and Sufi history who had
acquired considerable insight into Islam (here Islam appeared in discussion
as an unspecified category implying a closed set of standards for women),
Shari'a, and spiritual knowledge (*'ilm-i ruhani*). Several figures from Sufi
and Islamic history were recalled as examples of exceptional, highly gifted
women who had provided guidance and counsel to men and women alike.
In discourses about such women, spiritual authority and sainthood were
often linked with *parda* observance and related markers of what I have
referred to in the body of this work as an ideal of Muslim femininity. This
linking of the attainment of saintly virtue with conformity to what is prescribed and generally accepted as exemplary has been explored in John S.

Hawley's *Saints and Virtues*.[13] In Sufism as in Islam, the Prophet's example (*sunna*) functions as an overarching model of piety, and this example figured into my subjects' discussions about women in the ritual setting (in the form of anecdotes about the Prophet's stance toward women). In discussing women and spiritual authority as they were connected to saintly virtue, my Sufi subjects also emphasized the examples of Bibi Raziya, Bibi Kamalo, and the other daughters of Pir Jagjot (Sharaf al-din Maneri's paternal grandfather); the wives of the Prophet (especially Hazrat A'isha); the Prophet's daughter Fatima; and the ninth-century Sufi of Basra, Rabi'a al-'Adawiyya al-Basri.

Discourses surrounding the sainthood of these women pivoted upon two sets of ascriptions. First (with the exception of the Rabi'a), sainthood was linked to women's identity as members of a saintly lineage (particularly as the mothers and daughters of saintly men) and to the ways in which these women embodied ideal characteristics of Islamic femininity as my subjects articulated them. Such characteristics were *parda* observance as it exemplified modest behavior, female subordination to male authority, and women's separation from men unrelated to them. These linkages also underscored women's spiritual authority as being directly related to their saintly male relatives. Often such interpretations of female sainthood were provided by the men I spoke with, particularly the Bihar *pir*s, *pirzade,* and *khadims,* although one exception was that both male and female subjects ascribed the sainthood of the women of the Prophet's family to their association with him. (Within this exception lay another exception: Bibi Fatima's sainthood was linked both to the Prophet and to notions of her own inherent purity.)

Some women had achieved their saintly status, my male subjects reasoned, because they came from families of saints and thus had been raised in a milieu conducive to their being perceived as saintly. The women saints who fell into this category were the Prophet's wives; Bibi Raziya and two of her sisters; and Hazrat Bibi Fatima. For instance the *khadim*s at the *dargah* of Sharaf al-din Maneri consistently linked Bibi Raziya's spiritual authority to four criteria: her saintly lineage, which one *khadim* traced back to her maternal and paternal grandfathers; her knowledge of Islamic law (a concept that was again left unelaborated by my subjects but that implied a "general knowledge" of the rights and duties of women under Islam), imparted to her by her father, Pir Jagjot; her desire to raise children who were knowledgeable in matters of the law (Shari'a) as well as the spirit (*ruh*); and most important, Sharaf al-din's love and reverence of her. The wives of the Prophet were also identified as saints because of their marriage to him (his choosing of them serving to highlight their exceptionalness)

and because of their intimate knowledge of his life and of the history of the first generations of Muslims, knowledge that they disseminated orally and that has been encapsulated in the Hadis collections. Both men and women ascribed Fatima's spiritual authority to her father's love for her. In hagiography Fatima is described as the most beloved of all the Prophet's children, the only one to produce surviving grandsons (who carried on the Prophet's bloodline) and the closest to him from among her siblings. Devotion to Fatima was interpreted by both men and women as tantamount to performing an act that pleasing to the Prophet.

The figure of Fatima, however, stands at the crossroads of the two ascriptive categories I mentioned above, for while her spiritual authority comes from her identity as the beloved of the Prophet, her sainthood was also linked to her role as a powerful source of *barakat,* a kind of charisma conferring spiritual power. This role is manifested in practice by the vows both men and women make in her name, much as they would in the name of a Sufi saint. Another important source of her spiritual power and authority as articulated by my male subjects was her purity (*paki*). Fatima's physical purity (and concurrently the purity of her soul) recurred as an important theme in discussions about female sainthood. It was linked alternatively with her status as the Prophet's daughter and her unconditional and unwavering love for and obedience to him (in contrast to his wives, whom Hadis accounts maintain were at one point threatened with divorce because of their backbiting and jealousy toward each other) and with her spiritual "perfection," a gift bestowed by God. Fatima's purity was identified as a quality that allowed her to do things other women could not: as one *khadim* explained, she was so pure (here he referred to a tradition that says she did not menstruate) that she could go into the mosque without fear of reproach (although another *khadim* insisted that she could only do so when no man was present). Several others—*khadims* and *pirzade* men—explained that the food over which the *fatiha* prayer has been read in Fatima's name could only be consumed by women who were considered "pure" and "virtuous," and that she never used bad language or spoke ill of anyone (again an image that positions her in stark contrast to the Prophet's wives). In Sufi piety such reverence for Fatima—as the Prophet's beloved daughter and also as a paradigm of virtue and purity—is overlaid with Shi'a-inspired elements of devotion to the *ahl-i bait* as powerful intercessors with God.

Although Fatima stands at a crossroads whereby female sainthood is linked with ascription by kinship or marriage or through the female saint's own virtues, several other figures whose examples were highlighted in my discussions with Sufi men and women stood more firmly in the category of

sainthood by merit. As saints in their own right, these figures, Rabi'a al-'Adawiyya al-Basri and Bibi Kamalo, sometimes posed a problem for those of my subjects who found it difficult to reconcile female spiritual authority with autonomy and, in the case of Rabi'a, nonconformity to the ideals of Muslim womanhood that were articulated for the women in the first category mentioned above. Rabi'a's celibacy, for example, was seen as more problematic by men than women, for as several Bihari *pirzade* men and *khadims* pointed out, marriage is very important in Islam. Yet they made no attempt to reconcile Rabi'a's apparent violation of this normative value with the fact of her sainthood. On several occasions my male subjects dismissed the contradiction altogether, refusing to elaborate upon the disjunction between their discourses about a female sainthood that was reliant upon the embodiment of accepted social norms and the sainthood of Rabi'a, a woman who had neither husband, father, or children and who (according to tradition) associated freely with Sufi men, even instructing them on matters that they could not understand. A few male subjects did elaborate upon her status as guide as being in conformity with Sufi ideas about the limits of female spiritual authority by characterizing her "guidance" as being of an informal nature. In other words Rabi'a had no formally initiated disciples, according to them, but she did disseminate advice. Indeed Rabi'a emerged in discourse as a figure who could be made to conform to accepted standards for women in the Sufi milieu (as having spiritual power that was unlimited in its potential but bounded by social exigencies), while in other cases the problem of her identity as a woman uncontrolled by men was ignored or dismissed altogether.

Interestingly it was the *pirzade* women of the Gudri Shah order who emphasized Rabi'a's spiritual prowess as wholly independent and unlimited. In one story they related—a well-known hagiography involving Rabi'a in which her donkey dies on the road to Mecca and God resurrects the animal after she complains to him, so that she can continue her journey—the balance is shifted so that it is Rabi'a's spiritual power, rather than her piety and faith in God, that becomes the focus of the narrative. Nevertheless both men and women demonstrated ambivalence about the parameters of spiritual authority for women such as Rabi'a. As has been pointed out in an article on three Hindu *bhakti* saints, some types of sainthood serve to question accepted systems of ordinary moral propriety. They embody some kind of "higher," unharnessed and unharnessable, standard, although the social norms and rules constituting systems of ordinary moral propriety are not altogether dismissed in narratives about such saints.[14] This ambivalence, I believe, is closely tied to perceptions of the nature of

sainthood and spiritual power as being precarious and "wholly other," thus not entirely subject to the rules of social interaction that apply to ordinary men and women.

The figures mentioned above were in linked discourse with Prophetic Islam or "true" Sufism, and it was in part owing to such connections that their owing to sainthood was depicted by my subjects as "legitimate" and unquestioned. A more problematic figure in the category of female spiritual authorities, however, was what several Bihar interviewees referred to alternately as the female *maulana* and the "marketplace doctor." These terms referred to what seem to be localized instances of women establishing a clientele for whom they provide ritual services (most notably the effecting of cures and the distribution of amulets) and advice in matters both spiritual and personal. Such figures are often connected with Sufism or identified as Sufis, particularly if they operate in or near a Sufi shrine (an auxiliary shrine) or if they have (or claim to have) a connection with a Sufi *pir* (for example by having taken an oath of allegiance, or *bai'a*). In truth many of these figures seem to have a precarious (or even nonexistent) relationship with the establishment Sufi orders, although because I was able to access only one of these kinds of women, my supposition that this is the case lies on shaky ground and in fact comes more from what I have been told by my subjects (both Sufi and non-Sufi) about these women. I focused on two examples of such women in chapters 2 and 4: the female healer studied by the folklorist Joyce Flueckiger and Rafat, the woman I encountered in the *hujra gah* of Sharaf al-din Maneri in Bihar Sharif. My assessments of the role of these women as a group, therefore, is largely limited to their characterizations by others and does not adequately address questions such as the prevalence of such women, the scope of their authority vis-à-vis their clientele, or their self-perceptions. However, since I have chosen to focus on discourse, and particularly the discourses of the establishment Sufis, I will limit my analysis to the discrepancies found among these individuals.

Women such as Rafat and Amma represent a threat to the status quo, and it is this perspective I wish to highlight as one that emerged overwhelmingly in my discussions with others about these women. What also emerged from these discussions was the problematic of assessing the spiritual power of such women, in part because of the nature of sainthood and spiritual power itself. The disjunction between discourses about what constituted "false" and "true" Sufism (and Sufi practice) as seen in the example of women *pirs* (Amma) and ritual specialists (Rafat) was much more evident in women's than in men's explanations of how such women were able to do what they did. While men overwhelmingly characterized them as

"quacks" (to quote one *pirzade*) and charlatans preying on the ignorance of common people and seeking only monetary gain, women's attitudes were more ambivalent. The Gudri Shah *pirzade* women characterized Amma's practice as legitimate because it was sanctioned by a *pir* (in this case her husband, although in the first article published from this study Flueckiger implies that Amma's own *pir* did not sanction it) and because Amma's authority could readily appear subordinate to her husband's, who also worked with her in the healing context. Rafat, on the other hand, was characterized as "dangerous," but the Gudri Shah *pirzade* also admitted the possibility that such women were truly blessed with "spiritual gifts" (to quote the phrase one Gudri Shah disciple used). Rafat was seen as dangerous not only because she had entered into an arena that most women should not, but also because she was "mentally unstable" (notably this phrase was also applied by my subjects in Bihar to the wailing women at the *hujra gah* in Bihar Sharif, Rafat, and all women like her). Moreover Rafat's perceived "dangerous" nature was linked by my subjects in Ajmer to her use of the curse, with which she sought to do harm to others. Interestingly Sufi *pir*s will also use curses, as Desiderio Pinto's study of *piri-muridi* shows (although these are portrayed as rare cases), but Rafat's use of the curse was seen as evidence of her unpredictability and the shaky foundation upon which her knowledge rested. In Bihar the *pirzade* and *khadim*s characterized Rafat's knowledge as "misuse" (my phrase). In other words, as they explained, such women had merely gleaned information from *pir*s and books (such as the demotic texts available in the *bazar*s attached to Sufi shrines), and the knowledge these women professed therefore had no "truth" behind it. Such arguments posed these female ritual specialists as misguided (or corrupt) individuals operating in contrast to the laws of Islam and the Shari'a.

On the other hand, women were willing to admit the possibility that the basis of spiritual power upon which women such as Rafat and Amma relied for their authority and effectiveness was very real indeed. This admission points to the nature of spiritual power itself (encapsulated in the "sainthood" of the individual) as ambiguous, unpredictable, and indeterminate, which makes its characterization problematic, its explanation fraught with contradictions. Such contradictions in perceptions of Rafat became apparent in the reactions of others to her. In Bihar Sharif she was treated with reverence and respect by some of the women who came to the *hujra gah,* while in the marketplace most people seemed cowed by her raucous behavior. While my female subjects in Bihar and Ajmer at first assessed her (and women like her) as "crazy" or "disturbed," they were also willing to admit

that such women provided needed services and that they may indeed have been saintly. This ambivalence on the part of women brings to light the problems of using a dichotomy derived from Western discourse, in which madness or mental illness is interpreted as a measurable clinical condition and South Asians are characterized as usually assessing madness as a mark of divine favor. Two essays on *majzub*s have disputed such a notion.[15] Rather, I suggest that my subjects (particularly women) recognized that sainthood could not always be explained, rationalized, or understood and that some women may be recognized as spiritual authorities in spite of the fact that they stand outside accepted norms of behavior. The reluctance with which most of my interviewees dealt with such a subject showed that while the recognition of female spiritual authority as an accepted part of Islamic and Sufi faith could serve as proof of the appeal of such faith (in that it encompasses and embraces the contradictions), nevertheless such authority also threatens to undermine the hegemonic order (a hallmark of which is female subordination to male authority) by which most women defined themselves and their place in society, in the world of the Sufi orders and indeed in the wider world of Islam.

The interstices of discourse and practice suggest a fluidity that is germane to the notion of language as unlimited in its presupposition of given, continuous, temporal, or atemporal unities (as in the laws of the Qur'an or Shari'a) but bound by the particular contexts (and contextual meanings) of its occurrence. As a statement or set of statements seeking to conceptualize and constitute its object, discourse must be considered in light of the speaking subject's intention, the constraints that operate upon him or her in particular circumstances, and the relationship of discourse to the subject's self-perception.

While discourse as a prescriptive mode seeks to identify a normative system of values, beliefs, and practices, the precariousness of such normativity comes to light in the area of practice, wherein what constitutes the normative itself shifts or is "explained away." This precariousness points to the need to consider the power of discursive signification in both prescriptive and illustrative applications as rhetorical strategies that may simultaneously enable and inhibit, maintain a sense of group boundedness or exclusivity, and open up new avenues for participation. However, as I have argued, the apparent disjunction between discourse and practice should not be taken simply as evidence of contradiction or challenge, nor as an inherently destabilizing mechanism. The ambivalence of most observers toward the question of women as *pir*s, participants, or performers suggests a dialogic understanding of the prescriptive aspects of Muslim womanhood (in

this case the boundaries that prevent women from exercising agency in the shrine milieu) and the practical (the ways in which they can push those boundaries to exercise greater agency than discourse would suggest) that can reveal much about how structuring mechanisms are conceived, experienced, and enacted "on the ground."

# . Notes .

### Preface

1. Scholars have long used the word *saint* to refer to various types of holy men and women in Islam (such as Sufi, *darvish, faqir, marabout,* and *wali*). The relative singularity of the term's meaning in English belies the multivocality of the Arabic, Persian, and Urdu words for which it is substituted. Although *saint* is derived from its Christian sense and is used to refer to a phenomenon produced by quite different cultural factors, it has been co-opted by Sufis to refer to the holy among them. For this reason I use the term throughout this book.

2. The *pirs* of the Maner and Bihar Sharif branches of the Firdausi order are known as Shah Sahib. I will use this term to refer exclusively to them.

3. I have chosen to adopt the phrase "lived" religion instead of "popular" in order to avoid some of the pejorative connotations this term can carry and to emphasize instead the experiential aspects of Islam that were conveyed to me by the men and women who are featured in this study.

4. Metcalf, "Islam and Custom in Nineteenth-Century India,"64.

5. Salvatore, *Islam and the Political Discourse of Modernity;* Zaman, *The 'Ulama in Contemporary Islam: Custodians of Change.*

6. Brown, "Shari'a and State in the Modern Middle East, " 363–64; Asad, *The Idea of an Anthropology of Islam.*

7. Messick, *The Calligraphic State,* 3.

8. Nasr, *Traditional Islam in the Modern World,* 51–52.

9. Sanyal, *Devotional Islam and Politics in British India;* see chap. 6.

10. Metcalf, *Perfecting Women,* 5.

11. See 'Usmani, *Taqlid ki shari' haisiyat.*

12. See, for example, Arkoun, *Rethinking Islam;* Tibi, *Islam and the Cultural Accommodation of Social Change,* 59–75; Hassan, *Faithlines.*

13. Examples of works that have stressed the integration of these two approaches (in the study of Muslims and Islam) are Roff, "Islamic Movements"; Bowen, *Muslims through Discourse;* Bullock, *Rethinking Muslim Women and the Veil;* and Mahmood, *Politics of Piety.*

14. The Persian term *pir* means elder, holy man, or (sometimes) the head of a Sufi lineage. *Pirzade,* strictly speaking, refers to the offspring of a *pir.* Here I use the term in a wider sense to refer to the closest family members of the *pir. Khadim,* or servant, is the term used to refer to the hereditary functionaries attached to a shrine who claim blood and/or spiritual descent from the saint for whom the shrine is

named. The Urdu phrase *khadim log* (rhymes with "rogue") was also often used to refer to more than one person; no one I spoke with used the Arabic plural, *khuddam.*

15. That is to say, she is the sister of the Shah Sahib who succeeded their father soon after my first excursion to Bihar in 1996.

16. Quoted in Patel, "White Woman's Woe."

## Introduction

1. These studies include Mernissi, "Women, Saints, and Sanctuaries" (Morocco); Johnson, "A Sufi Shrine in Modern Tunisia" (Tunisia); Dwyer, "Women, Sufism and Decision-Making in Moroccan Islam" (Morocco); Hoffman, *Sufism, Mystics, and Saints in Modern Egypt* (Egypt); Ewing, *Arguing Sainthood* (India and Pakistan); Flueckiger, *In Amma's Healing Room* (India); Jeffery, *Frogs in a Well* (India).

2. Cornell, *Early Sufi Women;* Smith, *Muslim Women Mystics;* Roded, *Women in Islamic Biographical Collections;* Nurbakhsh, *Sufi Women;* Ernst, "Lives of Sufi Saints"; Eaton, "Sufi Folk Literature and the Expansion of Indian Islam."

3. Jeffery, *Frogs in a Well;* Hoffman, *Sufism, Mystics, and Saints;* Ewing, *Arguing Sainthood;* Mernissi, "Women, Saints, and Sanctuaries"; Flueckiger, *In Amma's Healing Room;* Abbas, *Female Voice in Sufi Ritual;* Raudvere, *Book and the Roses.*

4. Cadavid, trans., *Two Who Attained;* Roberts, trans., *The Subtle Blessings in the Saintly Lives of Abul-Abbas al-Nursi And His Master Abul-Hasan.*

5. Helminski, *Sufi Women;* Bakhtiar, *Sufi Women of America.* The terms *shaikh* and *pir,* Arabic and Persian (respectively) for elder and holy man, are often used synonymously in the Indian Subcontinent. I will use these terms indiscriminately as well, sometimes employing the feminine *shaikha* and *pirain* or *pirani* to refer to their female equivalents.

6. For example, O'Hanlon, "Recovering the Subject," and Chaturvedi, *Mapping Subaltern Studies.* See also Yang, *Crime and Criminality;* Siddiqi, "Review of Subaltern Studies III."

7. Guha, *Dominance without Hegemony;* Haynes and Prakash, *Contesting Power;* Scott, *Weapons of the Weak.*

8. See Prakash, "Becoming a Bhuniya."

9. Ibid., 169–70.

10. Guha, *Elementary Aspects of Peasant Rebellion,* 18–19.

11. Ibid., 33–34, 73–74.

12. Ibid., 1–2, 335–36.

13. Guha, *Dominance without Hegemony,* 5, 155.

14. Sanyal, *Devotional Islam and Politics in British India,* 6.

15. Arkoun, *Unthought in Contemporary Islamic Thought,* 251–52.

16. Several excellent studies have investigated these associations. See, for example, Chatterjee's *The Nation and Its Fragments;* Sarkar, *Hindu Wife, Hindu Nation;* and Hassan, *Forging Identities.*

17. See Robinson, *The 'Ulama of Farangi Mahall;* Metcalf, *Islamic Revival in British India;* and Nadvi, *Islamic Resurgent Movements in the Indo-Pak Subcontinent.*

18. See Robinson, "Islam and the Impact of Print in South Asia," in his *Islam and Muslim History in South Asia,* 66–104.

19. Buehler, *Sufi Heirs of the Prophet,* 90–96.

20. Pemberton, "Women *Pirs*," 73.

21. My sense of "middle class" here draws from two different understandings. One is framed by the consumer categories enumerated by Jan Nijman in a study of the rising middle class in contemporary Mumbai. See his article "Mumbai's Mysterious Middle Class." The second takes into consideration the cultural, social, and political capital wielded by the middle classes as explained by Leela Fernandes in *India's New Middle Class,* xviii–xix, xxix–xxxii, and the "producers and products of a new cultural politics" definition given by Sanjay Joshi in his *Fractured Modernity,* 7.

22. Varma, *The Great Indian Middle Class,* chap. 1; Fernandes, *India's New Middle Class,* esp. chap. 1; and Joshi, *Fractured Modernity,* 1–3.

23. Fernandes, *India's New Middle Class,* 157–59.

24. See, for instance, Minault, "Political Change"; Vreede de Stuers, *Parda;* and Vatuk, "Purdah Revisited." It should also be noted that for many Muslims of the lower classes, maintaining strict forms of *parda* is now seen as a mark of social mobility, much as it was for their middle- and upper-class compatriots in generations past.

25. This has been one of the criticisms leveled by Muslim women, particularly Islamic feminists today, against Western and/or secularist interpretations of Muslim women's subordination and oppression. Indeed as several recent studies have pointed out, Muslim women often feel that their non-Muslim counterparts in the West are oppressed by the objectification and sexualization of the female body.

26. Ernst and Lawrence address the persistence of "Sufism in decline" paradigms throughout the history of Sufism in *Sufi Martyrs of Love,* 1.

27. Werbner, *Pilgrims of Love,* 27–28, 140–44.

28. Gilmartin and Lawrence, *Beyond Turk and Hindu,* 2.

29. See, for example, Trimingham, *Sufi Orders in Islam;* Rahman, *Islam;* and Geertz, *Islam Observed.*

30. Travelers by rail on the Rajdhani Express from Delhi to Ajmer are now encouraged to visit the shrine complex of Mu'in al-din Chishti, which both underscores the shrine's continued importance in the region and points to a growth in the shrine's popularity as a tourist destination.

31. For a discussion of this analytical paradigm and the problems with it, see Mahmood, *Politics of Piety,* 8–9.

32. Ibid., 45.

33. Asad, *Genealogies of Religion,* 33, 36.

34. Graham, "Traditionalism in Islam," 496–97.

35. Cornell, *Early Sufi Women,* 54–57.

36. Ibid., 66–68.

37. *Ihya' 'ulum al-din.* Consulted English translation by Madelain Farah, "Book on the Etiquette of Marriage," online at http://www.ghazali.org/works/marriage .htm (accessed September 25, 2009). Quote from "Examination of the Husband's Rights," pt. 2 of chap. 3.

38. Ibid.

39. See Dallal, "Ghazali and the Perils of Interpretation."

40. For a wider discussion, see Malamud, "Sufi Organizations and Structures of Authority"; Wilkinson, "Life in Early Nishapur"; and Melchert, "Sufis and Competing Movements in Nishapur."

41. Malamud, "Sufi Organizations and Structures of Authority," and Lapidus, "Evolution of Muslim Urban Society." See also Chabbi, "Remarques sur le développement historique."

42. Lapidus, "Evolution of Muslim Society," 28–30.

43. Leila Ahmed makes this observation in her *Women and Gender in Islam*. See esp. chap. 4 of that work.

44. Chabbi, "Remarques sur le développement historique," 43–44. Prior to this period, it seems to have been primarily linked with the Qarmatians.

45. This trend seems to have increased after the thirteenth century. See Trimingham, *Sufi Orders in Islam*, 18.

46. Schimmel, *Mystical Dimensions of Islam*, 243.

47. See Abu al-Najib 'Abd al-Qahir al-Suhrawardi, *Kitab a dab al-Muridin*, 80–99.

48. Cornell, *Early Sufi Women;* Smith, *Muslim Women Mystics*, pt. 3; and Nurbakhsh, *Sufi Women*.

49. Malamud, "Sufi Organizations and Structures of Authority," 428–29.

50. From Bukhari's *Sahih*, vol. 8, bk. 73, no. 97. M. Muhsin Khan has provided an online translation of selections of this work at the USC-MSA Compendium of texts Web site (accessed September 25, 2009).

51. Cornell, *Early Sufi Women*, 26; Cornell, "Sufi Women's Spirituality," 170; Hodgson, *The Venture of Islam*, 2:201–2.

52. Trimingham, *Sufi Orders in Islam*, 67.

53. Schimmel, *My Soul Is a Woman*, esp. chap. 4; Murata, *The Tao of Islam*, 316–19.

54. These tropes are explored in Schimmel, *My Soul Is a Woman*.

55. Misunderstanding the social plane as identical, as opposed to derivative: that is to say, the social plane only faintly and incompletely resembles the cosmological plane of existence.

56. Murata, *The Tao of Islam*, 78.

57. By "inner circle" I refer to those disciples of an order who are closest to the *shaikh* among all his *murids* and who are privy to insights and knowledge that the average *murid* is not, both by virtue of their frequent presence in the company, or *suhbat*, of the *shaikh* and because many among them tend to be rather more well read in the classical texts of mystical Islam.

58. Lila Abu Lughod and Sherry B. Ortner discuss some of the problems with the resistance paradigm. See Abu Lughod, "Romance of Resistance," and Ortner, "Resistance and the Problem of Ethnographic Refusal."

59. This dynamic understanding of agency is put forward in considerable detail in Emirbayer and Mische, "What Is Agency?"

60. See the introduction to Pemberton and Nijhawan, *Shared Idioms*.

61. Lowe, *Critical Terrains,* ix–x, 5.

62. I treat this subject in more detail in chapter 1.

## Chapter 1. Perceptions of "Women's Religion" in Colonial India

1. Kumar, *Image of Patna,* 192.

2. Kumar's wording, "rank and file," seems to implicate the lower classes and castes of Hindus rather than the educated in the patronage of *dargah*s.

3. I use the term *Shari'a* in much the same manner as it was used by Marshall Hodgson and later Brickley Messick—that is, broadly to indicate a practical ideology for private and public living, rather than a particular form of law and jurisprudence in Islam. For the layperson this broad connotation is the most common use of the term in quotidian discourse.

4. Hardy, *Muslims of British India,* 31, 38–40, 41, 43–45. Hardy maintains that by and large Muslims in Bengal did not enjoy the benefits of such enfranchisement, despite their large numbers in the region, especially since the majority remained cultivators, while the system of *zamindari* enabled the enfranchisement of Hindu, more so than Muslim, landlords.

5. For critiques of this strategy, see the work of Shaikh, especially *Community and Consensus in Islam,* ch. 2, and Jalal, *Self and Sovereignty,* especially ch. 4.

6. The recording of women's presence in the "*Darvesh* castes" often served as an indicator of certain characteristics of these groups. For instance Sir Denzil Ibbetson's work on tribes and castes of the Panjab records the presence of women among the *darvish*es of the Batala, Pathankot, Amritsar, and Kapurthala districts as an index of whether or not caste formation had occurred among a group. The presence of large numbers of women within a group was noted by Ibbetson as evidence that conversion had ceased to occur and that group identity was based, rather, on descent. By contrast the presence of few women adherents of a group was explained by him as indicating that the group had not yet coalesced into a caste and was still recruiting members from outside. See his *Panjab Castes,* 229.

7. Ewing, *Arguing Sainthood,* 53–57.

8. Ibid., 31, 34–35, 49–53. For more in-depth studies of the Pindari wars and the role of the Sufi *shaikh* Sayyid Ahmad Barelwi and his followers, see Ahmad, *Wahhabi Movement in India,* and Nadvi, *Islamic Resurgent Movements.*

9. The women I refer to here are the wives, mothers, and other close female relatives of *pir*s.

10. By contrast, in the case of the Rahmaniyya *zawiya* in 1890s Algeria, the bid for directorship was split between Zainab bint Muhammad ibn Abiu'l Qasim and Muhammad ibn al-Hajj Muhammad, the daughter and the nephew of the departing *shaikh,* Muhammad ibn Abi'l Qasim (Sidi Muhammad). French authorities supported the claims of the nephew over and against those of Zainab, who was the more popular and influential figure among members of the order. She engaged in litigations against her cousin and the French administration for many years, finally

winning her case by default and remaining at the helm of the order until her death in 1904. According to Julia Clancy-Smith, the French authorities considered her a "dangerous woman" and sought to thwart her claims chiefly on the basis of her gender. It is also evident that Zainab's command of French legal procedures and Muslim law and her defiance of the colonial regime made her an impossible candidate for co-optation and control by the French authorities, unlike her cousin. See Clancy-Smith, "House of Zainab."

11. Buchanan-Hamilton remarked that the shrine was evidently in decline, as attested by the scarce number of pilgrims who patronized it. What is unusual in his account is that the shrine is described as belonging to the widow of the former *pir*. See Jackson, *Journal of Francis Buchanan,* 182.

12. See Eaton, *Rise of Islam and the Bengal Frontier,* especially ch. 6 and 7.

13. See Titus, "Mysticism and Saint Worship in India." On the whole, the first generation of British gazetteer and travelogue writers (for example Buchanan-Hamilton) seemed to take more of an interest in describing shrines and saint cults; some of these accounts many even be described as sympathetic. The writers of the later period ( J. J. D. La Touche, Col. James Tod, and Major Erskine, for instance) seem to have either disparaged or largely ignored important shrines in the areas they surveyed. The attitudes of the gazetteer writers toward local and regional customs and faith seems to accord with Sumanta Banerjee's findings in a study of elite and popular culture in nineteenth-century Calcutta. According to him, the British of the early nineteenth century participated in and took a more sympathetic view of popular culture, whereas those of the latter half of the century, along with indigenous members of the elite and middle classes, marginalized popular culture in favor of the cultural paradigms of the elite. See Banerjee, *Parlour and the Streets.*

14. Robinson, *Islam and Muslim History in South Asia,* 105; Salvatore, *Islam and the Political Discourse,* 42.

15. Eric Wolf cites the outbreaks of rebellion preceding the 1850s as a primary reason behind the change in attitude of the British colonial administration in this regard. See his *Europe and the People without History,* 251–52.

16. See note 6 above.

17. Hamilton, *East-India Gazetteer,* 485.

18. Ewing, *Arguing Sainthood,* 53–55; Freitag, "Collective Crime and Authority in British India."

19. Cohn, *Colonialism and Its Forms of Knowledge,* 5–11.

20. Eastwick, *Handbook of the Panjab,* 132–33. In other cases the works of company officials ignored the shrine altogether: for instance Col. James Tod's *Annals and Antiquities of Rajasthan,* which deals with Rajasthan's history, monuments, and legends, does not even mention the *dargah* of Mu'in al-din Chishti of Ajmer, although it is difficult to believe that its existence was unknown to him. Rather the shrine seems not to have interested Tod, since his *Annals* focuses more on the chronicles of the ruling Rajput groups than those of the Mughal dynasties, and on Hindu rather than Muslim religious establishments and ceremonies.

21. That Buchanan-Hamilton's attention to this subject was among the earliest is noted by Hardy in his "Modern European and Muslim Explanations," 72.

22. Jackson, *Journal of Francis Buchanan*, 167.

23. Gilmartin shows how this was especially true in the examples of the *sajjada nishin*s of Chishti shrines at Taunsa and Jalalpur in the Panjab. See his *Empire and Islam*, 65–71.

24. Gilmartin attributes this shift in part to the failure of the British to establish a viable structure of authority using the central symbolism of Muslim power, as had been the case with the Mughal Raj. *Empire and Islam*, 52–62.

25. Habib, *Agrarian System of Mughal India*. See esp. chaps. 7 and 8 for a more detailed description of these types of grants.

26. Ranajit Guha, "Dominance without Hegemony," 210.

27. Rizvi, *Muslim Revivalist Movements*, 18.

28. Habib, *Agrarian System of Mughal India*, 344n14, 349–50n41, 353n54, 355, 357n68.

29. Ibid., 222.

30. Lowe, *Critical Terrains*, 117–18.

31. Ewing, *Arguing Sainthood*, 49.

32. For instance in 1798 the British took over the regulation of license fees that pilgrims in Gaya (in the Bengal Presidency) used to pay to their priests. See Yang, *Bazaar India*, 123.

33. O'Malley, *Indian Civil Service*, 179–80. Directors, among other things, were responsible for providing the overseas passage of company servants. For information about the bureaucratic apparatus of the company up until around the mid–nineteenth century, see chaps. 1–3 of O'Malley's work.

34. Currie, *The Shrine and Cult of Muʻin al-Din Chishti*, 149.

35. Bayly, comp., *Chiefs and Leading Families in Rajputana*, 113.

36. This is pointed out by David Gilmartin in *Empire and Islam*, 48, although he also maintains that in some cases delegation of authority to the Court of Wards did not automatically entail its takeover by the British colonial administration.

37. Currie, *Shrine and Cult of Muʻin al-Din Chishti*, 166.

38. The various functionaries as well as administrative positions in the Ajmer *dargah* are discussed in chapter 2 of Currie's book.

39. Katherine Ewing made this observation in *Arguing Sainthood*.

40. Sprenger, *The Life of Muhammad;* Muir, *The Life of Mahomet*.

41. Muir's *Life of Mahomet*, which was reviewed by T. P. Hughes, author of the *Dictionary of Islam* and a missionary/scholar, is particularly relevant here. See Guenther, "Image of the Prophet," 44, for the impact of these biographies on missionaries' discourse about the Prophet Muhammad within the context of Christian-Muslim relations in India in the late nineteenth century.

42. Goldziher, "Cult of Saints in Islam," 302.

43. Ibid., 303.

44. Ibid., 307.

45. Oman, *Brahmans, Theists and Muslims of India*, 17.

46. Ibid., 281. Such views also extended to his treatment of Hinduism in *Brahmans, Theists and Muslims of India* and of Hinduism, Sikhism, and Buddhism in his earlier work, *Indian Life, Religious and General*. Here too he often associates what he understood to be the more dubious forms of popular worship with "women's spirituality," while his assessment of the popular veneration of deities and human and semidivine figures compared it unfavorably with the "systems" set forth by the "ancient" texts of the traditions and, in the case of Hinduism, with the "higher Hinduism" of the educated classes.

47. Ibid., 292, 301.

48. Kopf, *British Orientalism and the Bengal Renaissance*, 22.

49. This bias was also reflected in their treatment of contemporary Hindu and Sikh devotional and social practices.

50. Hodgson, *Venture of Islam*, 2:320–23, 334–35, 362–68.

51. Jahanpour, "Western Encounters with Persian Sufi Literature," 31–32.

52. Perhaps the most important work to follow Napoleon's invasion was the *Description de l'Egypte*, published between 1809 and 1822. It is a twenty-volume collection of scientific inquiries on Egyptian antiquities, sciences, music, literature, and ethnology. Other notable works published by French authors in the wake of Napoleon's Egyptian campaigns were Vivant Denon's 1802 *Le voyage de la basse et la haute Egypte pendant les campagnes du Général Bonaparte*, which was published in forty editions and translated into several languages, and J. F. Champollion's *Monuments de l'Egypte et de la Nubie* (1835). For a sampling of the contents of these texts, see the New York Public Library Digital Gallery at http://digitalgallery.nypl.org/nypldigital/index.cfm and the Bibliotheca Alexandria's Digital Assets Repository at http://www.bibalex.org (both accessed March 18, 2010).

53. Roe, "Thomas Roe's Journal," 718.

54. Tavernier, *Travels in India*, 2:299.

55. Ibid., 2:276, and Catrou, *Histoire générale de l'Empire du Mogol*, 238–39.

56. For a fuller account of this religious landscape in the Panjab, see Murphy, "Texts of the Guga Tradition," and in the south, see Assayag, *Au confluence de deux rivières*.

57. Manucci, *Storia do Mogor*, 2:213.

58. Tavernier, *Travels in India*, 1:312.

59. Ewing, *Arguing Sainthood*, 50, 52–57.

60. Tavernier, *Travels in India*, 2:139–41.

61. Oman, *Mystics, Ascetics, and Saints*, 271. See also Ewing, *Arguing Sainthood*, 59–61.

62. 'Ali, *Observations on the Mussulmauns of India*, 336, 337.

63. Ibid., 338, and note 1 for a description of *saalik*s and *majzub*s.

64. Ewing, *Arguing Sainthood*, 13.

65. This is pointed out by Guha in "Dominance without Hegemony," 212.

66. Minault, *Secluded Scholars*, 5.

67. This is particularly true of a text such as the *Bihishti Zewar*, which was initially written for women of the "respectable classes," and later came to be considered a text suitable not only for nonelite women but for men too.

68. Minault, *Secluded Scholars,* 231–33.

69. Sadiq, *History of Urdu Literature,* 347. For another view of the Urdu literary landscape of these times, see Pritchett, *Nets of Awareness.*

70. Minault, *Secluded Scholars,* 101–2.

71. Ibid., 76.

72. *Mangal kavya* and *vijay kavya* literature are versified homages to locally popular gods or goddesses. *Panchalika* is a genre of Bengali narrative folk song.

73. Roy, *Islamic Syncretistic Tradition in Bengal,* 89–91, 94–5. In Khan's *Maqtal* the story of Muhammad's birth and prophethood and his struggle against his Meccan enemies are depicted as a struggle against Hindu opponents.

74. See Varadarajan, *History of Tamil Literature.* The literature that emerged beginning in the 1930s from the Tani Tamizh Iyakkam movement in Tamil Nadu continued this trend of cultural critique: it provided a forum for Tamil women both to decry the imposition of Hindi and colonialism and to challenge traditional patriarchal structures and mores within their own community. For more information see Ramaswamy, "Tamil Separatism and Cultural Negotiations."

75. Ramakrishna, "Women's Journals in Andhra."

76. Mir, "Alternative Imaginings."

77. For a good overview of the different kinds of mass-print popular texts in Urdu, see Pritchett, *Marvelous Encounters.* In the context of Islamic ethical and religious literature in the Sufi milieu, see Sanyal, *Devotional Islam;* Buehler, *Sufi Heirs of the Prophet;* and comments in Schimmel, *Classical Urdu Literature,* 127–28, and Ahmad, *Wahhabi Movement in India,* 84.

78. This dichotomy is pointed out by Minault in *Secluded Scholars,* 6, and Metcalf, *Perfecting Women,* 1–2. Metcalf sees this as a transformation in attitudes, beginning in the twentieth century, toward women as preservers of tradition, in which the education of women in "mainstream Islamic teachings" was a prominent consequence.

79. Minault, *Secluded Scholars,* 172–73.

80. This was especially true of the Deobandi scholar-*shaikh* Maulana Ashraf 'Ali Thanawi.

81. This position was shared by Deobandis such as Thanawi and Barelwis such as Ahmad Riza Khan.

82. This was the position held by Ahmad Riza Khan Barelwi.

83. It is unlikely that the vast majority of these early reformers would have seen their goals as solidifying the Muslim community. Thanks are due to Barbara Metcalf for pointing this out to me.

84. Zaman, *The 'Ulama in Contemporary Islam,* chap. 1.

85. Mrs. Meer Hasan 'Ali's *Observations on the Mussulmauns of India* and Garcin de Tassy's *Mémoire sur des particularités de la religion musulmane dans l'Inde, d'après les ouvrages hindoustani* were republished under similar circumstances, under the auspices of the East India Company.

86. Gerhard Andreas Herklots, introduction to Sharif, *Islam in India,* xii.

87. Erskine, *Imperial Gazetteer of India,* 489. Anand Yang points out the appeal of popular pilgrimage festivals across religious, community, and sectarian lines. See

his *Bazaar India,* 155–60. For a discussion of the more popular fairs held in Bihar, see his chapter 3, "The Religious Places of Exchange," 112–60.

88. De Tassy, *Muslim Festivals in India and Other Essays,* 71.

89. Ibid., 82.

90. Subhan, *Sufism, Its Saints and Shrines,* 331.

91. Reverend Jones was principal of the Henry Martyn School, who along with his wife, Violet Rhoda, wrote a book on Muslim women in India intended for the education of young women missionaries from the West.

92. Subhan, *Sufism, Its Saints and Shrines,* 330–31.

93. O'Malley, *Bihar and Orissa District Gazetteers,* 67.

94. One such shrine is that of Shah Sultan in Muzaffargarh district. See David Gilmartin, *Empire and Islam,* 42n4.

95. Sharif, *Qanun-i Islam,* 139. Cf. descriptions of this ceremony in Titus, *Indian Islam,* 141, and Jones and Jones, *Woman in Islam,* 328. Jones and Jones also describe a ceremony in which women are possessed by the spirit of Bibi Fatima, the Prophet Muhammad's daughter, or the ninth-century saint of Basra, Rabi'a al-'Adawiyya, and in such a state perform similar functions as described in the *baithak* ritual above. *Woman in Islam,* 329.

96. Meaning shrines popularly considered Sufi, the identity of whose saints as such remains in dispute.

97. For information on *mujra* at the Loh Langar shrine in Mangalore, see Sharif, *Qanun-i Islam,* 145. For information on *mujra* at the Mu'in ud-din shrine, see Sarda, *Ajmer,* 102. For a general description of *mujra* see Jones and Jones, *Woman in Islam,* 325.

98. Jones and Jones, *Woman in Islam,* 314–15.

99. Jackson, *Journal of Francis Buchanan,* 182, cf.n.11.

100. Lina M. Fruzzetti suggests that within the context of saint cults, women who perform elaborate rituals to supplicate *pirs* are generally accorded a lower ritual status than men who perform such rituals in an exclusively male setting. More important, she implies that women are considered to have a lower ritual status when their activities are perceived as "un-Islamic" or as not having enough of an Islamic veneer. My studies of the performance of vows in the shrine setting also suggest that the use of Islamic "markers of authenticity" are an important consideration for the credibility of those who serve as "ritual specialists" performing services on behalf of clients. See Fruzzetti, "Ritual Status of Muslim Women in Rural India," 194, 200–201.

101. Jones and Jones, *Woman in Islam,* 309.

102. Robinson, *Islam and Muslim History,* 75–76.

103. Buehler, "Currents," 309.

104. Gilmartin, *Empire and Islam,* 59.

105. Salvatore, *Islam and the Political Discourse,* 47.

106. Metcalf and Metcalf, *Concise History of India,* 63.

### Chapter 2. *Piri-Muridi*

1. In literary examples as well as everyday parlance, the terms *pir* and *shaikh* are used synonymously.

2. There is a large amount of literature on the spiritual stations that may be attained by the adept. The order of these stations varies considerably, but they all suggest a similar trajectory of ascent through ever-more egoless levels of being, the summit being total absorption in God.

3. Ahmed, *Bengal Muslims 1871–1906;* Roy, *Islamic Syncretistic Tradition in Bengal;* Eaton, "Political and Religious Authority," and *Sufis of Bijapur;* Champion, "Wali Perempuan di India Bibi Kamalo di Kako"; Stewart, "Satya Pir"; Flueckiger, *In Amma's Healing Room;* Ansari, *Sufi Saints and State Power;* Ewing, *Arguing Sainthood;* de Munck, "Sufi, Reformist, and National Models of Identity"; Gardner, "Global Migrants and Local Shrines"; Assayag, *Au confluent de deux rivières;* Gaborieau, "Cult of Saints among the Muslims"; and Werbner, *Pilgrims of Love.* There have also been studies of women *pir*s in North Africa and the Middle East by scholars such as Pamela Ryden Johnson, Valerie Hoffman, Ruth Roded, Annemarie Schimmel, Julia Clancy-Smith, and Fatima Mernissi.

4. Here I refer to those texts that were particularly important for the Chishti and Firdausi Sufis from the fourteenth century. Aside from those texts written by (or in the name of) the principal *shaikh*s of the orders, these include al-Ghazali's *Ihya' 'ulum al-din,* al-Hujwiri's *Kashf al-Mahjub,* 'Abu Hafs 'Umar al-Suhrawardi's *A'warif al-Ma'arif,* al-Makki's *Qut al-Qulub,* and al-Qushayri's *Risala.* These and a number of others are identified as popular books read by Indian Sufis in the fourteenth-century historian Barani's *Tarikh-i Firuz Shahi,* and most of these texts continue to be cited in works written by Sufis in India today.

5. Again Shari'a should be understood in its broader ethicomoral connotations, not the narrow legal sense of *fiqh.* Some of these texts do specify that the adept should adhere to the law (this was particularly true in the case of Sharaf al-din Maneri's letters and discourses), but in most cases the meaning of Shari'a is articulated in much broader terms.

6. See Schimmel, *Islam in the Indian Subcontinent,* esp. chap. 1, and Digby, "Sufi Shaikh as a Source of Authority in Mediaeval India."

7. Katz makes a similar observation, focusing on Sufi hagiography, in *Dreams, Sufism, and Sainthood,* xv.

8. Some of these lexicons are the *Ihya' 'ulum al-din* by Abu Hamid al-Ghazali (d. 1111), the *Maktubat-i sadi* by Sharaf al-din Maneri (d. 1381), and the *Kashf al-mahjub* by Shaikh 'Ali al-Hujwiri (d. 1074). More generally they may be found in the letters and recorded discourses of prominent Sufi *shaikh*s within each order.

9. This second model was elaborated by Pir Shamim al-din Munammi of Mitan Ghat *dargah* in Patna. A Naqshbandi Sufi, he is related through marriage to the Firdausi Sufis of Bihar Sharif.

10. See, for instance, Trimingham, *Sufi Orders in Islam,* 166–68, 174, 177, and the work of Orientalist scholars of Sufism from early 1900s until the late 1960s, such as R. A. Nicholson and R. C. Zaehner.

11. Nizami, *Life and Times of Shaikh Nizamuddin Aulia,* 54. The quote is from the *Siyar al-Auliya,* by Mir Khvurd (d. 1328).

12. The diffusion of Sufism into all levels of society is characterized as a "degenerative" period in the works of such scholars of Sufism as A. J. Arberry, Ignaz

Goldziher, R. A. Nicholson, and J. S. Trimingham, among others. Ernst and Lawrence address the persistence of such views throughout the history of Sufism in *Sufi Martyrs of Love*, 12–13. The famous quote by the tenth-century Sufi 'Ali ibn Ahmad Bushanji about Sufism being a "name without a reality" underscores the persistence of this trope through time.

13. Mujeeb, *Indian Muslims*, 126–27. The quote is from the *Siyar al-Auliya*.

14. In Maneri, *Khwan-i pur ni'mat*, 77, Twentieth Assembly. See also Askari, "Maktubat of a Sufi of Firdausi Order of Bihar," 610.

15. As chapter 1 suggests, this trend continued into the colonial period, as British authorities provided land grants and other subsidies to families who could produce documentation demonstrating their connection with a shrine. Although this was not the trend in all parts of the Subcontinent, it was true in the Panjab, United Provinces, the Northwestern Provinces, and, in some respects, Bengal.

16. Eaton, *Rise of Islam and the Bengal Frontier*, 238. See also Ahmed, *Bengal Muslims 1871–1906*, 15–19, 25.

17. For a discussion of the varied and ambivalent meanings of the word *pir* in the Bengal context, see Roy, *Islamic Syncretistic Tradition in Bengal*, 50–51.

18. Ibid., 44–46.

19. Eaton, *Rise of Islam and the Bengal Frontier*, 232–34, 236, 238, 249, 256. See also his earlier work, *Sufis of Bijapur*, chap. 8.

20. It must be noted that since at least the eighth century, the terms used to signify a spiritual guide were rather fluid, and even where they were associated with Sufism in some circles (as in the term *wali* Allah), they also had broader meanings of pious behavior or that did not necessarily signal acceptance of Sufi beliefs or worldviews. For a more comprehensive discussion of this topic, see Cornell, *Realm of the Saint*, 5–9.

21. See Cornell, *Realm of the Saint*, 162, 190, 257; other useful sources that discuss this role of *pir*s in Morocco include Westermarck, *Ritual and Belief in Morocco;* Dermengham, *Culte des saints dans l'Islam maghrébin;* Geertz, *Islam Observed;* and Eickelman, *Moroccan Islam*.

22. On the conflict between the French colonial authorities and Sufis in then Maghreb, see Julia Clancy-Smith, "Saints, Mahdis, and Arms," and *Rebel and Saint*, esp. chap. 7.

23. Hiskett, *Development of Islam in West Africa*, 244–56.

24. Mack and Boyd, *One Woman's Jihad*, 16.

25. For details about Raushan Ara, her devotees, and political patronage of her shrine, see Dey, *Sufism in India*, 8–10.

26. Roded, *Women in Islamic Biographical Collections*, 106.

27. Firdausi, *Mirat al-kaunain*, 235–36.

28. See Maneri, *Khwan-i pur ni'mat*, 144, Fortieth Assembly, and Diwarkar, *Bihar through the Ages*, 443.

29. Dihlavi, *Akhbar al-akhyar;* see the appendix on female saints.

30. Ernst and Lawrence, *Sufi Martyrs of Love*, 130.

31. See Pemberton, "Ritual, Reform, and Economies of Meaning at a South Asian Sufi Shrine," 175–77.

32. Robert Rozehnal, *Islamic Sufism Unbound,* 95.

33. Ibid., 41–42.

34. In the Qur'an sura 2:30, *khalifa* is used for Adam and may connote his status either as representative of the angels who lived on Earth prior to his existence or as the representative of God. It is also used of the prophet-king David in Sura 38:26, apparently in reference to his capacity as representative of God's rule on Earth. The first caliph, Abu Bakr, apparently did not assume the term, but for his successor, 'Umar, it was used to connote the caliph's assumption of the activities and authority of the Prophet Muhammad, not including his prophetic role. Under the 'Abbasids the term acquired the added meaning of protector of the religion of Islam and patron of the *'ulama.* Later the scholars al-Mawardi (974–1058), in his *al-Ahkam al-Sultaniyya,* and Ibn Khaldun (1332–1406), in his *Muqaddima,* chaps. 25–28, elaborated the prevalent doctrines of their eras concerning the character and role of the political *khalifa.*

35. See the translation of Nizam al-din Auliya's discourses, as recorded by his disciple Amir Hasan Sijzi, in Lawrence, *Nizam ad-din Awliya,* 15, 29, 30. See also Mir Khwurd, *Siyar al-Auliya,* 288.

36. See Currie, *Shrine and Cult of Mu'in al-Din,* 22–24.

37. Ibid., 84. The *Dalil al-'arifin,* attributed to Qutb al-din Bakhtiyar Khaki, is purported to be the discourses of Khwaja Mu'in al-din Chishti. The *Siyar al-aqtab* is the first full treatment of the legend of the saint, according to Currie. *Bazm-i Sufiya* (1971), by 'Abdurrahman Sabah al-din, is a biography of Indian Sufis.

38. Jones and Jones, *Woman in Islam,* 309n7; Subhan, *Sufism, Its Saints and Shrines,* 206.

39. Askari, "Hazrat Abdul Quddus Gangohi," 16.

40. Umar, *Islam in Northern India,* 80, 83; Bowen, *Muslims through Discourse,* 7.

41. Mauss, "Techniques of the Body," 458; Bourdieu, *Outline of a Theory of Practice,* 74.

42. See Hirschkind, *Ethical Soundscape,* esp. the introduction and page 101.

43. These ideas may be found in Ibn Sina's *Kitab al-Mahda wa'l Ma'ad* (Book on the Origin and the Return), and *Kitab al-Najat,* al-Farabi's *Kitab al-Huruf,* and al-Kindi's *Fi Hudud al-ashya' wa-rusumiha.*

44. Personal interview with Naila Firdausi (first paragraph) and the wife of 'Ali Imam (second paragraph), elder sister of Naila Firdausi, Sultanganj, Patna City, April 10, 1998. My translation.

45. An excellent study of this is Peirce's *Imperial Harem.*

46. Strictly speaking, *pirzade* means "born of a *pir,*" but here I use the term in a wider sense to refer to the closest relatives—mothers, sisters, aunts, uncles, cousins, nieces, and nephews—of a *pir.* These relatives often make up the extended family unit that resides within, or close by, the *pir*'s residence.

47. Beginning in the late 1940s, a series of land reforms, among which were the Bihar State Acquisition of Zamindaris Bill of 1947 and its successor, the 1950 Bihar Land Reforms Act, provided for the takeover of large, hereditary estates by the government. See Diwarkar, *Bihar through the Ages,* 790–91.

48. Ashraf, *Muslim Elite,* 64, and Diwarkar, *Bihar through the Ages,* 452.

49. Jackson, "Perceptions of the Dargahs of Patna," 99.

50. The term *Uwaysi* refers to a Muslim mystic who receives spiritual blessing and instruction from the spirit of a deceased saint, although there are also scattered historical references to an Uwaysi order. It originated with the name of a contemporary of the Prophet Muhammad, Uways, who is supposed to have communicated with the Prophet psychically. Although the Uwaysi tradition tends to be either marginalized or incorporated into the framework of one of the Sufi *silsilas,* it is nevertheless recognized by most of the orders as an authentic tradition. For more information on the Uwaysis, see Baldick, *Imaginary Muslims.* The book also contains a section on female Sufis.

51. Notably the social status and moral authority of the *pir*s and *pirzade* of both lineages surveyed here are partly predicated on widespread perceptions of them as *both* social and spiritual elites who are bound to uphold impeccable behavioral standards (they are *sayyids,* or members of the highest social class for Muslims) and to adhere to a code of spiritual ethics in which service to the surrounding community—especially its poor and dispossessed members—is of great importance. The characterization of "true" Sufis as ones who are concerned with the welfare of the poor and unfortunate, and who make it their duty to serve them, is one I encountered almost universally during my initial excursions to shrines across North and Central India in the summer of 1996.

52. Besides these properties the Gudri Shahs also own a shrine complex in Mehrauli, just outside of Delhi, and a village in Moradabad, U.P.

53. For a description of its activities and mission of promoting communal harmony and social uplift, see the school's Web site, http://www.Sufisaintschool.org.

54. Nawab is a title that came to be used broadly to refer to Muslim nobles. Originally it referred to a provincial governor or viceroy of a region in the Mughal Empire.

55. Forged or false claims to Sayyid or *shaikh* status, however, are not uncommon. The closing chapters of Tehmina Durrani's 1998 novel, *Blasphemy,* demonstrate how the importance in Pakistan of Sayyid lineage for Sufi *pir*s has led some to forge ancestral claims.

56. For instance the hereditary properties of the landholding classes, of which Sayyids formed a large part, have been greatly reduced in India since Partition, while the same was not true in Pakistan.

57. In hagiographical accounts both Mu'in ud-din Chishti and Sharaf al-din Maneri are described as belonging to the Sayyid classes. In fact the first lines of the section on Sharaf al-din in the biography *Mirat al-kaunain* emphasize the saint's descent from the Prophet Muhammad's own tribe, the Quraish. See Firdausi, *Mirat al-kaunain,* 350.

58. Saints are believed to possess, wield, and leave behind *barakat* after their deaths. While *bij* implies person-to-person transmission, *barakat* is a force that may be manipulated by others through contact with the people or inanimate objects in which it resides.

59. The importance of a chain of spiritual succession linking the *pir*s in an order to the Prophet Muhammad should not be understated. Most Sufi *silsila*s in existence today document, or claim to have, such a link. Consanguineous links to the Prophet tend to be less important, while such links between outgoing and incoming *pir*s seem to be more important in the eyes of most of those interviewed for this study. By some accounts the failure of a *pir* to name his successor does not prevent the transmission of *bij* to his offspring, and thus the leadership of an order may be assured (though it may be hotly disputed among its members, causing orders to splinter into two or more groups). Often the recipient is a son or other close male relative, although stories of transmission to the daughter of a *pir* are not unknown. It is not uncommon for a *pir* to name a nonrelative as his successor, particularly in cases of childlessness (or incompetence of the son), but among the majority of the Sufis I have interviewed in North and Central India and the Panjab in Pakistan, it is widely considered more appropriate that succession pass to the son of a *pir*.

60. See Maneri, *Maktubat-i sadi*, 289–93.

61. However, *taqlid-i shaikh*, or "imitation" of the *shaikh*, has been criticized by many Sufi masters. See, for instance, Chittick, *Sufi Path of Love*, 125–28. This does not apply to the Prophet Muhammad's example, however, which should be followed closely. In fact Sharaf al-din Maneri, among many of his contemporaries and successors, underscored the imitation of the Prophet Muhammad's example as being key to the spiritual perfection of Sufi masters. See his *Khwan-i pur ni'mat*, 8.

62. These states are temporary and do not necessarily represent advancement along the Sufi path. On the other hand, they can help the disciple cultivate the proper receptive spiritual disposition for a traveler along the path to God. They are said to "descend" upon the disciple from the unseen world.

63. In the case of the Gudri Shah *pir-ma*, this is demonstrated by her visitation of shrines, along with her father, at a young age; her knowledge of the writings and teachings of eminent Sufi masters—in part through her own initiative and in part through interactions with her father and husband; and her practices of Qur'an reading, nonobligatory prayers, and various forms of mystical contemplation of God and the unseen, which she presumably learned from her parents.

64. These ideas are explored in greater detail in chapter 3.

65. Smith, "Experience of Muslim Women," 90. See also Hegland, "Political Roles of Aliabad Women." In this essay Hegland argues that the association of female with the private realm and male with the public is an ideology that has enabled men to control and manipulate women's political activities.

66. See Shems Friedlander, "The Coat."

67. Sikand, "Changing Nature of Religious Authority."

68. The *pir-ma*'s role in the selection of the next *pir* and *pir-ma* should not be underestimated; in the Firdausi order at least, she can exercise considerable influence over her husband in both choices.

69. The blood associated with menstruation and childbirth is considered to make women particularly vulnerable to the influence of harmful forces.

70. Ewing, *Shari'at and Ambiguity*, 2.

71. Hawley, *Saints and Virtues*, xiv.

72. Ansari, *Hazrat Maulana Shahbaz*, 17. Musammat Bibi Nusrat Marhuma is also mentioned in *Tazkira-yi sadiqa*, according to Ansari. Bhagalpur is a town located east of Patna, near the confluence of the Ganga and the Badua rivers.

73. Personal interview with *pirzada* Shamim al-din Munammi, Mitan Ghat *dargah*, Patna, February 19, 1998.

74. See Flueckiger, *In Amma's Healing Room*, 5, 138–39, 151.

75. Personal interview with *khadim* Manzar ul-Haque, *dargah* of Sharaf al-din Maneri at Bihar Sharif, May 10, 1998. My translation.

76. Sharib, *Culture of the Sufis*, 37, and Mujeeb, *Indian Muslims*, 138.

77. Personal interview with *pirzada* Shamim al-din munammi, Mitan Ghat *dargah*, Patna, April 19, 1998. My translation.

78. For contemporary examples see Ewing's *Arguing Sainthood*, esp. her description of the female *majzub* Bava Sahib in chap. 7; Basu, "Hierarchy and Emotion," 18, 120–22, 133–34; and the story of Sufi Baba in Mehta, *Work, Ritual, Biography*, chap. 7.

79. Personal interview with *khadim* Manzar ul-Haque, *dargah* of Sharaf al-din Maneri at Bihar Sharif, April 17, 1998. My translation.

80. Pugh, "Divination and Ideology," 293–94.

81. Flueckiger, "Vision Was of Written Words," 264.

82. In fact they say that they "soak in the colors of all the *silsilas*." They carry the name Qadiri. Since the death of Amma's husband in 1998, the name Chishti has been included in the inscription on his mausoleum. Joyce Flueckiger, e-mail to the author, March 9, 2000. These affiliations have been noted in Flueckiger's book, published after this correspondence.

83. Flueckiger, "In Anna's Healing Room, 11–13.

84. Flueckiger, "Vision Was of Written Words," 275.

85. This book by Hakim Azhar Dihlavi may be readily purchased at a number of the *bazars* attached to Sufi *dargah*s.

86. Personal interview with Shakila Khatoon Begum in Ajmer, Rajasthan, Sharib House (Gudri Shah *khanaqah*), March 11, 1998. It should be noted that such books were not the *basis* for Amma's learning but rather supplemented her already formidable understanding of the mechanisms and psychology of healing in the Sufi context. The reactions of my interviewees to Amma's work evoked essentially the same negative reactions that Flueckiger recorded from Muslims who were told about Amma's healing practice.

87. Flueckiger, *In Amma's Healing Room*, 12–13.

## Chapter 3. Singing and Reciting

1. Personal interview with Shamim al-din Munammi, Naqshbandi *pirzada* Mitan Ghat *dargah*, Patna City, Bihar, February 19, 1998. My translation.

2. From *Journey towards the Friend*, January 1998, pt. 3 (a newsletter published by the Society of Mystics under the auspices of the Gudri Shahi Sufi order of Ajmer).

3. In 1997, the year of my attendance, this date fell on November 10.

4. Actually many of the members of the inner circle of *murid*s are the disciples of the *pir*'s father, Zahur al-Hasan Sharib, who died in the late spring of 1996.

5. 'Usman Haruni was the spiritual guide of Mu'in al-din Chishti.

6. For a discussion of this process, see Qureshi, *Sufi Music of India and Pakistan,* 127, 138.

7. For a discussion of the role of the *zakira* in Shi'i Islam today, see D'Souza, "Gendered Ritual and the Shaping of Shi'i Identity."

8. Abbas, *Female Voice in Sufi Ritual,* 35.

9. See the work of Helene Basu, especially "Hierarchy and Emotion," 130, 133 and "Music and the Formation of Sidi Identity," 164, 171, 172, 174.

10. *Qawwali* originated in Persia in the ninth century, but *qawwali* in the form that we know it today can be traced to the fourteenth century, and in particular to Amir Khusrau, the disciple of the Chishti *shaikh* Nizam al-din Auliya, who fused Persian and indigenous South Asian musical forms. The *mahfil-i sama'* in Indo-Pakistan today, then, primarily refers to *qawwali* performance and connotes, further, the devotional setting as opposed to the purely commercial venue.

11. Although India, Pakistan, and Bangladesh have yet to produce female Qur'an reciters that have become as globally renowned as women reciters from Egypt, Malaysia, and Indonesia, the popularity of such vocalists as Umm-e Habiba (known for her a cappella renditions of *na't* and *hamd*) among pious Muslims suggests that female reciters of the Qur'an are well-received in the Subcontinent. For more information see Gade, *Perfection Makes Practice,* 1, 303; Rasmussen, "Qur'an in Indonesian Daily Life"; and Nelson, *Art of Reciting the Qur'an,* 202.

12. See D'Souza, "Gendered Ritual and the Shaping of Shi'ah Identity," 197, 202–4

13. Schimmel, *Islam in the Indian Subcontinent,* 24n124.

14. See Post, "Professional Women in Indian Music," 98–99.

15. Ibid., 98. Moti Chandra notes the term *veshya* as the (Hindi) name of a quarter where prostitutes lived. Chandra gives other names for the different kinds of prostitutes: *sadharanastri* (strumpet), *varamukhya* (chief courtesan), *kuttani* (bawd), *shambhali* (prostitute), *panapanyangana* (a woman who could be enjoyed for a *pana*). The officer in charge of the women was known as *veshyacharya*. For more information on these types of women, see Chandra, *World of Courtesans.* For a detailed, fictionalized treatment of a real courtesan's life and trade, see the famous novel by Mirza Mohammad Hadi Ruswa, *Umrao Jan Ada* (Delhi: Orient Paperbacks, 2005), originally published as *Umrao Jan Ada* (Lucknow: Munshi Gulab Singh and Sanz Press, 1889).

16. See Newman, *Life of Music in North India,* 100. There are different classes of courtesans, as Newman describes, some of whom are vocalists and others of whom specialize in instrumental music alone. Newman also maintains that even today, when an increasing number of female vocalists are not courtesans, some of the more prominent ones still are. His description also contains many pertinent details about the social hierarchies within courtesan communities and how they were regarded within broader circles of musicians.

17. Thanawi and others also identify other kinds of female singer-dancers who perform at weddings: *randi* (prostitutes, who Thanawi says performed for men) and *domni* and *mirasin* (both described as "vagabond singers" performing in the women's quarters), none of whom enjoy the same social status and prestige as did *tawa'ifs*. See Metcalf, *Perfecting Women,* 93.

18. Qureshi, "Islamic Music," 46. It is interesting to note that many of the women who sing in devotional assemblies seem to be of socially "marginalized" groups. Qureshi maintains that it is seen as socially acceptable for amateurs from "respectable" families to perform in the *majlis* setting, since it is a devotional setting. I agree with her observation, but not with her reasoning. Writing in the early nineteenth century, Mrs. Meer Hasan 'Ali described the women who recited the *majlis* in all-women gatherings in Lucknow thus: "These educated females are chiefly daughters of poor Syaads, who have not been married for the lack of a dowry; they live devoutly in the service of God, according to their faith. They are sometimes required, in the families of the nobility, to teach the Khoraun to the young ladies, and, in that capacity, they are called Oustaardie (Ustadji), or more familiarly Artoojee" (*Observations on the Mussulmauns of India,* 29).

19. Sharar, *Lucknow,* 269.

20. Prajnanananda, *Historical Study of Indian Music,* 217.

21. The fact that courtesans were largely responsible for preserving classical Indian music traditions in the late nineteenth and early twentieth centuries, and that many of the early *ghazal* superstars, such as Begum Akhtar, came from courtesan backgrounds, also serves to strengthen the associations between courtesans and singing for all-male or mixed-gender audiences in the minds of many people.

22. *Mujra* sometimes refers to when the singer squats on the floor or ground while singing. Veena Talwar Oldenburg describes *mujra* as *nach,* or dancing and singing performances, especially those performed in the salons of the upper classes and other classes of means. See Oldenburg, *Making of Colonial Lucknow,* 134–37.

23. Sarda, *Ajmer,* 102. It is unclear as to the exact period when these kinds of performances were taking place, and Sarda does not provide any relevant details. Generally speaking, though, British- and English-educated Indian elites' attitudes toward many aspects of popular culture helped to undermine such things as *nach* performances. This argument is put forward in Banerjee, *Parlour and the Streets.* See Oldenburg, *Making of Colonial Lucknow,* 134–42, 200–202, and Newman, *Life of Music in North India,* chapter 4, for more detailed discussions of the courtesan classes and their decline.

24. Sharif, *Qanun-i Islam,* 145.

25. Subhan, *Sufism, Its Saints and Shrines,* 115–16.

26. Details about the lives and spiritual careers of the Gudri Shah *pir*s are found in the order's newsletter, *Journey towards the Friend,* printed by the Society of Mystics in Ajmer. See especially the January 1998 (pt. 3) and July 1998 (pt. 4) issues. See also the "Gudri Shah Sufi Order" online at http://www.sufiajmer.org (accessed June 29, 2010).

27. Qureshi notes that many *tawa'ifs* have turned to religious singing nowadays because of changing times and circumstances that have virtually eliminated their role in former contexts. "Islamic Music," 46.

28. This is a common circumstance for courtesans today. Their withdrawal from the arts traditionally associated with their profession has also been hastened by the emergence of female musicians from nonhereditary families, who have come to be increasingly accepted by Indian society. Many courtesans have disappeared from public view for a number of reasons, among which Post identifies loss of patronage, increasing age, awareness of their low social position, and a diminished demand for their music. See "Professional Women in Indian Music," 106. As for Munni Bai, she is likely deceased since the family lost contact with her in the late 1990s.

29. Sharib House, where the Gudri Shah *khanaqah* is located, is a large dwelling that can accommodate an extended family household. The first level contains, among other things, a dwelling that is rented by individuals or families from time to time. *Murid*s and other guests of the *khanaqah,* however, are given free lodging and food.

30. Sayyids are considered the highest social order among Muslims. They are descended from the Prophet Muhammad's family.

31. Qureshi talks about the expression of social and spiritual hierarchies in the *mahfil-i sama‘* setting. She also highlights the placement of the body—seating arrangements, expression of spiritual ecstasy, movements or lack of during the assembly—as an indicator of social and spiritual differences among participants. See *Sufi Music of India and Pakistan,* 103–31.

32. This word is used to indicate that they are highly spiritually advanced individuals.

33. Personal interview with Apa, mother, and Meher Nur, sister, of the *pir,* Gudri Shah Baba V, Inam Hasan, Sharib House (Gudri Shah *khanaqah*), Ajmer, March 11, 1998. My translation.

34. Ibid. The Gudri Shah *pirzade* women do not attend these events. In my first few years of knowing the Gudri Shah women, I was regularly teased by the *pir's* sisters for wanting to attend *sama‘* assemblies with men (as was the youngest sister of the *pir,* who attended with me and other women so that we would not be alone). The teasing was all in good-natured fun, and I was never discouraged from attending.

35. The *milad* (a general term for commemorative celebrations) can be observed on many different festive occasions, such as a birth, marriage, and Ramzan, or even on particular days of the weeks, such as Fridays. For a fuller explanation, see Schimmel, *Islam in the Indian Subcontinent,* 124–25. At times I would visit the *parda*-observing (*parda-nishin*) ladies of the Firdausi *khanaqah* in Bihar Sharif, and they would recite *na‘t, hamd,* and *salam* poetry for me while I taped their performances (with the understanding that they would not be played in front of unrelated men). The Shah Sahib referred to these impromptu assemblies as *milad.*

36. The birth of *qawwali* in the Indian Subcontinent is traditionally attributed to Amir Khusrau, the fourteenth-century courtier and disciple of Nizam ud-din Auliya. Sufiana *kalam* (the sayings of the Sufis), said to have originated in Iran in the fifteenth century, was first popularized in Kashmir. While *qawwali* music is typically

sung in ensemble format, Sufiana *kalam* features a solo performance, usually in the vernacular, while *qawwali* makes use of Persian, Urdu, and vernacular forms. Women are more likely to perform Sufiana *kalam,* which is considered a folk form. For more details on these two performance genres, see Abbas, *Female Voice in Sufi Ritual,* 54–55.

37. One interesting headline in Delhi's *Asian Age* (April 19, 1997) describes her as the "Pakistani Sufi Queen."

38. Strangely none of those I spoke with could name any famous female *qawwali* singers in India, although they knew the names of a few Pakistani singers. Except for Munni Bai, the other singers in the *mahfil-i rindan*—Jori Firdausi Tabassum of Jaipur, Kaunsar Parvin of Baroda, Salma Tabassum of Nagpur, Jaba Qawwal of Mumbai, and the duo Rumbina-Shabina of Mumbai—are all reputed to be well-known *qawwals,* as well as *murids* who perform for both commercial and devotional venues, according to the article that appeared in the Ajmer newspaper *Dainik Navjyoti* on November 11, 1997, and according to In'am Hasan, the current *pir* of the Gudri Shah order. An article in the *Indian Express* (New Delhi) that appeared on February 2, 1995, states that female *qawwali* singers are a recent phenomenon given impetus by the *qawwals* of Mumbai. I believe that there have been others throughout history, although references to them in the available textual sources are sparse.

39. For information about these singers, refer to the following articles: Vaish, "Resonant Strain from the Past"; Khan, "Rediscovering the Qawwali Tradition"; Parwar, "Qawwali 's Reigning Begum"; Kumar, "Shastriya sangeet hamari sanson sa juda he"; and Sharma, "Songs of the Sufis."

40. When we met, it was the father of this *pir* who was the head of the order, based in Mitan Ghat *dargah* in Patna City, the old quarter of Patna, in Bihar.

41. There is a marked disdain for giving cash payments for religious services within the Sufi circles to which I had access. In the *mahfil* setting, the *pir*'s act of "blessing" the *nazrana* that is given to *qawwali* performers is seen as transforming the negative taint associated with the cash transaction into a positive act of charity and devotion. Qureshi explains this process more thoroughly in her *Sufi Music of India and Pakistan,* 127, 138. See also (for a different context) Pinto, *Piri-Muridi Relationship,* 154–55.

42. All the Sufis I spoke with shared the opinion that in many cases, *muridi,* or allegiance to a *pir* and a Sufi order, was no more than a "social setup" that merely involved performing certain rituals without any real knowledge of the meanings and purposes behind the acts, and attending select festivals, particularly the *'urs.* Interestingly Qureshi views the performers in the *sama'* setting as merely a category of service professionals. Even if they are disciples of a *pir,* they are not, according to her, considered Sufis or devotees. I do not entirely agree with this opinion, as it seems to have been the response of her subjects and not reflective of a wider range of opinions. Further, in light of the difficulty of naming just who is and is not a Sufi (a difficulty acknowledged by most Sufis I interviewed), I am reluctant to see Qureshi's statement regarding performers in the *sama'* setting as indicative of a general order. See Qureshi, "Sufi Practice in the Indian Context," 143.

43. See Rozehnal, "'Proving Ground' for Spiritual Mastery," 657, 661. For an alternative perspective on "professional" Sufi singers who also perform in shrine settings, see ul-Huda, "Memory, Performance, and Poetic Peacemaking in Qawwali."

44. My use of the term *sama'* here refers specifically to the act of listening to music or recited poetry and not to the other meanings found in the classical literature of Sufism and outlined in Avery, *Psychology of Early Sufi Sama',* esp. chap. 3.

45. Several Hadis deal specifically with the Prophet Muhammad's equivocal attitude toward women singing. On the battlefield female singers from the Quraysh opposed to the Prophet performed war songs and satirized the nascent Muslim community, using reproaches and invective to demean their enemies. It is perhaps no surprise, then, that most references in early Islamic literature to these kinds of women are negative. However, the Prophet Muhammad came to harness this powerful medium in the cause of Islam, as seen in the example of al-Khansa. She began her career performing at weddings, births, and funerals, but after the death of her beloved brother in battle, she assumed the role of poet on the battlefield to arouse male and female fighters for Islam. According to the transmitters of another Hadis report, the Prophet invited a female singer from a tribe famous for music to come and perform for him and his wife, A'isha. After hearing the woman's song, the Prophet remarked, "Surely Shaitan [Satan] has blown into her nostrils." While those opposed to music interpreted this as a condemnation of the woman's singing, others, such as Hadis scholar Maulana Wahi al-din Nu'mani (in his work *Rafi' al-ghina*), have surmised that the phrase *nafakha al-shaitan* refers to the singer's excellence. Nu'mani argued that although Shaitan may be considered the inventor of the arts, such a reference to Shaitan having inspired the singer does not necessarily convey that singing in itself (or by implication singing by women in mixed company) is unlawful. Elsewhere Hadis report that the Prophet had expressed his disapproval of women's performances, as when he forbade Shirin, the handmaid of Hasan ibn Thabit, to sing. See Choudhury, "Music in Islam," 67, and Nicholson, *Literary History of the Arabs,* ch. 3. For a broader treatment of how early Sufi authors used Prophetic traditions in their arguments for *sama',* see Avery, *Psychology of Early Sufi Sama'.*

46. Al-Hujwiri, *Kashf al-Mahjub,* 418–19.

47. Dihlavi, *Fawa'id al-Fu'ad,* 435, *majlis* 20.

48. Maneri, *Maktubat-i sadi,* 390–91.

49. Ahmad, *Makhdoom Sharaf al-din Ahmad Yahya Maneri,* 318. My translation.

50. Ibid. My translation.

51. Al-Ghazali, *Ihya' 'ulum al-din,* 229.

52. Ibid., 235–36; emphasis added.

53. Ibid., 235.

54. One notable exception was the Persian *shaikh* Abu Sa'id Abi'l Khair (d. 1048), who felt that *sama'* was highly beneficial to beginners. See Lewisohn, "Sacred Music of Islam," 11.

55. Haq, "Sama' and Raqs of the Darwishes," 29.

56. Ahmad, *Makhdoom Sharaf al-din Ahmad Yahya Maneri,* 319.

57. Maneri, *Maktubat-i sadi,* 385.

58. Al-Hujwiri, *Kashf al-Mahjub,* 402–3.

59. Lawrence, *Nizam ad-din Awliya,* 118–19.

60. The best-known work in this area of study is that of Catherine M. Bell, whose *Ritual* provides a number of theoretical and practical discussions of the topic. See also Phelan, "Practice, Ritual and Community Music," and the chapters in part 2 of Pemberton and Nijhawan's *Shared Idioms.*

61. This *mahfil khana* was built in 1888 by the wealthy Hyderabadi noble Sir Asman Jah and is located west of the *dargah's* main entrance gate. Sarda, *Ajmer,* 14. Despite the restrictions and the efficiency of security staff in policing this space, it is very common to see women repeatedly attempting to enter the *mahfil khana* when the guards have their backs turned. Other examples suggest that women are often assertive in expressing their desire to attend these *mahfils,* and the servants of shrines (*khadim log*) are often responsive to these desires. For example in Bihar Sharif, one servant at the *dargah* of Sharaf al-din Maneri told me that women frequently hover around the edges of the *sama'* assembly during the time of the *'urs,* and although he and his fellow servants do not approve of the women's presence, they also do not have the heart to turn them away. And in Maner, the son-in-law of the Firdausi Shah Sahib explained that although they do not condone women's attendance at *sama'* assemblies, arrangements are sometimes made for women to listen from outside of the audition hall.

62. *Hazari dena* means literally to "give one's presence" but connotes, in the case of musical performance, "being present" in one's music. The term bears some similarity to the concept of *seva* (service) in Hindu devotion, especially in the idea of spiritual merit that accrues to the performer as a consequence of the performance. The performance that is called *hazari dena* often takes on particular characteristics that distinguish it form other types of *sama'* performances. It is "dedicated" to the saint and consists of prayers, Qur'anic recitations, and songs of praise (*manqabat*) to the Sufi saint. Most important, it is (ideally) given without expectation or hope of financial reward.

63. Personal interview with Vidya Rao, Indian International Centre, New Delhi, January 10, 1998.

64. Compare Qureshi, *Sufi Music of India and Pakistan,* 104–5. Qureshi notes that in the Nizam al-din Auliya *dargah* in Delhi, special (*khas*) assemblies are held inside chambers located inside the *dargah* complex, such as the private prayer chamber (*hujra*) or seclusion chamber (*chilla*).

## Chapter 4. The Work of Petitioning

1. From interview with Azara Husain (Dadiji) Farhat Arshad (first and third passages) and friend (second passage), Bihar Sharif, February 6, 1998. My translation.

2. To borrow a term used by Susan Star Sered in her book, *Women as Ritual Experts.*

3. On the importance of writing in the Islamic healing context, see Flueckiger, "Vision Was of Written Words," 255–57, and the book that emerged from this study, *In Amma's Healing Room.*

4. I am not certain what she meant here, although I would hazard to guess that she was referring to a particular form of devotional poetry to the Prophet Muhammad.

5. 'Ali is the cousin and son-in-law of the Prophet Muhammad and was the fourth caliph of Islam. Many Sufi orders claim a line of spiritual descent originating with him. Fatima is his wife and the favorite daughter of the Prophet. Hasan and Husain are their sons, each of whom was murdered as a young man. The names of the *panj-i pak* appear on all the amulets I have ever seen in India and Pakistan. Moreover these five names are written on the entryways to all but the smallest and most obscure Sufi shrines I have visited in India.

6. Such imagery is common in Muslim devotional prayers. In 'Abd al-Qadir al-Jilani's *Hizb al-fawatihi 'l-basa'ir,* one prayer reads, "We, Thy destitute, weak and poor servants are standing at the threshold of the courtyards of Thy Majesty" (author's translation). See Padwick, *Muslim Devotions,* 216.

7. She referred to herself as Rafat Nisha. *Nisha* is a vernacular pronunciation of the Arabic *nisa',* which means woman. She always referred to me as Akila, despite my initial efforts to get her to pronounce my name correctly.

8. Sher Shah Suri, the Afghan ruler who dominated the region in the sixteenth century, is buried in an elaborate mausoleum in the town of Sasaram, located in Shahabad district on the Grand Trunk Road, roughly 150 kilometers southwest of Patna. I did not get the opportunity to visit the shrine, which Rafat told me she visited frequently. It would merit further investigation to see whether or not this tomb, like various graves of Sufi saints (of genuine and of questionable identity), other holy men and women, and even British soldiers, has become the object of veneration for local residents.

9. Constance Padwick notes a prayer for Shi'a pilgrims to the tomb of the Imam 'Ali al-Rida at Mashhad that bears some similarities to Rafat's petition. It reads in part:

Let me enter, O God!
Let me enter, O Apostle of God!
Let me enter, O our Lord, Commander of the Faithful.
Let me enter, O our Lady Fatima the Fair, mistress of the women of the
    two worlds.
Let me enter, our lord Hasan, son of 'Ali.
Let me enter, our lord Husain, son of 'Ali.
Let me enter, our lord 'Ali, son of Husain, ornament of worshippers.
Let me enter, our lord Muhammad, son of 'Ali
Let me enter, our lord Ja'far, son of Muhammad
Let me enter, our lord Musa, son of Ja'far.

Let me enter, our lord 'Ali, son of Musa

Let me enter, our lord Muhammad, son of 'Ali

Let me enter, our lord Hasan, son of 'Ali

Let me enter, our lord Hujjat, son of Hasan, lord of the age.

Let me enter, O ye angels on duty, standing, surrounding, guarding this noble and blessed precinct, and the mercy of God and His blessings be upon you.

See Padwick, *Muslim Devotions*, 238–39.

10. Qureshi, *Sufi Music of India and Pakistan*, 86.

11. The left hand is considered unclean.

12. These are to be the names of my two sons. As the week came to a close, Rafat had decided that I should have three children: two boys and a girl. She gave me a third *ta'wiz* for this petition, which I had not in fact asked for, but which she evidently saw fit to add to my requests.

13. This is her approximation of where Sharib House is located.

14. It is unclear why she specified this amount. It possibly has something to do with the practice of giving odd-numbered amounts (in terms of gifts of money or other measurable substances) to the bride and bridegroom, as these are seen as being more auspicious than even-numbered amounts.

15. She would not elaborate, but I assume she meant that she would take them to his shrine to burn or bury them.

16. She simply laughed and brushed off my protest that I was Christian and might encounter some family opposition to giving my children Muslim names.

17. A few people told me that petitions could even be performed in one's home, but this opinion was rare. Most agreed that it was necessary to carry out the ritual in some shrine or sacred place. The reason for this necessity is that such places are imbued with the spiritual power (*barakat*) of the saint(s) buried therein. The presence of servants at the burial shrine of Sharaf al-din Maneri, and their disapproval of this kind of petitioning, in which the women operated autonomously rather than through the medium of the *khadim* or *pir*, seemed to obviate the likelihood of these kinds of rituals being performed wholly at the *dargah* or *khanaqah*. The importance of concluding the ritual by making an offering to Sharaf al-din Maneri at his mausoleum, however, should not be understated.

18. I was struck by the fact that she rarely called upon the name of the Sufi *shaikh* at whose shrine we were performing this ritual. Makhdum Sahib's name, rather, was one of many she included in a litany of appeals to the saints.

19. The importance of reciting Qur'anic passages at the beginning and end of the *mahfil-i sama'*, for similar reasons as I note here, is underscored in Qureshi's *Sufi Music of India and Pakistan*, 115–16.

20. As regards the female petitioners in Bihar Sharif, I interviewed four types of people: the Shah Sahib of Bihar Sharif and his male relatives (the *pirzade* men); the hereditary servants of Sharaf al-din Maneri's mausoleum; prominent local (Muslim) women, mostly from the middle class; and the poor and middle-class women (Hindu and Muslim) who frequent Sharaf al-din's prayer cell (*hujra gah*) and mausoleum.

21. This is also demonstrated in the Chinese bureaucratization of religion, which is much more complex and structured than is devotion to local Sufi saints. See, for instance, Yang, *Religion in Chinese Society*, esp. chaps. 5 and 7. As in the Chinese model, the hierarchy that is demonstrated in ritual and spiritual status differentials within a Sufi order bears some structural similarities (and similarities in nomenclature) to hierarchies of political authority.

22. To paraphrase one *khadim* at the Nizam al-din *dargah* in New Delhi who explained the concept of petitioning a Sufi saint: "If you want to talk to the prime minister, you wouldn't go to him yourself. You would send a message through someone who was close to him. Only then could you be sure that your message would be heard, and that he would respond favorably." Desiderio Pinto also describes this kind of reasoning in his study of *piri-muridi* at the Nizam al-din shrine in Delhi. See his *Piri-Muridi Relationship*, 137.

23. The tension between hierarchical and horizontal sources of authority has been noted cross-culturally, in several studies on cults of saints. See, for instance, Brown, *Cult of Saints*, 123–24.

24. Although the performances of dancing women at major shrines (such as the mausoleum of Mu'in al-din Chishti) have been noted in colonial-era sources, it is apparent that their presence was commissioned by the functionaries attached to the shrines. Unlike "ritual agents" such as Rafat, dancing (*nach*) women do not work independently and without the permission of the shrine's authorities in such places.

25. The *khadim* told me that they generally let women come to the *dargah* and pray as they like, except when they perceive that the women are tapping into the spiritual power (*barakat*) of the saint in order to engage in black magic (*jadu*), for example by bringing jars of water to the shrine to be placed near the saint's grave and thus absorb its *barakat*. Disdain for these kinds of practices is common among many Sufis. When I told the women of the Gudri Shah *pir*'s family in Ajmer about my work with Rafat in Bihar Sharif, they warned me not to associate with such dangerous people. One of the *pirzade* women was familiar enough with the curse Rafat had uttered against her enemies to repeat it verbatim, without my having recited the words for her on any previous occasion.

26. Personal interview with *pirzada* Sayyid Shahab al-din Firdausi, *khanaqah-i mu'azzam*, Bihar Sharif, February 26, 1998. My translation.

27. Personal interview with *khadim* Anwar Iqbal, *dargah* of Sharaf al-din Maneri, Bihar Sharif, February 22, 1998. My translation.

28. Personal interview with *khadim* Manzar ul-Haque, *dargah* of Sharaf al-din Maneri, Bihar Sharif, May 1, 1998. My translation.

29. This seemed to be the general consensus on both the women who frequented the *hujra gah* and those who performed the work of petitioning.

30. Personal interview with *pirzada* Sayyid Shahab al-din Firdausi, *khanaqah-i mu'azzam*, Bihar Sharif, February 26, 1998. My translation.

31. Personal interview with *khadim* Manzar ul-Haque at the *dargah* of Sharaf al-din Maneri, Bihar Sharif, May 2, 1998. My translation.

32. Personal interview with Azara Husain (Dadiji), Farhat Arshad, and friend in Bihar Sharif, February 6, 1998. Quote from Azara Husain. My translation.

33. Personal interview with *pirzada* Sayyid Shahab al-din Firdausi, *khanaqah-i mu'azzam*, Bihar Sharif, February 26, 1998. My translation.

34. Personal interview with *khadim* Manzar ul-Haque at the *dargah* of Sharaf al-din Maneri, Bihar Sharif, April 17, 1998. My translation.

35. Personal interview with *khadim* Manzar ul-Haque at the *dargah* of Sharaf al-din Maneri, Bihar Sharif, May 2, 1998. My translation.

36. These comments were in response to my reference to an earlier conversation we had, on the subject of women being forbidden (according to my interviewee's understanding of Islam) to sing in front of men who were unrelated to them. Personal interview with *khadim* Manzar ul-Haque at the *dargah* of Sharaf al-din Maneri, Bihar Sharif, May 2, 1998. My translation.

37. Personal interview with Azara Husain (Dadiji), Farhat Arshad, and friend, Bihar Sharif, February 6, 1998. Quote from Farhat Arshad. My translation.

38. Ibid. Quotes from Azara Husain. My translation.

39. Although not an exact analogy, June McDaniel's distinctions between spontaneous and ritual ecstasy in the Bengal setting are helpful for the description I have offered above. See McDaniel, *Madness of the Saints,* 17–20.

40. Despite the general truth of this statement, the poor tend to be especially vulnerable to the teachings of reformist groups such as the Tablighi Jama'at and the Jami'at-i Islami Hind, who encourage a "return" to the "pure" teachings of Islam, among which are touted a strict observation of *parda* among women. Such views become especially salient in times of trouble, when sustained social, economic, and/ or political crises in Muslim-majority countries are interpreted by these groups as resulting from the community's neglect of the letter of Islamic rules. John L. Esposito quite thoroughly discusses this mind-set from a political standpoint in his *Islamic Threat,* esp. chap. 1. See also Hermansen, "Religious Literature and the Inscription of Identity."

41. Valerie Hoffman's study of Sufism in Egypt today suggests the same. See *Sufism, Mystics, and Saints,* 28.

42. See, for instance, Madani, *Impact of Hindu Culture,* 86. Imtiaz Ahmad's work on caste among Muslims in India has also investigated these trends.

43. For more information on these Muslim castelike occupational groups, see Madani, *Impact of Hindu Culture,* 86–89; Khan, *John Marshall in India,* 393; Imtiaz Ahmad, *Caste and Social Stratification;* Askari and Ahmad, *Comprehensive History of Bihar,* vol. 2, pt. 2: 378–79; Shadbano Ahmad, "Methodological Problems in the Study of Muslim Women"; Faridi and Siddiqi, *Social Structure of Indian Muslims;* and Schimmel, *Islam in the Indian Subcontinent.*

44. Madani, *Impact of Hindu Culture,* 89–90, 93–96; Ahmad, "Methodological Problems in the Study of Muslim Women"; Askari and Ahmad, *Comprehensive History of Bihar,* vol. 2, pt. 2: 379–80.

45. Madani, *Impact of Hindu Culture,* 90–91. This remains true even today.

46. Faridi and Siddiqi, *Comprehensive History of Bihar,* 2:68.

47. Ewing, "Pir or Sufi Saint in Pakistan," 150.

48. Ibid., 153–55.

49. Desiderio Pinto, *Piri-Muridi Relationship*, 157.

50. Schimmel, *Islam in the Indian Subcontinent*, 19. For a more comprehensive study of the *malang*s and Qalandars today (and popular perceptions of them), see Ewing, "*Malang*s of the Punjab" and *Arguing Sainthood*, 201–52.

51. See Parry, *Death in Banaras*, 227.

52. Interestingly Qureshi notes that it is elderly devotees of low social status who are most likely to engage in ecstatic dancing during the *mahfil-i sama'*, while high-status listeners control their body movements, even when an ecstatic state (*hal*) has descended upon them. See Qureshi, *Sufi Music of India and Pakistan*, 129.

53. See, for instance, McDaniel, *Madness of the Saints*, 8.

54. More often than not, it is young women who are possessed. This was explained to me by several people as a consequence of women's monthly "impurity," that is, menstruation.

55. Pinto, *Piri-Muridi Relationship*, 166.

56. Personal interview with Yasser 'Ali at his house, Patna, March 31, 1998; my translation.

## Conclusion

1. Foucault, *Archaeology of Knowledge*, 66.

2. Ibid. Foucault cogently makes this argument in pt. 2, chap. 6, and pt. 4, chaps. 2–5.

3. Salvatore, *Islam and the Political Discourse*, 48.

4. Gudri Shah Baba III, Nawab Sahib, and Gudri Shah Baba IV, Zahur ul-Miyan.

5. I make this assumption based on the ways in which my subjects referred to the example of past *pir*s of the order as a model for current attitudes and practices. The third and fourth Gudri Shah *pir*s remain very much a living presence for the current members of the order. One needs only to spend a few days with the Gudri Shahs to realize this fact. By contrast the Firdausis never spoke of *pir*s of the recent past (either anecdotally or by way of explanation for current practices and attitudes) in my presence. Rather Sharaf al-din Maneri and his immediate family members were cited by both Maner and Bihar Sharif Firdausis as the preeminent Sufi saints of the order, and as such their examples served as key reference points.

6. That he intended his letters to be instructive for contemporary and future generations is cited by Sharaf al-din in his work, as well as indicated in the introduction to Paul Jackson's translation to the *Maktubat-i sadi*.

7. In marked contrast to the Maner Firdausis, within the all-female assemblies held by the Firdausi women of Bihar Sharif, neither general *milad*s nor the *milad sharif* seem to necessitate the Shah Sahib's presence. The sister of the current Shah Sahib of Bihar Sharif stated emphatically that it was women who made all the arrangements for these assemblies and that women alone were the ones who decided upon the materials to be recited for the event. I have come to believe that the absence of the *pir* in the women's quarters in Bihar Sharif on the occasion of the

Prophet's birthday may be in part explained by the fact that the order does not possess any of the Prophet's relics.

8. Compare the following two characterizations of the *majzub:* Denny, "Prophet and *Wali*," esp. 86, and Jürgen Wasim Frembgen, "*Majzub* Mama Ji Sarkar."

9. The *pirzade* women did not tell me this story until after I had come to know them over a period of years, although they were well aware that I was in search of this kind of research material. In fact the telling of Khala's story struck me as both spontaneous and calculated: spontaneous because it seemed to come out of nowhere as I sat with the women in their bedroom, conversing about a totally different topic, and calculated because it was revealed to me at a point in time when I had begun to express openly frustration at not having been able to get the very type of information they provided. The story of Khala was told in the instance of a single afternoon—I had neither tape recorder nor notebook at the time (perhaps another reason why the women were willing to reveal the information when they did) and had to rely on memory to record what they told me. Afterward I rushed to my room to write down Khala's story. When I later asked for further elaboration, though, the *pirzade* women were extremely reluctant to comply. I did manage to solicit some information from the *shaikh* in order to fill in areas of the story that I was uncertain of having correctly recorded and to get a sense of how he, as the head of the order but also as a man, conceived of this woman. Like his mother and siblings, he presented the figure of Khala as extraordinary, her story an impressive and memorable part of the history of the Gudri Shah order. However, neither Inam Hasan nor the *pirzade* women gave the impression that Khala's example was one to be followed by other women.

10. The notion of ambivalence rather than strategy as a way of looking at the disjunction between dominant and subordinate discourses has been argued in an article on sainthood and "divine madness" as part of family history in Ewing, "*Majzub* and His Mother."

11. Compare Feldman, "(Re)presenting Islam," 35.

12. The idea of the *bazar* may be conceived as a concept or as a physical space. Many of those I interviewed referred more broadly to the *bazar* as any place that is the site of commercial (particularly merchant) activity, whether a single storefront or an open market.

13. Hawley, *Saints and Virtues.* The author makes this connection in his preface, xiv.

14. Ibid., xvi and chap. 4. See also Hawley's chap. 2, "Morality beyond Morality," in *Three Bhakti Voices.*

15. See Ewing, "*Majzub* and His Mother," 161, and Frembgen, "*Majzub* Mama Ji Sarkar," 145.

# . Glossary .

Most of the definitions included here reflect particular uses relevant to the Sufi context. They are not intended to be exhaustive. The spelling of terms is based on Urdu orthography.

*adab:* rules of comportment or etiquette; a greeting; good manners

*ahl-i bait:* "people of the house," or members of the Prophet's family, especially his wives, offspring, and their descendants

*astana:* tomb, grave, or shrine of a holy person

*'itr:* oil-based perfume

*bai'at:* the oath of allegiance made by a prospective disciple to a spiritual guide; the ritual act that establishes a relationship of *piri-muridi*

*barakat:* the spiritual power that *pir*s or other spiritually potent people are said to possess; *dargah*s are believed to be imbued with the *barakat* of the Sufi saints buried within.

*bazari tabib:* "marketplace doctor," a pejorative term for *piri-muridi*

*bismillah:* name of the invocation *bismillah-i r-rahman-i r-rahim* ("in the name of God, the merciful, the compassionate")

*burqa':* a loose-fitting garment worn by women in *parda; burqa'*s worn in India today usually consist of one (in the form of a cloak) or two (a cloak and skirt) long pieces of cloth for covering the body (except for the hands and feet) and one piece for covering the head, face, and breast.

*buzurg; buzurgan-i din:* the ancestors; deceased spiritual masters

*chaiti:* originally seasonal folk music, now more stylized and included in the *dadra* vocal style

*chilla:* a forty-day retreat during which the adept engages in particularly difficult spiritual exercises

*chilla gah:* a place—often a cave that has had a structure erected over it—where a Sufi adept stays during a *chilla*

*chiragh:* a small wick lamp, often made of clay

*dadra:* a light, classical vocal form of music; also the cycle of six beats (*matra*) in which it is performed

*daf:* a kind of bass tambourine without cymbals

*dargah:* a place that contains the tomb of the saint for whom it is named, as well as the tombs of the saint's disciples and family

*dargah bazar:* the open-stall market surrounding the *dargah* of Mu'in al-din Chishti in Ajmer

*darvish:* mendicant, wandering person, especially one who claims to be or is perceived as pursuing a spiritual path (as in Sufi).

*diwan:* the highest ranking functionary in charge of a Sufi shrine

*Domni:* feminine for *Dom,* a caste of singer-musicians; the women of this caste are said to perform for female audiences.

*du'a:* an informal prayer (as opposed to the prescribed prayers, *namaz*), usually of petition

*dupatta:* a long cloth used by women to cover their heads, shoulders, and chests

*durud:* a devotional prayer form that is intended to invoke blessings on the Prophet Muhammad

*fatiha:* the first *sura,* or chapter, of the Qur'an, a prayer recited in many different contexts

*gaddi:* "throne," a term used in Sufi circles to refer to the spiritual inheritance (particularly the *barakat*) that is said to be automatically passed down through the ranks of spiritual successorship

*ghair mahram:* anyone to whom the women's quarters are not open; a term used to describe men outside of one's family

*ghazal:* a love poem of no fewer than five and not more than twelve *baits* (verses, distichs), with a single rhyme

Hadis: reports of the first generation of Muslims that transmit the *sunna* ("traditions") of the Prophet and his companions; Shi'a Muslims have their own Hadis that report the sayings of the *imams.*

*hal:* a spiritual "state" that is said to descend upon the believer during moments of ecstasy

*hamd:* poem of praise to God

*hazari dena:* literally to "give one's presence," but connoting, in musical performance for example, "being present" in one's music. The term bears some similarity to the concept of *seva* in Hindu devotion.

*hujra gah:* a private prayer cell

*ijazat:* permission; authority; license; also *ijazat nama,* a document that grants permission to take on disciples or to pass on the teachings of one's *shaikh*

*imam:* prayer leader; one of the leaders of the Shi'a community, descended from the Prophet Muhammad's bloodline and beginning with 'Ali, the Prophet's cousin and son-in-law

*imambara:* sacred building commemorating the Shi'a *imams*; in Sufi shrines an *imambara* is used primarily during festivals such as Muharram and the birthday of Hazrat Imam 'Ali.

*jadu:* black magic

*jinn:* "genie"; a class of spirits that are made from smokeless fire (according to the Qur'an [55:15]); they are often, but not always, mischievous or evil; some are Muslim.

*karamat:* miracle, especially one performed by a *wali* or saint, as opposed to miracles performed by a Prophet; miracle-working power

*khadim:* (Ar. pl. *khuddam*): "servant," a term used to describe hereditary attendants at Sufi shrines

*khalifa:* "deputy"; the spiritual delegate of a *pir* or *shaikh,* authorized to make disciples and spread the *pir*'s teaching; the leader of the global Muslim community; the position was officially abolished in the 1920s.

*khanaqah:* residential teaching center for Sufis that emerged in Iran in the late tenth or eleventh century and later developed ritual and other functions; it may also be the place where the *pir* and his family live.

*kurta-pyjama:* style of dress consisting of long pants tied with a drawstring and a shirt that reaches to or below the knees

*langar:* free kitchen open to the public at many Sufi shrines, especially during major commemorative events

*madrasa:* establishment of learning where Islamic (especially Qur'anic) studies are taught; a college for higher studies; in the tenth and eleventh centuries, it functioned as a school for law, other Islamic sciences, and literary and philosophical subjects.

*mahfil-i sama':* musical assembly of devotional songs

*mahfil-khana:* the building or room in which the *mahfil-i sama'* takes place

*malfuzat:* the collected discourses of a Sufi *shaikh* or *pir*

*manqabat:* poem of praise to a deceased Sufi *shaikh* or *pir*

*maulana:* a Sunni scholar, one who has attained competence in a field of Islamic learning to teach, deliver sermons, and conduct necessary rituals; the term also sometimes connotes, in addition to "religious scholar," a person who is skilled in making *ta'wiz* or *naqsh* (amulets) or offering other kinds of remedies for spiritual ailments.

*maulwi:* similar to *maulana*

*mihrab:* the niche in the wall of a mosque or prayer space that orients worshippers in the direction of Mecca

*milad:* birthday celebration

*milad al-nabi* (called *mawlid* in the Arabic-speaking world): the celebration of the Prophet's birthday

*murid:* the disciple of a Sufi *shaikh* or *pir*

*murshid:* spiritual guide

*musha'ira:* assembly held for the recitation of poetry

*mutawalli:* "trustee"; administrative position at the *dargah* of Mu'in al-din Chishti in Ajmer

*nach* (sometimes written in English as *nautch*): singing and dancing performances, especially those once performed in the salons of the moneyed classes

*nafil namaz:* a type of prayer beyond the daily prayers required of Muslims

*nafs:* the lower or base soul

*namaz:* the prayers Muslims must perform five times a day

*naqsh:* a type of amulet

*nasab nama:* genealogical tree of spiritual descent

*na't* or *na't-i rasul:* poem of praise to the Prophet Muhammad

*nazrana:* an offering or donation of money as part of religious devotion

*Nazim Dargah:* administrative post at the *dargah* of Mu'in al-din Chishti in Ajmer

*panj-i pak:* the "five pure ones": the Prophet Muhammad, his cousin and son-in-law 'Ali, his daughter Fatima, and Hasan and Husain, the sons of 'Ali and Fatima; these names appear often in Sufi symbolism and are often inscribed on amulets and Sufi shrines.

*parda:* often translated as the veiling and seclusion of females; actually a complex term referring to a somewhat variable code of ethics and physical behavior that emphasizes modesty, female subordination to senior male authority, and gender segregation

*parda nishin:* "sitting in *parda*," a term used to describe a woman who practices a strict form of *parda*

*pir:* general term for spiritual guide

*pirani:* a female *pir;* the wife of a *pir* (also *pirain, pir-ma*).

*piri-muridi:* the master-disciple relationship

*pirzada* (pl. *pirzade*): "born of a *pir*," the children of a *pir* or Sufi *shaikh.* I also use this term to refer to those relatives of a *pir* or Sufi *shaikh* who are actively involved in the order.

*qawwali:* Indo-Pakistani Sufi music; a type of Hindustani light classical music set to mystical poetry that is recited in Persian (Farsi), Urdu, Hindi, and vernacular dialects and is performed at Sufi shrines

*rakheli:* term used for a type of "common" prostitute who has not been schooled in the arts

*ribat:* a Sufi retreat or hospice (a term often used in North Africa)

*sadhu:* holy man, particularly a mendicant; this term is usually applied to Hindus.

*sahih:* authentic; also the name of one of the ninth-century collections of Hadis by al-Bukhari or Imam Muslim

*sajjada nishin:* "he who sits on the prayer carpet"; same as *ja nishin* and *gaddi nishin*

*salam:* benedictions on the Prophet Muhammad that are sung during the month of Ramzan and on auspicious occasions

*shalwar-kamiz:* dress for women in South Asia, consisting of long pants tied with a drawstring and a top that reaches below the knees

*sama':* "audition"; in Sufism a musical assembly of devotional songs

Shah Sahib: the term used for the heads of two of the branches of the Firdausi *silsila*s in Maner and Bihar Sharif

*shaikh:* a man more than fifty years old; term of respect given to men of distinction and/or learning, Sufi adepts and/or heads of a Sufi order, Qur'anic scholars, jurists, and prayer leaders

Shari'a: Islamic law as based on the Qur'an, *sunna,* and the doctrines of the schools of Islamic law; may also be used in a general sense to refer to ethical and moral framework by which believing Muslims live

*shajara:* a genealogical table of the saints and holy predecessors of a Sufi order

*sifarat or sipara:* the single chapters of the Qur'an used to facilitate teaching

*silsila:* "chain"; denotes a continuous chain of spiritual descent; through it the *pir* is connected with the order's founder and back through 'Ali ibn Abi Talib (or sometimes Abu Bakr) and the Prophet Muhammad.

*subhat:* "companionship," "keeping company," especially with a Sufi *shaikh* or *pir*

*sunna:* "custom," "way of acting," "sayings," especially of the Prophet Muhammad as handed down by tradition; obligatory religious duties; the prayers enjoined by the Prophet Muhammad

*tabarruk:* the sweetmeats or any other edible object that is said to be imbued with the *barakat* of a Sufi shrine or saint

*tariqa:* the Sufi way or path; a method of spiritual discipline; term used for Sufi order

*ta'wiz:* an type of amulet, often inscribed with magic formulas or one of the ninety-nine names of Allah

*tawa'if:* a courtesan, particularly one who is highly trained in the arts

*tazkira:* a biographical memoir

*thumri:* a romantic vocal form that often explores themes of *viraha,* the pain of separation from the beloved

*'ulama'* (s. *'alim*): the learned class of religious and legal scholars

*'urs:* "wedding"; the death-day anniversary celebration held in honor of a deceased Sufi *shaikh, pir,* or holy person

*veshya:* Sanskrit term for prostitute; also used to describe a quarter where prostitutes lived; a type of "common" prostitute who has not been schooled in the arts

*wali* (f. *waliya*): "friend" of God; term used to describe holy men and women, often translated as "saint"

*waqf:* institutional, permanent, tax-free lands, which are usually not inheritable by the descendants of the original grantee

*wuzu:* ritual ablution before prayer

*zanana* or *zanankhana:* the women's quarters

*zawiya:* a Sufi hospice (a term used mostly in North and West Africa)

*zikr:* ritualized repetition of the names of God or of some other prayer formula

*ziyarat:* "pilgrimage"; also used to describe the display of relics said to have belonged to the Prophet Muhammad

# . Bibliography .

Primary Sources: Urdu, Persian, Hindi,
and English Translations

Ahmad, Sayyid Zamir al-din. *Makhdoom Sharaf al-din Ahmad Yahya Maneri: Ahwal o afkar* (Life and Thoughts). Patna: Khuda Bakhsh Oriental Public Library, 1994. Reprint of *Sirat al-sharaf* (A Noble Way), 1951.

al-Badaoni, 'Abdul-Qadir ibn-i Muluk Shah. *Muntakhab al-tawarikh*. 3 vols. English translation by George S. A. Ranking. Calcutta: Baptist Mission Press, 1898. Reprint, Karachi: Karimsons, 1976–78.

Barani, Ziya al-din. *Tarikh-i Firoz Shahi*. Edited by Shams Siraz Afif and Vilayat Husain. Calcutta: Asiatic Society of Bengal, 1891.

Chishti, Ilah Diya. *Siyar al-aqtab*. N.p., 1913.

Dihlavi, Amir Hasan 'Ala Sijzi. *Fawa'id al-fu'ad*. English translation by Ziya ul-Hasan Faruqi as *Fawa'id al-Fu'ad: Spiritual and Literary Discourses of Shaikh Nizam ud-din Awliya*. New Delhi: D.K. Printworld, 1996.

Dihlavi, Shaikh 'Abdul Haq Muhaddis. *Akhbar al-akhyar*. Urdu translation by Maulana Iqbal al-din Ahmad. Karachi: Dar al-Isha'at, 1973.

Firdausi, Maulwi Ghulam Nabi. *Mirat al-kaunain*. Lucknow: Matba' nama Munshi Nawal Kishore, n.d.

al-Ghazali, Abu Hamid Muhammad. *Ihya' 'ulum al-din*, book 18. Translated by Duncan Black MacDonald as "Emotional Religion in Islam as Affected by Music and Singing: Translation of a Book of the Ihya 'Ulum al-Din." *Journal of the Royal Asiatic Society of Great Britain and Ireland* (1902): 195–252. Available online at http://www.ghazali.org/articles/gz-music.pdf (accessed February 16, 2010).

al-Hujwiri, 'Ali 'Usman. *Kashf al-mahjub*. English translation by R. A. Nicholson. Lahore: Islamic Book Foundation, 1976.

Jamali, Hamid bin Fazl ullah. *Siyar al-'arifin*. Urdu translation by Muhammad Ayub Qadiri. Lahore: Central Urdu Board, 1976.

Khan, Muhammad Zafrullah. *The Qur'an: Arabic Text with a New Translation*. New York: Olive Branch, 1997.

Khwurd, Mir. *Siyar al-Auliya*. Urdu translation by 'Ijaz al-Haq Quddusi. Lahore: Central Urdu Board, 1980.

Lawrence, Bruce B. *Notes from a Distant Flute: The Extant Literature of Pre-Mughal Indian Sufism*. Tehran: Imperial Iranian Academy of Philosophy, 1978.

Maneri, Sharaf al-din. *Maktubat-i sadi*. English translation by Paul Jackson as *Letters from Maneri, Sufi Saint of Medieval India*. Mahwah, N.J.: Paulist, 1980.

———. *Khwan-i pur ni'mat*. English translation by Paul Jackson as *Khwan-i pur ni'mat: A Table Laden with Good Things*. Delhi: Idara-i A'dabiyat-i Dilli, 1986.

Roberts, Nancy, trans. *The Subtle Blessings in the Saintly Lives of Abu al-'Abbas al-Mursi and His Master Abu al-Hasan*. Louisville, Ky.: Fons Vitae, 2005.

Sabah al-Din, 'Abd al-Rahman. *Bazm-i Sufiyya*. A'zamgarh: Dar al-Musannifin, 1949.

al-Suhrawardi, Abu al-Najib. *Kitab adab al-muridin*. English translation by Menahem Milson as *A Sufi Rule for Novices: Kitab Adab al-Muridin of Abu al-Najib al-Suhrawardi*. Cambridge, Mass.: Harvard University Press, 1975.

al-Sulami, Abu 'Abd al-Rahman. *Dhikr al-niswa al-muta'abbidat al-sufiyyat*. Translated, with an introduction, by Rkia Cornell as *Early Sufi Women: Dhikr an-niswa al-muta'abbidat al-sufiyyat*. Louisville, Ky.: Fons Vitae, 1999.

Thanawi, Maulana Ashraf 'Ali. *Bihishti Zewar*. Excerpts translated by Barbara D. Metcalf as *Perfecting Women: Maulana Ashraf 'Ali Thanawi's "Bihishti Zewar."* Berkeley and Los Angeles: University of California Press, 1990.

## Secondary Sources

Abbas, Shemeem Burney. *The Female Voice in Sufi Ritual: Devotional Practices of Pakistan and India*. Austin: University of Texas Press, 2002.

Abu Lughod, Lila. "The Romance of Resistance: Tracing Transformations of Power through Bedouin Women." *American Ethnologist* 17 (1990): 41–55.

Ahmad, Imtiaz. *Caste and Social Stratification among Indian Muslims*. New Delhi: Munshiram Manoharlal, 1978.

Ahmad, Qeyamuddin. *The Wahhabi Movement in India*. 2nd ed. Delhi: Manohar, 1994.

Ahmad, Shadbano. "Methodological Problems in the Study of Muslim Women." In *Muslim Women in India*, ed. Mohini Anjum, 24–28. New Delhi: Radiant, 1992.

Ahmed, Leila. *Women and Gender in Islam*. New Haven: Yale University Press, 1992.

Ahmed, Rafiuddin. "Conflict and Contradictions in Bengali Islam: Problems of Change and Adjustment." In *Shari'at and Ambiguity in South Asian Islam*, ed. Katherine Ewing, 114–42. Berkeley: University of California Press, 1988.

———. *The Bengal Muslims 1871–1906: A Quest for Identity*. Delhi: Oxford University Press, 1981.

Ajmal, Mohammad. "A Note on Adab in the *Murshid-Murid* Relationship." In *Moral Conduct and Authority: The Place of Adab in South Asian Islam*, ed. Barbara D. Metcalf, 241–51. Berkeley: University of California Press, 1984.

Ansari, Abdul Ghaffar. *Hazrat Maulana Shahbaz Muhammad Devari sum Bhagalpuri*. Bhagalpur: Muhammad Mu'in Daftary, 1982.

Ansari, Sarah F. D. *Sufi Saints and State Power: The Pirs of Sind, 1843–1947*. Cambridge: Cambridge University Press, 1992.

Arkoun, Mohammad. *Rethinking Islam: Common Questions, Uncommon Answers*. Boulder, Colo.: Westview, 1994.

———. *The Unthought in Contemporary Islamic Thought*. London: Saqi, 2002.

Asad, Talal. *Genealogies of Religion: Discipline and Reasons of Power in Christianity and Islam*. Baltimore: Johns Hopkins University Press, 1993.

———. *The Idea of an Anthropology of Islam*. Washington, D.C.: Center for Contemporary Arab Studies, Georgetown University, 1986.

Ashraf, 'Ali. *The Muslim Elite*. New Delhi: Atlantic, 1982.

Askari, Syed Hasan. "Hazrat Abdul Quddus Gangohi." *Patna University Journal* 11, nos. 1–2 (1957): 1–74.

———. *Islam and Muslims in Medieval Bihar*. Patna: Khuda Bakhsh Oriental Public Library, 1989. Reprint, 1998.

———. "The Maktubat of a Sufi of Firdausi Order of Bihar." In *Khuda Bakhsh Lectures, Indian and Islamic,* 1:565–92. Patna: Khuda Bakhsh Oriental Public Library, 1993.

———. *Medieval Bihar: Sultanate and Mughal Period*. Patna: Khuda Bakhsh Oriental Public Library, 1990.

Askari, Syed Hasan, and Qeyamuddin Ahmad, eds. *The Comprehensive History of Bihar*. 3 vols. Patna: Kashi Prasad Jayaswal Research Institute, 1974–87.

Assayag, Jackie. *Au confluent de deux rivières: Musulmans et hindous dans le sud de l'Inde*. Paris: École Française d'Extrême-Orient, 1995.

Avery, Kenneth S, *A Psychology of Early Sufi Sama'*. London and New York: Routledge/Curzon, 2004.

Bakhtiar, Laleh. *Sufi Women of America: Angels in the Making*. Chicago: Institute for Traditional Psychoethics and Guidance, 1996.

Baldick, Julian. *Imaginary Muslims: The Uwaysi Sufis of Central Asia*. New York: New York University Press, 1993.

Baljon, J. M. S. "Shah Waliullah and the Dargah." In *Muslim Shrines in India: Their History, Character, and Significance,* ed. Christian W. Troll, 1517–25. Delhi: Oxford University Press, 1989.

Banerjee, Sumanta. *The Parlour and the Streets: Elite and Popular Culture in Nineteenth Century Calcutta*. Calcutta: Seagull, 1989.

Basu, Helene. "Hierarchy and Emotion: Love, Joy, and Sorrow in a Cult of Black Saints in Gujarat, India." In *Embodying Charisma: Modernity, Locality, and the Performance of Emotion in Sufi Cults,* ed. Pnina Werbner and Helene Basu, 51–75. New York: Routledge, 1998.

———. "Music and the Formation of Sidi Identity in Western India." *History Workshop Journal* 65 (2008): 161–78.

Begg, Mirza Wahiduddin. *The Holy Biography of Hazrat Khwaja Muinuddin Hasan Chishti, the Holy Saint of Ajmer*. Ajmer: Begg, 1960.

Bell, Catherine M. *Ritual: Perspectives and Dimensions*. New York: Oxford University Press, 1997.

Bourdieu, Pierre. *Outline of a Theory of Practice*. Cambridge: Cambridge University Press, 1977.

Bowen, John. *Muslims through Discourse: Religion and Ritual in Gayo Society*. Princeton: Princeton University Press, 1993.

Brown, Nathan. "Shari'a and State in the Modern Middle East." *International Journal of Middle East Studies* 29, no. 3 (1997): 359–76.

Brown, Peter. *The Cult of Saints: Its Rise and Function in Latin Christianity*. Chicago: University of Chicago Press, 1981.

Buehler, Arthur F. "Currents of Sufism in Nineteenth- and Twentieth-Century Indo-Pakistan: An Overview." *Muslim World* 87, no. 3–4 (2007): 299–314.

———. *Sufi Heirs of the Prophet: The Indian Naqshbandiyya and the Rise of the Mediating Sufi Shaikh.* Columbia: University of South Carolina Press, 1998.

Cadavid, Leslie, trans. *Two Who Attained: Twentieth-Century Sufi Saints, Fatima al-Yashrutiyya and Shaykh Ahmad al-'Alawi.* Louisville, Ky.: Fons Vitae, 2005.

Chabbi, Jacqueline. "Remarques sur le développement historique des mouvements ascétiques et mystiques au Khurasan." *Studia Islamica* 46 (1977): 5–72.

Champion, Catherine. "Wali Perempuan di India Bibi Kamalo di Kako." In *Ziarah dan wali di dunia Islam,* ed. Henri Chambert-Loir and Claude Guillot, 261–67. Jakarta & Paris: École Française d'Extrême-Orient, 2007.

Chandra, Moti. *The World of Courtesans.* Delhi: Vikas, 1973.

Chatterjee, Partha. *The Nation and Its Fragments: Colonial and Postcolonial Histories.* Princeton, N.J.: Princeton University Press, 1993.

Chaturvedi, Vinayak, ed. *Mapping Subaltern Studies and the Postcolonial.* London: Verso, 2000.

Chittick, William C. *The Sufi Path of Love: the Spiritual Teachings of Rumi.* Albany: State University of New York Press, 1983.

Choudhury, M. L. Roy. "Music in Islam." *Journal of the Asiatic Society Letters* 23, no. 2 (1957): 43–102.

Clancy-Smith, Julia. "The House of Zainab: Female Authority and Saintly Succession in Colonial Algeria." In *Women in Middle Eastern History,* ed. Nikki R. Keddie and Beth Baron, 254–74. New Haven: Yale University Press, 1991.

———. *Rebel and Saint: Muslim Notables, Populist Protest, Colonial Encounters: Algeria and Tunisia, 1800–1904.* Berkeley: University of California Press, 1997.

———. "Saints, Mahdis, and Arms: Religion and Resistance in Nineteenth-Century North Africa." In *Islam, Politics, and Social Movements,* ed. Edmund Burke III and Ira M. Lapidus, 60–80. Berkeley: University of California Press, 1988.

Cohn, Bernard S. *Colonialism and Its Forms of Knowledge: The British in India.* Princeton: Princeton University Press, 1996.

Cornell, Rkia Elaroui. "Sufi Women's Spirituality: A Theology of Servitude." In *Voices of Islam: Voices of the Spirit,* ed. Vincent J. Cornell, 167–74. Westport, Conn.: Praeger, 2007.

Cornell, Vincent. *Realm of the Saint: Power and Authority in Moroccan Sufism.* Austin: University of Texas Press, 1998.

Currie, P. M. *The Shrine and Cult of Mu'in al-Din Chishti of Ajmer.* Delhi: Oxford University Press, 1992.

Dallal, Ahmad. "Ghazali and the Perils of Interpretation." *Journal of the American Oriental Society* 122 (2002): 773–87.

Davies, Philip. *A Penguin Guide to the Monuments of India.* 2 vols. London & New York: Viking Penguin, 1989.

De Munck, Victor C. "Sufi, Reformist, and National Models of Identity: The History of a Muslim Village Festival in Sri Lanka." In *Muslim Communities of South Asia: Culture, Society, and Power,* ed. T. N. Madan, 555–78. New Delhi: Manohar, 1995.

Denny, Frederick M. "Prophet and *Wali:* Sainthood in Islam." In *Sainthood: Its Manifestations in World Religions,* ed. Rickard Kieckhefer and George D. Bond, 69–97. Berkeley: University of California Press, 1988.

Dey, Amit. *Sufism in India.* Calcutta: Ratna Prakashan, 1996.

Digby, Simon. "The Sufi Shaikh as a Source of Authority in Mediaeval India." In *Islam et Société en Asie du Sud,* ed. Marc Gaborieau, 57–77. Paris: Colléctions Purusartha, 1986.

Diwarkar, R. R., ed. *Bihar through the Ages.* Bombay: Orient Longman, 1959.

D'Souza, Diane. "Gendered Ritual and the Shaping of Shi'i Identity." In *Shared Idioms, Sacred Symbols, and the Articulation of Identities in South Asia,* ed. Kelly Pemberton and Michael Nijhawan, 188–211. New York: Taylor & Francis, 2008.

Durrani, Tehmina. *Blasphemy.* Delhi: Viking Penguin, 1998.

Dwyer, Daisy Hilse. "Women, Sufism and Decision-Making in Moroccan Islam," in *Women in the Muslim World,* ed. Lois Beck and Nikki Keddie, 585–98. Cambridge, Mass.: Harvard University Press, 1978.

Eaton, Richard M. "Court of Man, Court of God: Local Perceptions of the Shrine of Baba Farid, Pakpattan, Punjab." *Contributions to Asian Studies* 17 (1982): 44–61.

———. "The Political and Religious Authority of the Shrine of Baba Farid." In *Moral Conduct and Authority: The Place of Adab in South Asian Islam,* ed. Barbara D. Metcalf, 333–56. Berkeley: University of California Press, 1983.

———. *The Rise of Islam and the Bengal Frontier, 1204–1760.* Berkeley: University of California Press, 1996.

———. "Sufi Folk Literature and the Expansion of Indian Islam" [1974]. In *Essays on Islam and Indian History,* 189–99. Delhi: Oxford University Press, 2000.

———. *The Sufis of Bijapur: Social Roles of Sufis in Medieval India.* Princeton, N.J.: Princeton University Press, 1978.

Eickelman, Dale. *Moroccan Islam.* Austin: University of Texas Press, 1976.

Elias, Jamal. "Female and Feminine in Islamic Mysticism." *Muslim World* 78:3–4 (July–October 1988): 209–24.

Emirbayer, Mustafa, and Anne Mische, "What Is Agency?" *American Journal of Sociology* 103 (January 1998): 961–1023.

Ernst, Carl W. *Eternal Garden: Mysticism, History, and Politics at a South Asian Sufi Center.* Albany: State University of New York Press, 1992.

———. "Lives of Sufi Saints," in *Religions of India in Practice,* ed. Donald S. Lopez Jr., 495–506. Princeton, N.J.: Princeton University Press, 1995.

Ernst, Carl W., and Bruce B. Lawrence, *Sufi Martyrs of Love: The Chishti Order in South Asia and Beyond.* New York: Palgrave Macmillan, 2002.

Esposito, John L. *The Islamic Threat: Myth or Reality?* New York: Oxford University Press, 1992.

Ewing, Katherine Pratt. *Arguing Sainthood: Modernity, Psychoanalysis, and Islam.* Durham, N.C.: Duke University Press, 1997.

———. "The Dream of Spiritual Initiation and the Organization of Self-Representations Among Pakistani Sufis." *American Ethnologist* 17 (1990): 56–74.

———. "A *Majzub* and His Mother: The Place of Sainthood in a Family's Emotional Memory." In *Embodying Charisma: Modernity, Locality, and the Performance of Emotion in Sufi Cults,* ed. Pnina Werbner and Helene Basu, 160–83. New York and London: Routledge, 1998.

———. "*Malang*s of the Punjab: Intoxication or *Adab* as the Path to God?" In *Moral Conduct and Authority: The Place of Adab in South Asian Islam,* ed. Barbara D. Metcalf, 357–71. Berkeley: University of California Press, 1984.

———. "The Pir or Sufi Saint in Pakistan." Ph.D. diss., University of Chicago, 1980.

———, ed. *Shari'at and Ambiguity in South Asian Islam.* Berkeley: University of California Press, 1988.

Faridi, F. R., and Siddiqi, M. M. *The Social Structure of Indian Muslims.* New Delhi: Institute of Objective Studies, 1992.

Faruqi, Ziya ul-Hasan. *The Deoband School and the Demand for Pakistan.* Bombay: Asia Publishing House, 1963.

Feldman, Shelley. "(Re)presenting Islam: Manipulating Gender, Shifting State Practices, and Class Frustrations in Bangladesh." In *Appropriating Gender: Women's Activism and Politicized Religion in South Asia,* ed. Patricia Jeffery and Amrita Basu, 33–52. New York & London: Routledge, 1998.

Fernandes, Leela. *India's New Middle Class: Democratic Politics in an Era of Economic Reform.* Minneapolis: University of Minnesota Press, 2006.

Flueckiger, Joyce Burkhalter. *In Amma's Healing Room: Gender and Vernacular Islam in South India* Bloomington: Indiana University Press, 2006.

———. "'The Vision Was of Written Words': Negotiating Authority as a Female Muslim Healer in South India." In *Syllables of Sky,* ed. David Shulman, 250–82. Delhi: Oxford University Press, 1995.

Foucault, Michel. *The Archaeology of Knowledge.* Translated by A. M. Sheridan Smith. New York: Pantheon, 1972.

Freitag, Sandria B. "Collective Crime and Authority in British India." In *Crime and Criminality in British India,* ed. Anand A. Yang. Tucson: University of Arizona Press, 1985.

Frembgen, Jürgen Wasim. "The *Majzub* Mama Ji Sarkar: 'A Friend of God Moves from One House to Another.'" In *Embodying Charisma: Modernity, Locality, and the Performance of Emotion in Sufi Cults,* ed. Pnina Werbner and Helene Basu. New York and London: Routledge, 1998.

Friedlander, Shems. "The Coat." *Parabola* 2, no. 4 (1977): 26–31.

Fruzzetti, Lina. "Ritual Status of Muslim Women in Rural India." In *Women in Contemporary Muslim Societies,* ed. Jane I. Smith, 186–208. Cranbury, N.J.: Associated University Presses, 1975.

Gaborieau, Marc. "The Cult of Saints among the Muslims of Nepal and Northern India." In *Saints and Their Cults,* ed. Stephen Wilson, 291–307. Cambridge: Cambridge University Press, 1985.

Gade, Anna M. *Perfection Makes Practice: Learning, Emotion, and the Recited Qur'an in Indonesia.* Honolulu: University of Hawaii Press, 2004.

Gardner, Katy. "Global Migrants and Local Shrines: The Shifting Geography of Islam in Sylhet, Bangladesh." In *Muslim Diversity: Local Islam in Global Contexts,* ed. Leif Manger, 37–57. Richmond, Surrey, U.K.: Curzon, 1998.

Geertz, Clifford. *Islam Observed.* New Haven, Conn.: Yale University Press, 1968.

Gilmartin, David. *Empire and Islam: Punjab and the Making of Pakistan.* Berkeley: University of California Press, 1988.

Gilmartin, David, and Bruce B. Lawrence, eds., *Beyond Turk and Hindu: Rethinking Religious Identities in Islamicate South Asia.* Gainesville: University Press of Florida, 2000.

Graham, William A. "Traditionalism in Islam: An Essay in Interpretation." *Journal of Interdisciplinary History* 23 (1993): 495–522.

Goldziher, Ignaz, "The Cult of Saints in Islam." *Moslem World* 1 (1911): 302–12.

Guenther, Alan M. "The Image of the Prophet as Found in Missionary Writings of the Late Nineteenth Century." *Muslim World* 90 (2000): 43–70.

Guha, Ranajit. "Dominance without Hegemony and Its Historiography." In *Subaltern Studies: Writings on South Asian History and Society,* vol. 6, ed. Ranajit Guha, 210–309. Delhi: Oxford University Press, 1989.

———. *Dominance without Hegemony: History and Power in Colonial Asia.* Cambridge, Mass.: Harvard University Press, 1997.

———. *Elementary Aspects of Peasant Rebellion.* Delhi: Oxford University Press, 1983.

Habib, Irfan. *The Agrarian System of Mughal India, 1556–1707.* 1963. New York: Oxford University Press, 1999.

Haq, Sirajul. "Sama' and Raqs of the Darwishes." *Islamic Culture* 18 (1944): 124–36.

Hardy, Peter. "Modern European and Muslim Explanations of Conversion to Islam in South Asia: A Preliminary Survey of the Literature." In *Conversion to Islam,* ed. Nehemia A. Levtzion, 88–99. New York: Holmes, 1979.

———. *The Muslims of British India.* Cambridge: Cambridge University Press, 1972.

Hassan, Riaz. *Faithlines: Muslim Conceptions of Islam and Society.* New York: Oxford University Press, 2002.

Hassan, Zoya. *Forging Identities: Gender, Communities and the State in India.* Boulder, Colo.: Westview, 1994.

Hawley, John S., ed. *Saints and Virtues.* Berkeley: University of California Press, 1987.

Hawley, John Stratton. *Three Bhakti Voices: Mirabai, Surdas, and Kabir in Their Times and Ours.* New York: Oxford University Press, 2005.

Haynes, Douglas, and Gyan Prakash, eds., *Contesting Power: Resistance and Everyday Social Relations in South Asia.* Berkeley: University of California Press, 1991.

Hegland, Mary. "Political Roles of Aliabad Women: The Public-Private Dichotomy Transcended." In *Women in Middle Eastern History,* ed. Nikki R. Keddie and Beth Baron, 215–30. New Haven: Yale University Press, 1991.

Helminski, Camille Adams. *Sufi Women: A Hidden Treasure.* Boston: Shambhala, 2003.

Hermansen, Marcia K. "Religious Literature and the Inscription of Identity: The Sufi *Tazkira* Tradition in Muslim South Asia." *Muslim World* 87 (1997): 315–29.

Hirschkind, Charles. *The Ethical Soundscape: Cassette Sermons and Islamic Counter-publics.* New York: Columbia University Press, 2006.

Hiskett, Mervyn. *The Development of Islam in West Africa.* New York: Longman, 1984.

Hodgson, Marshall G. S. *The Venture of Islam: Conscience and History in a World Civilization.* 3 vols. Chicago: University of Chicago Press, 1974.

Hoffman, Valerie J. "Muslim Sainthood, Women, and the Legend of Sayyida Nafisa." In *Women Saints in World Religions,* ed. Arvind Sharma, 107–44. Albany, N.Y.: SUNY Press, 2000.

——. *Sufism, Mystics, and Saints in Modern Egypt.* Columbia: University of South Carolina Press, 1995.

ul-Huda, Qamar. "Memory, Performance, and Poetic Peacemaking in Qawwali." *Muslim World* 97 (2007): 678–700.

Ikramullah, Begum Shaista S. *From Purdah to Parliament.* London: Cresset, 1963.

Jackson, Paul. "Perceptions of the Dargahs of Patna." In *Muslim Shrines in India: Their History, Character, and Significance,* ed. Christian W. Troll, 98–110. Delhi: Oxford University Press, 1989.

——. *The Way of a Sufi: Sharafuddin Maneri.* Delhi: Idara-i Adabiyat-i Delli, 1987.

Jahanpour, Farhang. "Western Encounters with Persian Sufi Literature." In *The Heritage of Sufism,* vol. 3, ed. Leonard Lewisohn and David Morgan, 28–62. Oxford: Oneworld, 1999.

Jalal, Ayesha. *Self and Sovereignty: Individual and Community in South Asian Islam since 1850.* New York: Routledge, 2000.

Jeffery, Patricia. *Frogs in a Well: Indian Women in Purdah.* London: Zed, 1979.

Johnson, Pamela Ryden. "A Sufi Shrine in Modern Tunisia" (Ph.D. Diss., University of California, Berkeley, 1979).

Joshi, Sanjay. *Fractured Modernity: Making of a Middle Class in Colonial North India.* Delhi: Oxford University Press, 2001.

Junaid, Sydra Raza. "Thousand-Gated City of the Self: Parveen Shakir's Poetry of Defiance." Ph.D. diss., Columbia University, 2009.

Katz, Jonathan Glustrom. *Dreams, Sufism, and Sainthood: The Visionary Career of Muhammad al-Zawawi.* Leiden: Brill, 1996.

Kopf, David. *British Orientalism and the Bengal Renaissance: The Dynamics of Indian Modernization.* Berkeley: University of California Press, 1969.

Lapidus, Ira M. "The Evolution of Muslim Urban Society." *Comparative Studies in Society and History* 15 (1973): 21–50.

Lawrence, Bruce B., trans. *Nizam ad-din Awliya: Morals for the Heart.* New York: Paulist, 1992.

Lewisohn, Leonard. "The Sacred Music of Islam: Sama' in the Persian Sufi Tradition," *British Journal of Ethnomusicology* 6 (1997): 1–33.

Liebeskind, Claudia. *Piety on Its Knees: Three Sufi Traditions in South Asia in Modern Times.* Delhi: Oxford University Press, 1998.

Lowe, Lisa. *Critical Terrains: French and British Orientalisms.* Ithaca, N.Y.: Cornell University Press, 1991.

Mack, Beverly B., and Jean Boyd. *One Woman's Jihad: Nana Asma'u, Scholar and Scribe.* Bloomington: Indiana University Press, 2000.

Madani, Mohsen Saeidi. *Impact of Hindu Culture on Muslims.* New Delhi: M.D. Publications, 1993.

Mahmood, Saba. *Politics of Piety.* Princeton, N.J.: Princeton University Press, 2005.

Malamud, Margaret. "Sufi Organizations and Structures of Authority in Medieval Nishapur." *International Journal of Middle East Studies* 26 (1994): 427–42.

Mauss, Marcel. "Techniques of the Body." In his *Techniques, Technology and Civilization,* ed. Nathan Schlanger, 77–96. New York: Durkheim/Berghahn, 2006.

McDaniel, June. *The Madness of the Saints: Ecstatic Religion in Bengal.* Chicago: University of Chicago Press, 1989.

Mehta, Deepak. *Work, Ritual, Biography: A Muslim Community in North India.* New Delhi: Oxford University Press, 1997.

Melchert, Christopher. "Sufis and Competing Movements in Nishapur." *Iran* 39 (2001): 237–47.

Mernissi, Fatima. "Women, Saints, and Sanctuaries." *Signs* 3 (1977): 101–12.

Messick, Brinkley Morris. *The Calligraphic State.* Berkeley: University of California Press, 1993.

Metcalf, Barbara D. "Islam and Custom in Nineteenth-Century India: The Reformist Standard of Maulana Thanawi's *Bihishti Zewar.*" *Contributions to Asian Studies* 17 (1982): 62–78.

——. *Islamic Revival in British India: Deoband, 1860–1900.* Princeton, N.J.: Princeton University Press, 1982.

Metcalf, Barbara D., and Thomas R. Metcalf. *A Concise History of India.* Cambridge: Cambridge University Press, 2002.

Minault, Gail. "Political Change: Muslim Women in Conflict with Parda: Their Role in the Indian Nationalist Movement." In *Asian Women in Transition,* ed. Sylvia A. Chipp and Justin J. Green, 199–202. University Park: Pennsylvania State University Press, 1980.

——. *Secluded Scholars: Women's Education and Muslim Social Reform in Colonial India.* Delhi: Oxford University Press, 1998.

Mir, Farina. "Alternative Imaginings: Shared Piety in Punjabi Popular Narrative, c. 1850–1900." Unpublished paper presented at the Association of Asian Studies Annual Meeting, Washington, D.C., April 5, 2002.

Mujeeb, Mohammad. *The Indian Muslims.* New Delhi: Munshiram Manoharlal, 1967. Reprint, 1995.

Muradullah Sahib, Sayyid Shah Muhammad. *Asar-i Maner.* Bankipur: Patna High Commission Press, 1992.

Murata, Sachiko. *The Tao of Islam.* Albany: State University of New York Press, 1992.

Murphy, Anne. "Texts of the Guga Tradition: Diversity and Continuity in Changing Contexts." Master's thesis, University of Washington, 1995.

Nadvi, Syed Habibul Haq. *Islamic Resurgent Movements in the Indo-Pak Subcontinent.* Durban, South Africa: Academia, the Centre for Islamic, Near and Middle Eastern Studies, Planning and Publication, 1987.

Narain, V. A. "Position of Women in Bihar; Marriage Laws and Customs; Dress, Costumes, and Ornaments." In *The Comprehensive History of Bihar,* vol. 3, pt. 2, ed. Kali Kinkar Datta. Patna: Kashi Prasad Jayaswal Research Institute, 1976.

Nasr, Seyyed Hossein. *Traditional Islam in the Modern World.* London & New York: Kegan Paul International, 1990.

Nelson, Kristina. *The Art of Reciting the Qur'an.* Cairo: University of Cairo Press, 2001.

Newman, Daniel M. *The Life of Music in North India: The Organization of an Artistic Tradition.* Detroit: Wayne State University Press, 1980.

Nicholson, R. A. *A Literary History of the Arabs.* Cambridge: Cambridge University Press, 1930. Reprint, 1953.

Nijman, Jan. "Mumbai's Mysterious Middle Class." *International Journal of Urban and Regional Research* 30 (2006): 758–65.

Nizami, K. A. *The Life and Times of Shaikh Nizamuddin Aulia.* Delhi: Idara-yi Adabiyat-i Delli, 1991.

Nurbakhsh, Javad. *Sufi Women.* New York: Khaniqahi-Nimatullahi, 1983.

O'Hanlon, Rosalind. "Recovering the Subject: Subaltern Studies and Histories of Resistance in Colonial South Asia." *Modern Asian Studies* 22 (1988): 189–224.

Oldenburg, Veena Talwar. *The Making of Colonial Lucknow 1856–1877.* Princeton, N.J.: Princeton University Press, 1984.

Oman, John Campbell. *Indian Life, Religious and General.* London: Unwin, 1889.

———. *The Mystics, Ascetics, and Saints of India: A Study of Sadhuism, with an Account of the Yogis, Sanyasis, Bairagis, and Other Strange Hindu Sectarians.* London: Unwin, 1903.

Ortner, Sherry B. "Resistance and the Problem of Ethnographic Refusal." *Comparative Studies in Society and History* 37 (1995): 173–93.

Padwick, Constance. *Muslim Devotions, a Study of Prayer-Manuals in Common Use.* London: SPCK, 1961.

Papanek, Hanna, and Gail Minault. *Separate Worlds: Studies of Purdah in South Asia.* Delhi: Chanakya, 1982.

Parry, Jonathan P. *Death in Banaras.* Cambridge: Cambridge University Press, 1994.

Peirce, Leslie P. *The Imperial Harem: Women and Sovereignty in the Ottoman Empire.* New York: Oxford University Press, 1993.

Pemberton, Kelly. "Ritual, Reform, and Economies of Meaning at a South Asian Sufi Shrine." In Pemberton and Nijhawan, *Shared Idioms,* 166–87.

———. "Women *Pir*s, Saintly Succession, and Spiritual Guidance in South Asian Sufism." *Muslim World* 96 (January 2006): 61–87.

Pemberton, Kelly, and Michael Nijhawan, eds. *Shared Idioms, Sacred Symbols, and the Articulation of Identities in South Asia.* New York: Routledge, 2009.

Phelan, Helen. "Practice, Ritual and Community Music: Doing as Identity." *International Journal of Community Music* 1 (2008): 143–58.

Pinto, Desiderio. *Piri-Muridi Relationship: A Study of the Nizamuddin Dargah.* Delhi: Munshiram Manoharlal, 1995.

Post, Jennifer. "Professional Women in Indian Music: The Death of the Courtesan Tradition." In *Women and Music in Cross-Cultural Perspective,* ed. Ellen Koskoff, 97–110. Westport, Conn.: Greenwood, 1987.

Prajnanananda, Swami. *A Historical Study of Indian Music.* Calcutta: Anandadhara Prakashan, 1965.

Prakash, Gyan. "Becoming a Bhuniya: Oral Traditions and Contested Domination in Eastern India," in Haynes and Prakash, *Contesting Power,* 159–74.

Pritchett, Frances W. *Marvelous Encounters.* New Delhi: Manohar, 1985.

———. *Nets of Awareness: Urdu Poetry and Its Critics.* Berkeley: University of California Press, 1994.

Pugh, Judy F. "Divination and Ideology in the Banaras Muslim Community." In *Moral Conduct and Authority: The Place of Adab in South Asian Islam,* ed. Barbara D. Metcalf, 288–305. Berkeley: University of California Press, 1983.

Qureshi, Regula Burckhardt. *Sufi Music of India and Pakistan: Sound, Context and Meaning in Qawwali.* Chicago: University of Chicago Press, 1986. Reprint, 1995.

———. "Islamic Music in an Indian Environment: The Shi'ah *Majlis.*" *Ethnomusicology* 25 (1981): 20–48.

———. "Sufi Practice in the Indian Context." *Islam and the Modern Age* 17, no. 3 (1986): 130–50.

Rahman, Fazlur. *Islam.* Chicago: University of Chicago Press, 1979.

Ramakrishna, V. "Women's Journals in Andhra during the Nineteenth Century." *Social Scientist* 19, nos. 5–6 (1991): 80–87.

Ramaswamy, Vijaya. "Tamil Separatism and Cultural Negotiations: Gender Politics and Literature in Tamil Nadu." *Social Scientist* 26, nos. 5–6 (1998): 61–83.

Rashid, A. *Society and Culture in Medieval India, 1206–1556 A.D.* Calcutta: Firma K. L. Mukhopadhyay, 1969.

Rasmussen, Anne K. "The Qur'an in Indonesian Daily Life: The Public Project of Musical Oratory." *Ethnomusicology* 45 (2001): 30–57.

Raudvere, Catharina. *The Book and the Roses: Sufi Women, Visibility and Zikr in Contemporary Istanbul.* London: Tauris, 2003.

Rizvi, S. A. A. *Muslim Revivalist Movements in Northern India in the Sixteenth and Seventeenth Centuries.* Agra: Agra University Press, 1965. Reprint, Delhi: Munshiram Manoharlal, 1995.

Robinson, Francis. *Islam and Muslim History in South Asia.* Delhi: Oxford University Press, 2000.

———. *The 'Ulama of Farangi Mahall and Islamic Culture in South Asia.* Delhi: Permanent Black, 2001.

Roded, Ruth. *Women in Islamic Biographical Collections: From Ibn Sa'd to Who's Who.* Boulder: Lynne Rienner, 1994.

Roy, Asim. *The Islamic Syncretistic Tradition in Bengal.* Princeton, N.J.: Princeton University Press, 1983.

Rozehnal, Robert. *Islamic Sufism Unbound: Politics and Piety in Twenty-First Century Pakistan.* New York: Palgrave Macmillan, 2007.

———. "A 'Proving Ground' for Spiritual Mastery: The Chishti Sabiri Musical Assembly." *Muslim World* 97 (2007): 671–72.

Sadiq, Muhammad. *A History of Urdu Literature,* 2nd ed. Delhi: Oxford University Press, 1984.

Salvatore, Armando. *Islam and the Political Discourse of Modernity.* Reading, U.K.: Garnet, 1997.

Sanyal, Usha. *Devotional Islam and Politics in British India: Ahmad Riza Khan Barelwi and His Movement, 1870–1920.* Delhi: Oxford University Press, 1996.

Sarkar, Tanika. *Hindu Wife, Hindu Nation: Community, Religion, and Cultural Nationalism.* Bloomington: Indiana University Press, 2002.

Schimmel, Annemarie. *And Muhammad Is His Messenger: The Veneration of the Prophet in Islamic Piety.* Chapel Hill: University of North Carolina Press, 1985.

———. *Classical Urdu Literature from the Beginning to Iqbal.* Wiesbaden: Otto Harrassowitz, 1975.

———. *Islam in the Indian Subcontinent.* Leiden: Brill, 1980.

———. *My Soul Is a Woman: The Feminine in Islam.* New York: Continuum, 1997.

———. *Mystical Dimensions of Islam.* Chapel Hill: University of North Carolina Press, 1975.

Scott, James. *Weapons of the Weak: Everyday Forms of Peasant Resistance.* New Haven, Conn.: Yale University Press, 1985.

Sered, Susan Star. *Women as Ritual Experts: The Religious Lives of Elderly Jewish Women in Jerusalem.* New York: Oxford University Press, 1992.

Shaikh, Farzana. *Community and Consensus in Islam: Muslim Representation in British India, 1860–1946.* New York: Cambridge University Press, 1989.

Sharar, Abdul Halim. *Lucknow: The Last Phase of an Oriental Culture.* Translated and edited by E. S. Harcourt and Fakhir Hussain. London: Elek, 1975.

Sharib, Zahurul Hassan. *The Culture of the Sufis.* Southampton, U.K.: Sharib Press, 1999.

Siddiqi, Majid Hayat. "Review of Subaltern Studies III." *Indian Economic & Social History Review* 22, no.1 (1985): 92–95.

Sikand, Yoginder. "The Changing Nature of Religious Authority in Twentieth Century South Asian Islam." *Journal of the Henry Martyn Institute* 16 (January–June 1997): 5–22.

Smith, Jane I. "The Experience of Muslim Women: Considerations of Power and Authority." In *The Islamic Impact,* ed. Yvonne Yazbeck Haddad, Byron Haines, and Ellison Findly, 89–112. Syracuse: Syracuse University Press, 1984.

Smith, Margaret. *Muslim Women Mystics: The Life and Work of Rabi'a and Other Women Mystics in Islam.* Oxford: Oneworld, 1994. Reprint, 2001.

Sprenger, Aloys. *The Life of Mohammad from Original Sources.* Allahabad: Presbyterian Mission Press, 1851.

Stewart, Tony. "Satya Pir: Muslim Holy Man and Hindu God." In *Religions of India in Practice,* ed. Donald S. Lopez, 578–97. Princeton, N.J.: Princeton University Press, 1995.

Subhan, John A. *Sufism, Its Saints and Shrines.* Lucknow: Lucknow Publishing House, 1938. Reprint, New York: Weiser, 1970.

Tibi, Bassam. *Islam and the Cultural Accommodation of Social Change.* Boulder, Colo.: Westview, 1990.

Trimingham, J. S. *The Sufi Orders in Islam.* Oxford: Clarendon, 1971. Reprint, Oxford: Oxford University Press, 1998.

Umar, Mohammad. *Islam in Northern India during the Eighteenth Century.* New Delhi: Munshiram Manoharlal, 1993.

'Usmani, Muhammad Taqi. *Taqlid ki shari' haisiyat*. Karachi: Zam Zam, 1998.

Varadarajan, M. *A History of Tamil Literature*. Translated by E. Sa. Viswanathan. Madras: Sahitiya Akademi, 1988.

Varma, Pavan. *The Great Indian Middle Class*. New Delhi: Viking, 1998.

Vatuk, Sylvia. "Purdah Revisited: A Comparison of Hindu and Muslim Interpretations of the Cultural Meaning of Purdah in South Asia." In *Separate Worlds: Studies of Purdah in South Asia*, ed. Hanna Papanek and Gail Minault, 54–78. Delhi: Chanakya, 1982.

Vreede de Stuers, Cora. *Parda: A Study of Muslim Women's Life in Northern India*. Assen, Netherlands: Van Gorcum, 1968.

Werbner, Pnina. *Pilgrims of Love: The Anthropology of a Global Sufi Cult*. Bloomington: Indiana University Press, 2003.

Werbner, Pnina, and Helene Basu, eds. *Embodying Charisma: Modernity, Locality, and the Performance of Emotion in Sufi Cults*. New York: Routledge, 1998.

Wolf, Eric. *Europe and the People without History*. Berkeley: University of California Press, 1982.

Yang, Anand. *Bazaar India: Markets, Society, and the Colonial State in Bihar*. Berkeley: University of California Press, 1998.

———, ed. *Crime and Criminality in British India*. Tucson: University of Arizona Press, 1985.

Yang, C. K. *Religion in Chinese Society*. Berkeley: University of California Press, 1961.

Zaman, Muhammad Qasim. *The 'Ulama in Contemporary Islam: Custodians of Change*. Princeton, N.J.: Princeton University Press, 2002.

## Reference Works

Lewis, B. Ch. Pellat, and J. Schacht, eds. *The Encyclopaedia of Islam*. Leiden: Brill, 1965.

Chaturvedi, Mahendra, and Tiwari, B. N. *A Practical Hindi-English Dictionary*. 18th ed. Delhi: National Publishing House, 1991.

Cowan, J. M., ed. *Wehr's Arabic-English Dictionary*. Ithaca, N.Y.: Spoken Language Services, 1976.

Fallon, S. W. *A New Hindustani-English Dictionary: With Illustrations from Hindustani Literature and Folklore*. Banaras, 1879. Reprint, Delhi & Madras: Asian Educational Services, 1989.

Haq, Abdul. *Urdu-English Dictionary*. Delhi: Star, 1996.

Houtsma, M. Th., A. J. Wensinck, and H. A. R. Gibb, eds. *The Encyclopedia of Islam: A Dictionary of the Geography, Ethnology, and Biography of the Muhammadan Peoples*. Leiden: Brill, 1927.

MacGregor, R. S. *The Oxford Hindi-English Dictionary*. New York: Oxford University Press, 1997.

Platts, John T. *A Dictionary of Urdu, Classical Hindi, and English*. 2nd ed. Delhi: Munshiram Manoharlal, 1988.

Steingass, F. *A Comprehensive Persian-English Dictionary: Including the Arabic Words and Phrases to Be Met with in Persian Literature*. Delhi: Munshiram Manoharlal, 1996.

### Gazetteers, Surveys and Journals, Census Reports, Government Reports, Mission Literature

Bayly, C. S. comp. *Chiefs and Leading Families in Rajputana.* Calcutta: Office of the Superintendent of Government Printing, 1894.

Eastwick, Edward B. *Handbook of the Panjab, Western Rajputana, Kashmir, and Upper Sindh.* Vol. 4. London: Murray, 1883.

Erskine, Maj. K. D. *Imperial Gazetteer of India. Provincial Series: Rajputana.* Calcutta: Superintendent of Government Printing, 1908.

Hamilton, Walter. *The East-India Gazetteer.* London: Murray, 1815.

Ibbetson, Sir Denzil. *Panjab Castes: Being a Reprint of the Chapter on "The Races, Castes, and Tribes of the People" in the Report on the Census of the Panjab Published in 1883 by the Late Sir Denzil Ibbetson, K.C.S.I.* Patiala: Languages Dept. Punjab, 1970.

Jackson, V. H., ed. *Journal of Francis Buchanan (Afterwards Hamilton) Kept during the Survey of the Districts Patna and Gaya in 1811–12.* Patna: Superintendent, Government Printing, Bihar and Orissa, 1925.

Kumar, Nagendra. *Gazetteer of India: Bihar, Patna.* Patna: Government of Bihar, Gazetteers Branch, Revenue Department, 1970.

——. *Image of Patna: A Supplement to Patna District Gazetteer, 1970.* Patna: Government of Bihar, Gazetteers Branch, Revenue Department, 1971.

La Touche, J. J. D. *Gazetteer of Ajmer-Merwara, in Rajputana.* Calcutta: Office of the Superintendent of Government Printing, 1875.

O'Malley, L. S. S. *Bihar and Orissa District Gazetteers. Patna.* Reprint of 1912–16 series. Revised by J. F. W. James, I.C.S. Patna: Superintendent, Bihar and Orissa Government Printing, 1924.

——. *The Indian Civil Service, 1601–1930.* London: Murray 1931. Reprint, London: Cass, 1965.

Punjab Government. *Gazetteer of the Peshawar District 1897–1898.* Lahore: Sang-i Meel, 1989.

——. *Punjab District Gazetteers: Multan District 1923–1924.* Lahore: Superintendent, Government Printing, 1926.

Sarda, Har Bilas. *Ajmer: Historical and Descriptive.* Ajmer: Scottish Mission Industries, 1911. Reprint, 1967.

——. *Ajmer: The Last Capital of the Hindu Empire in India.* Ajmer: Scottish Mission Industries, 1923.

Watson, C. C., I.C.S. *Rajputana District Gazetteers. Ajmer-Merwara.* Vol. I-A. Ajmer: Scottish Mission Industries, 1904.


### Travel Literature, Early European Histories, Works of Cultural Preservation, and Early Orientalist Scholarship

'Ali, Mrs. Meer Hasan. *Observations on the Mussulmauns of India.* 1832. Reprinted with notes and an introduction by William Crooke. London: Oxford University Press, 1917.

Arnold, T. W. *The Preaching of Islam: A History of the Propagation of the Muslim Faith.* London: Constable, 1913.

Catrou, Pere François, trans. *Histoire générale de l'Empire du Mogol: Depuis sa fondation.* Paris: Guillaume de Voys, 1708.

Dermenghem, Emile. *Le culte des saints dans l'Islam maghrébin.* Paris: Gallimard, 1954.

Jones, V. R., and L. Bevan Jones. *Woman in Islam.* Lucknow: Lucknow Publishing House, 1941.

Khan, Shafaat Ahmad, ed. *John Marshall in India: Notes and Observations in Bengal, 1668–1672.* London: Oxford University Press, 1927.

Manucci, Niccolao. *Storia do Mogor; or, Mogul India, 1653–1708, by Niccolao Manucci.* Edited and translated by William Irvine. 4 vols. London: Murray, 1907–8.

Muir, Sir William. *The Life of Mahomet: From Original Sources.* 3rd ed. London: Smith, Elder, 1894.

Oman, John Campbell. *The Brahmans, Theists and Muslims of India: Studies of Goddess-Worship in Bengal, Caste, Brahmaism, and Social Reform, with Descriptive Sketches of Curious Festivals, Ceremonies, and Faquirs.* London: Unwin, 1907.

Roe, Thomas, "Sir Thomas Roe's Journal, Giving an Account of His Voyage to India, and His Observations in That Country, and Particularly at the Court of the Great Mogul, Where He Resided as Ambassador from James the First King of England." In *A Collection of Voyages and Travels, Some Now First Printed from Original Manuscripts, Others Now First Published in English.* London: Churchill, 1732.

Sharif, Ja'far. *Qanun-I Islam.* 1921. Translated by Gerhard Andreas Herklots, revised by William Crooke as *Islam in India.* Delhi: Oriental Books Reprint, 1972.

Tassy, Garcin de. *Muslim Festivals in India and Other Essays.* Translated and edited by M. Waseem. Delhi: Oxford University Press, 1995. Originally published as *Mémoire sur des particularités de la religion musulmane dans l'Inde, d'après les ouvrages hindoustani.* Paris, 1831.

Tavernier, Jean-Baptiste. *Travels in India.* Translated by V. Ball. 2 vols. London: Oxford University Press, 1925.

Titus, Murray. *Indian Islam: A Religious History of Islam in India.* London: Oxford University Press / Humphrey Milford, 1930.

———. "Mysticism and Saint Worship in India." *Moslem World* 12 (1922): 129–41.

Tod, James. *Annals and Antiquities of Rajasthan, or the Central and Western Rajpoot States of India.* 2 vols. London: Smith, Elder, 1829–1832.

Westermarck, Edward. *Ritual and Belief in Morocco.* London: Macmillan, 1926.

Wilkinson, Charles K. "Life in Early Nishapur," *Metropolitan Museum of Art Bulletin 9*, no. 2 (1950): 60–72.

Newspapers, Journals, and Online Sources

*Journey towards the Friend,* parts 3 and 4 (January and July 1998).

Khan, M. Muhsin, trans. and ed. Al-Bukhari's *Sunan.* Online at http://www.usc.edu/dept/MSA/fundamentals/hadithsunnah/bukhari/073.sbt.html#008.073.097 (accessed March 18, 2010).

Khan, Sameera. "Rediscovering the Qawwali Tradition." *Times of India* (Mumbai), April 6, 1997.

Kumar, Ajay. "Shastriya sangeet hamari sanson sa juda he." *Dainik Hindustan* (Delhi), April 8, 1996.

Parwar, Yogesh. "Qawwali's Reigning Begum." *Indian Express* (Mumbai), April 2, 1997.

Patel, Bhaichand. "White Woman's Woe." *Outlook India,* February 4, 2008. Available online at http://www.outlookindia.com/article.aspx?236621 (accessed March 18, 2010).

Sharma, Ashish. "Songs of the Sufis." *Indian Express* (New Delhi), February 2, 1995.

Vaish, Rashmi. "A Resonant Strain from the Past." *Metropolis* (Mumbai), April 6, 1997.

Zahuri, Jamiluddin Morris. "Some Brief Notes Introducing the Subject of 'The Sufi Way' to American College Students." *The Zahuri Sufi* Web site. September 16, 1998. Online at http://www.j-morris.dircon.co.uk/article1border.htm (accessed November 15, 2008).

# . Index .

MW01105344